Dealing with Diversity

Edited by

George B. Graen

Southwest Tennessee Community College
Gill Center Library
3833 Mountain Terrace
Memphis, TN 38127

INFORMATION AGE
PUBLISHING

80 Mason Street
Greenwich, Connecticut 06830

Library of Congress Cataloging-in-Publication Data

Dealing with diversity / edited by George B. Graen.
  p. cm. – (LMX leadership)
Includes bibliographical references.
  ISBN 1-930608-48-9 (pbk.) – ISBN 1-930608-49-7 (hardcover)
  1. Diversity in the workplace–United States. I. Graen, George B. II. Series.
  HF5549.5.M5D43 2003
  658.3'008–dc22
                                         2003021157

Copyright © 2003 Information Age Publishing

All rights reserved. No part of this publication may be reproduced, stored on a retrieval system, or transmitted, in any form or by any means, electronic, mechanical, photocopying, microfilming, recording or otherwise, without written permission from the publisher.

Printed in the United States of America

CONTENTS

	List of Contributors	*vii*
	Preface *George B. Graen*	*ix*
	Foreword *George B. Graen*	*xi*
1	Role Making onto the Starting Work Team Using LMX Leadership: Diversity As An Asset *George B. Graen*	*1*
2	LMX and Teamwork: The Challenges and Opportunities of Diversity *Nathan J. Hiller and David V. Day*	*29*
3	Organizational and Social Influences on Leader-Member Exchange Processes: Implications for the Management of Diversity *Ceasar Douglas, Gerald R. Ferris, M. Ronald Buckley, and Michael J. Gundlach*	*59*
4	LMX and Mentoring Diverse Followers: Finding the Competitive Advantage for Each *S. Gayle Baugh, Terri A. Scandura, and Claudia C. Cogliser*	*91*
5	The Narrative Basis of Leader-Member Exchange *Gail T. Fairhurst and Stephanie Rhea Hamlett*	*117*

6	Interpersonal Workplace Theory at the Crossroads: LMX and Transformational Theory as Special Cases of Role Making in Work Organizations *George B. Graen*	*145*
7	The New Conduct of Business: How LMX Can Help Capitalize on Cultural Diversity *Diane M. Sullivan, Marie S. Mitchell, and Mary Uhl-Bien*	*183*
8	LMX and Organizational Citizenship Behavior: Examining the Links within and Across Western and Chinese Samples *Rick D. Hackett, Jiing-Lih Farh, Lynda J. Song, and Laurent M. Lapierre*	*219*

LIST OF CONTRIBUTORS

S. Gayle Baugh	University of West Florida
M. Ronald Buckley	University of Oklahoma
Claudia C. Cogliser	University of Oklahoma
David V. Day	Pennsylvania State University
Ceasar Douglas	Florida State University
Gail T. Fairhurst	University of Cincinnati
Jiing-Lih Farh	Hong Kong University of Science and Technology
Gerald Ferris	Florida State University
George B. Graen	University of Louisiana
Michael J. Gundlach	Bond University
Rick D. Hackett	McMaster University
Stephanie Rhea Hamlett	University of Missouri
Nathan J. Hiller	Pennsylvania State University
Laurent M. Lapierre	University of Ottawa
Marie S. Mitchell	University of Central Florida
Terri A. Scandura	University of Miami
Lynda J. Song	Hong Kong University of Science and Technology
Diane M. Sullivan	University of Central Florida
Mary Uhl-Bien	University of Central Florida

PREFACE

George B. Graen

Diversity in the workplace has made significant progress in United States companies. Unfortunately, much of the apparent progress has been at the surface-level of diversity (Hiller & Day, 2004), where readily visible characteristics identify people of varying genders, ages, ethnicity, and religions. What are needed are prescriptions, based on solid theory and research, that will allow the deep-level diversity to transform well intentioned affirmative action programs from their old reliance on surface-level diversity to a new reliance on deep-level diversity.

It is our hope that this volume will stimulate the scholarly activity needed to make progress toward the above stated goal of making deep-level diversity the benchmark of human progress in the workplace.

I would like to thank the contributors to this volume for their great work. Special thanks go to our second reviewers David Day and Jerry Ferris, and to Gail Fairhurst and Stephanie Rhea Hamlett for stepping in when Mitsuru Wakabayashi became ill. Thanks also go to George Johnson, Publisher of Information Age for his guidance, patience, and production assistance. Finally, Joan Graen was the driving force, word processor, and organizer of this volume.

Dealing with Diversity
A Volume in: LMX Leadership: The Series, pages ix–x.
Copyright © 2003 by Information Age Publishing, Inc.
All rights of reproduction in any form reserved.
ISBN: 1-930608-49-7 (hardcover), 1-930608-48-9 (paperback)

This volume started out with my life-long research partner and best friend as a major contributor. Sadly, Dr. Mitsuru Wakabayashi (Wak), could not complete his contribution to this volume due to a serious illness. On behalf of the contributors to this project, I would like to dedicate this research volume to Wak.

FOREWORD

George B. Graen

Beginning with this volume, I will serve as General Editor of *Dealing with Diversity, LMX Leadership: the Series*. Future volumes will focus on theory and research that enrich our understanding of the deep-level processes of workplace leadership, followership, and partnership. For example, volume two will include topics such as new dimensions of deep-level LMX, TMX as a meta-LMX theory, deep-third culture LMX, LMX and fairness, LMX and workplace bonding, LMX and mentoring, and LMX in Germany, among others.

The volumes will be original scholarly papers. Inquires, suggestions, and proposals for future volumes are invited.

Dealing with Diversity
A Volume in: LMX Leadership: The Series, page xi.
Copyright © 2003 by Information Age Publishing, Inc.
All rights of reproduction in any form reserved.
ISBN: 0-000000-00-0 (hardcover), 0-000000-00-0 (paperback)

CHAPTER 1

ROLE MAKING ONTO THE STARTING WORK TEAM USING LMX LEADERSHIP
Diversity As An Asset

George B. Graen

Diversity may be an asset or a liability depending on how it is integrated into an organization. As pointed out by Hiller and Day (2003), diversity exists at different levels from the surface-level to the deep-level. Moreover, as relationships develop in the workplace, the influence of surface-level diversity declines and that of deep-level diversity grows. This leads to the recommendation that people enrich their deep-level diversity and search out deep-level diversity in others. Relying on surface-level diversity (stereotypes) tends to produce dysfunctional results for both individuals and their organization. This chapter explores the process of mutual selection, negotiation, and development in the workplace based on deep-level diversity. Clearly, both parties must work to make it mutually satisfying.

Wherever you work, your organization at its core is split into "players" and "supporters." "Players" are those who make the rules, estab-

Dealing with Diversity
A Volume in: LMX Leadership: The Series, pages 1–28.
Copyright © 2003 by Information Age Publishing, Inc.
All rights of reproduction in any form reserved.
ISBN: 1-930608-49-7 (hardcover), 1-930608-48-9 (paperback)

lish the standards, and bring about change when needed. They are cleared for inside information, given critical assignments, and entrusted with the future of the organization. Most are good folks who are trying to do the right thing. "Supporters," in sharp contrast, are those whose work is more routine, who receive little inside information, are given mostly standard assignments, and only can make small contributions to the future direction of the organization. Also, they are good folks who are trying to do the right thing.

In career terms, "players" are on the fast track to promotions, wealth, and happiness. They shoot up rapidly and are rewarded with sometimes embarrassingly valuable material and social rewards. Plum assignments are offered to them on a routine basis. They make real contributions. "Supporters" remain on the slow track, often without understanding how they opted out of the competition by taking the wrong turns.

How does one get to be a "player"? Let me mention five ways. They are:

1. Political favoritism;
2. Family connections;
3. Educational advantage;
4. Friendships; and
5. Leader-Member Exchange (LMX) skills, including performance on team skills.

"Godfathers" know that many more ways exist, but they shall not be mentioned for fear that someone might get desperate and try one or more. If one doesn't possess the first four, don't worry, the fifth is still available and recommended to become a "player." This book focuses on the fifth way: Getting the opportunity and developing the partnership skills that can help one get inside without compromising ethics.

Political Favoritism varies from minimum help in one's career (e.g., sage advice, a letter or e-mail of reference, a telephone call, a mention of your name during golf, tennis, or racquetball), to maximum payoffs to a prospective employer. An example is Eastern prep school networks in which children of privilege form politically favorable bonds that endure throughout their lives.

Family Connections include extended family such that one can be fortunate to be born into a powerful family, be adopted into it, or marry into it. Family influence with employers also varies from the minimum, (e.g., the Graens') to a maximum, (e.g., the Fords' and the Rockefellers').

Educational Advantage is the way many people crack the inside of the corporation. The problem is getting the right educational specialty for the time. Unless one keeps current and anticipates the next demanded specialty, one becomes obsolete and loses the educational advantage. Even now the value of a popular MBA is being openly questioned at Stanford University (Pfeffer & Fong, 2002.)

Friendships can be made on the job. Earning a friendship is usually based on nonwork activities (e.g., sports, entertainment, or leisure). Bringing friendships into work-related issues is dangerous and may backfire. It is not recommended as a basis for career success.

LMX Partnering Skills including Performance on Team Skills can be learned and applied by most people who can hold a job. These skills are not learned in most Business Schools even by the MBA or the more mature EMBA. They are learned in the school of hard knocks on the job, with mentors or by trial and error. Some learn the process of getting inside by themselves and acquire the necessary skills, but most never learn the process and give up trying. They settle for taking orders that they don't fully understand, and their performance suffers. They are told to let the "players" do all the thinking, because only they understand what the organization is trying to do and only they can be trusted to do the right things. "Supporters" sometimes protest that this is unfair, but few take them seriously. Women and minorities may feel the inequality of opportunity and often chalk it up to the Old Boy's Club. But they need to stop cursing the darkness and begin lighting candles to light their way inside.

This chapter will not help one with political favors, family connections, educational advantage, or friendships. Gaining these keys to the inside is beyond the scope of this book. This book explores how to become a player without selling out, and using a fair, honest, and ethical process to do so. Some people believe that they cannot do this without selling out their ethics, but this often is only an easy excuse for not persisting. It can be done ethically, but it's more difficult.

THE MISSION

This monograph is a 21st Century primer for research on workforce diversity to prepare minorities with partnering skills to become dependable players. Three Rs of Read'n, Rit'n, and Rithmatic are used to describe in detail how the three processes operate in the workplace. Although these processes continue to be illuminated by solid past research, they are unknown to many people because they are scattered among many different scientific journals. Equally important, this approach not only tells minorities how these processes work, but also helps them to become players and still be good people. This is "meta affirmative action." Women and minorities can get into the executive suites and board rooms by using this theory. Moreover, they can earn their ticket to ride the private fast track elevator to the executive suite. Women, minorities, and even historically favored white males can benefit greatly from learning about these informal leadership processes.

Consider some facts: At 500 of the largest companies, women held 12.5 percent of corporate office positions in 2000 and 12.4 percent of the board seats in 2001 as reported by Catalyst in New York; from 1995 to 2000, women managers in several fields made even less than men, and the salary gap widened in 7 of the 10 sectors employing 71 percent of all females according to the General Accounting Office report 2002.

Women executives have told the author that they cannot play by the same rules because they are judged by different standards than men. When this happens, I tell them that until women help write and regulate the standards this will be the case. And the path to this is marked "players only."

Federal and State laws against unfair discrimination in the workplace do not apply to these informal processes. Lawmakers choose not to address these processes and thus do not. By understanding these processes, one can open the doors and go inside. Becoming a player means negotiating workplace partnerships with everyone who works with you (i.e., 360 degrees).

As stated above, this partnering program involves three separate underlying processes—the three Rs—Read'n, Rit'n, and Rithmatic. Read'n is the process of discovering what a prospective partner really seeks from a workplace partner. This process includes studying the potential partner and delivering free samples of what is sought (e.g., going the extra miles). This skill matures into consistently delivering the goods beyond expectations. Once the Read'n process is developed sufficiently and you are picked by a prospective partner, the Rit'n process begins.

In this process, a partnership is negotiated over time between the parties. Partners may be coworkers with more, less, or the same power in their jobs (Generally, one starts with his/her immediate supervisor). After the agreement negotiation is well along (it is seldom final), the Rithmatic process begins. This is the partnership managing process in which both parties work to keep both process and outcome fair. Once one builds a mature partnership with one's boss, one needs to do the same with peers and colleagues, upstairs, downstairs, and across the hall (i.e., 360 degrees). In this way, one carefully constructs a personal "competence network" (i.e., a network of competent partners who will help when needed).

In sum, a player is a person who is always looking for opportunities to form the building blocks of "competence networks," namely, working partnerships that are the interpersonal agreements that characterize the players. In contrast, the supporters tend to be hired hands and form mainly acquaintanceships at work. Only when supporters discover these working partnerships can they become respected by players and have a chance to work themselves into players.

Workplace minorities continue to ask the hard questions: How do I get moved ahead at work and make a difference? Must I "sell out" to get ahead? Why are some people blessed with opportunities and others not? It isn't fair, or is it? We shall explore these questions in the volume.

WHAT IS LEADERSHIP IN ORGANIZATIONS?

Leadership is a complex concept that includes at least a team leader, a team member, and an exchange relationship between—a Leader, a Member, and an Exchange (i.e., Leader-Member Exchange or LMX). Without any one of these elements leadership cannot be claimed. A leader must have at least one follower and a trusting, respectful, and committed "give and take" relationship with that follower.

The hallmarks of a leadership relationship involved the control of social influence, social meaning, and social emergence based on the interactions of a leader and a member. The basis for these leadership processes are produced by:

1. bonding to build mutual trust of, respect of, and commitment to the other, which generates social influence,
2. bonding discussions about, and actions modeling team values that produce new meanings,
3. bonding, creating, and enabling conditions by which new opportunities may emerge.

By definition leadership includes the above three elements of L, M, X, and the above three leadership outcomes of social influence, social meaning, and social emergence. Moreover, these three leadership outcomes are produced by bonding emotionally, cognitively, and behaviorally. Two people can generate leadership outcomes when they bond in these three ways.

Once leadership outcomes are realized by two people, they can unite to collect new resources, build new leadership networks, and improve fitness and innovation. Using this powerful, extra-organizational process called leadership, two or more people can create emergent outcomes that are impossible to duplicate with hierarchical bureaucracy and managerial roles.

Two types of leadership theories are the focus of this volume. They are traditional leadership theory (Bass, 1990) and Leader-Member Exchange (LMX) theory (Graen & Uhl-Bien, 1995; Uhl-Bien, Graen, & Scandura, 2000). The main differences between these two leadership theories are the following:

1. Traditional is top-down and LMX is bottom-up.
2. Traditional is leader controlled and LMX is controlled by emergence.
3. Meaning is controlled by leader's core vision under traditional and is controlled by team values under LMX.
4. Emergence is controlled by leader delegated follower empowerment under traditional and by enabling follower under LMX.

LMX theory focuses on diversity issues due to the above differences. Because LMX theory is bottom up, it depends on the diversity in human assets available for development. Because LMX is controlled by emergence, it seeks diversity to stimulate innovation and fitness. Because LMX meaning within the team is controlled by team values, it capitalizes on incorporating diversity. Finally, because

LMX is controlled by enabling followers, it depends on embedded talents and cultural differences.

LMX leadership is thus different than traditional leadership in several important respects. LMX seeks a match between the growth needs of a leader and a member and attempts to build a leadership relationship on their communality. LMX leaders foster the emergence of growth need fulfilling opportunities for their followers, which are tailored to the growth needs of the particular person. In this way, people grow out of the confines of their job descriptions and into emergent leadership relationships. Thus, followers may grow in a variety of directions with a variety of foci. Therefore, LMX leadership allows more diversity of people, ideas, and behavior in terms of input, process, and outcomes than traditional leadership.

Leadership appears to be a lottery situation in that you must buy a ticket and hope that one's number is selected. Both traditional and LMX leadership share this characteristic, but the bases of winning the lottery are different. For traditional leadership, the opportunity is extended to those who commit to the leader's vision, mission, and practices. In contrast, for LMX leadership, the opportunities are offered to those who negotiate a mutual growth need-based relationship with their leader. Thus, traditional leaders develop and sell their vision, mission, and practices to their members, and only those who "buy in" become players. Those who fail to commit are not players, but only supporters doing their prescribed job. In contrast, LMX leaders also develop their vision, mission, and practices, but negotiate these with their people based on mutual growth needs and emergent opportunities, and those who complete the process become players. Both leaders and members must buy into the joint vision. Those who fail to complete the process are supporters doing their prescribed jobs.

Unlike a lottery, under LMX leadership, people can improve their odds of success by understanding the process of development. Once people understand the process, they can develop their vision, mission, and practices based on their growth needs and their opportunities, and proceed to negotiate an LMX relationship (Graen, 1989). After people have done their homework, they are prepared to initiate or invite a development process. The questions become how to get picked to become a participant and grow into a "player." It is to this question we turn next.

EARLY INVESTIGATIONS ON THESE QUESTIONS

In one of our early investigations of these workplace progress questions (Graen, 1976), we studied the development of project teams from their outset as groups of workplace strangers to their maturity as players and nonplayers ten months later. In this study, we were present at the invitation of the project CEO at the first meeting of all 60 managers and professionals. Over the life of the overall project, we interviewed all managers and professionals separately as leaders and as followers using a patterned interview schedule. This was done at four different times over ten months. This was a large project team and the entire life of the team was ten months. This was an ideal setting for our probing investigations.

We were interested in finding partnerships that were most effective in terms of generating mutual incremental influence, reciprocal trust, respect, commitment, outgrowing jobs, and becoming partners in terms of communications and ethics. Our research literature at that time suggested that a particular style was most effective. We found that some people outgrew their jobs and became players while others did not and were not. When we attempted to relate this success of individuals to their respective work groups, we failed abysmally. All work groups had some people who became players with their bosses, but all also had a number of people who did not. In sum, outgrowing of one's job and becoming a player was not related to the boss' leadership style in the work unit, but it was strongly related to being picked for development. All units encouraged *some* of their people to become players, but few encouraged *all*.

Encouragement of some people and not others suggested to us that units were "cherry picking" those most ready for development. Those "ready" people would be developed first in the initial wave of partner making. Those ready people were similar to their leaders in respect to ambitions and readiness for partnership. The plan was that those next most ready would be developed in the second wave, then the third wave, and so on. Unfortunately, no second wave was initiated. They settled for a low level of human resource investment, and it ended after the first wave. The reason given for this was that the project team was too busy. By the end of the study, most of those picked in the first wave had developed into players, but the others had received no encouragement to outgrow their jobs and did not develop beyond supporters.

The final partnership development process was predictable based on the follower's initial (two months) development. The stronger the early development, the higher the frequency of later development in terms of encouraged outgrowing of one's job. In addition, greater development at the beginning was related to greater need satisfaction, better communications, and higher agreement on ethics at the end of the process. Clearly, opportunity was achieved by some but not others in the same unit. Not all of those passed over were happy about the process or the result. More people could have been developed without too much trouble, but it did not happen. Executives agreed that this was an unfortunate waste of human talent. Many more partnerships could have been developed thereby creating greater strategic assets for the project. During those critical times when the project needed more players, they were not available as human assets because they had not been developed and development takes time.

When we interviewed the executives about this waste, they said that it was not their intention to stop with the first group, however, later they found that they could spare no time for further development. They had what they needed at a minimum to deal with most unusual problems. They did not mean to limit the diversity of the partners as the process did. Also, the Director took the pressure off development too soon, and the program was truncated due to lack of encouragement from the top down. In fact, later developmental efforts could not be charged against a unit's time budget. In any case, the development was not completed. Reactions of those left out of this development ranged from apathy to resentment. Those completing the development outgrew their jobs through more challenging "player" projects. In general, those left outside did not blame their more fortunate peers, but they did blame their leaders and their organization.

Results of this truncated development process were workplace units with both player bonds and supporter bonds. Not all of those left in the supporter status wanted to just do their job and go home. Clearly, more player bonds could have been developed, but they were not. This may not be a bad strategy if the budget is tight. Also, this is an example of developing only the minimum diversity necessary. This may prove to be a false economy, because when a corporation really needs all of its people, they may not all be there. This is not a good time to find out. Perhaps, had the project lasted longer, more people would have been developed. Left to their own devices, units tend to develop only the most "ready" to become partners and players. Although cherry picking is better than letting all ripe cherries rot on the trees, it is a common practice, and the wise candidate will become noticeably ready.

IN SEARCH OF WORKPLACE PARTNERSHIP

After two additional long-term, panel studies failed to produce consistent leadership style results by which we could characterize a leader's behavior toward all members of the unit, we developed an alternative model now called LMX, a workplace partnership model (Graen & Cashman, 1975). This model assumes that the heart and soul of development emerge through the growth exchanges between two people. In these exchanges, leaders offer people opportunities to outgrow their current jobs and grow into more responsible positions and their leader's leader offers leaders opportunities to do the same upstairs. As these exchanges mature the nature of the exchange moves from economic to social.

Economic exchanges by their nature are more socially distant than partnership exchanges and require more bookkeeping in the interest of fair exchange. Moreover, during this development, the two parties grow mutual respect, trust, commitment, influence, communications, and ethics, and they move from self-interest to team interest. In this way, additional team players as strategic human assets are produced for the team and the organization.

Not only are players more likely to perform beyond expectation and become natural partners, but also they are more likely to contribute some of their chips earned with people outside of the unit or organization. These chips are products of exchanges with outside people, and often give a team a competitive advantage. Workplace teamwork appears to begin in the two-person exchanges and spread to an entire team. However, if the two-person exchanges are violated, the damage to the exchanges also may spread to the team (Phillips, 1996). In contrast, when they are maintained properly, they facilitate team building by aiding the development of peer partnerships and team commitments.

LMX partnership thrives in the rich soil of United States society as we shall see. It is not who your parents are or where you went to school (i.e., surface-level), but what you are in terms of ability and motivation (i.e., deep-level). According to this model, partnership grows out of the interactions of two or more people, (a dyad or team), and it all begins with challenges. These challenges call for the person to grow out of their present job expectations and go beyond them in terms of exercising ability, motivation, and capitalizing on opportunity. Such challenging opportunities may be offered several times before they are accepted (Graen & Uhl-Bien, 1995). Often good people need to be courted before they can commit.

Once accepted, the process of development begins. Both parties learn their new roles gradually over time. They learn to teach, to reward, and to challenge each other in the proper way at the appropriate times. This process of reciprocally going beyond expectations gradually builds partnership in the form of mutual trust, respect, and commitment. What begins as economic exchange of material-based rewards for goal attainment is transformed into social exchanges based on mutually satisfying relations. Under economic exchanges, people are rewarded with things of clear economic value (cash & carry), whereas under social exchanges, people are rewarded with internalized commitment. Economic exchanges are unstable over time as a base. If they fail to be transformed into social exchanges, they can deteriorate quickly. The process begins with material rewards and moves on to either social rewards or regresses to earlier stages. This doesn't mean that as individuals assume greater responsibilities, they forgo the material rewards. They get them also as part of the reward package. Players generally get much more of the goodies of every kind.

Those leader and follower dyads that are transformed successfully into social exchanges (i.e., natural partners) tend to be stable over time. This is the highest state. Partner's promises to their partners are fulfilled faithfully as are partners' promises to them. No one gets cheated. It is a "win-win" relationship. Cheating damages trust and may destroy the partnership.

These challenges are offered to the most ready first. The process is not severely limited by the numbers of partners unless the time and resources available are too short. It may take longer to transform larger numbers but it is well worth the effort. Ideally, everyone ready is extended some challenge. Unfortunately, not all coworkers will accept the challenge and earn their spurs. This is accepted as the American way. Those who demure are held to their job expectations. They do not want to grow out of their jobs, and that is their choice. Of course, they forgo the joys and benefits and have no gripe later when their peers are promoted far faster and further.

They can be late bloomers and accept their second chance, but they must then play catch up (Graen, Dharwadkar, Grewal, Wakabayashi, & Hui, in press).

To review, under this LMX workplace partnership model leaders offer challenges to coworkers to outgrow their jobs. If they accept, leaders come to understand that this means teaching, motivating, and challenging the partner and accepting teaching, rewarding, and challenging from the partner. The partner's role is the reciprocal. Over time, exchanges are transformed from those characterized as economic "cash and carry" to committed teammates. As a result, the outcomes of trust, respect, and commitment grow from minimum to a maximum. All parties go from self-interest to team interest. As a result, these units are the building blocks of teams. The mortar, which bonds these blocks together, is LMX partnership.

JOB EXPERIENCES: HOW INVESTMENT LEADS TO THE FAST TRACK

In another study we asked: How does career investment lead to greater career progress? The answer to this question is vital to career success. If people can recognize the ways in which investment provided job experiences that lead to the fast track, they can more actively control their careers. They can seek out career-enhancing experiences and avoid career threatening mistakes. To answer this question, Graen (1989) randomly selected and studied the careers of 50 fast-track and 50 slow-track managers in an engineering division of a multinational consumer products corporation. The managers we studied were college graduates with at least 5 (and as many as 15) year's service with the company. They represented all levels of the management hierarchy in the division.

Few Succeed Alone

When we focused on the managers' first four jobs after joining the organization, we found that seven types of job experiences were much more common for the fast-track managers than for their slow track colleagues:

1. They received career investments from at least one immediate superior;
2. Careers were influenced in a positive manner by an average of four superiors;
3. They gained technical expertise from several superiors;
4. They learned how to influence others, and partnership building from several superiors;
5. Their career development was opportunistic and active regarding specific job experience;
6. They moved to different job assignments at appropriate intervals;
7. They applied their education and training in their first job.

Clearly, the first four of the seven kinds of job experiences depend entirely on having at least one superior invest in the subordinate's career during the first four job assignments. Even the fifth, sixth, and seventh job experiences also rely heavily on being offered the opportunity to gain those experiences. For a subordinate to gain these job experiences, the subordinate had to get at least one superior to invest substantially in her or his career.

Further, we found that managers who did not receive these enriching job experiences during the first four job assignments were unlikely to be in the fast-track group later. Those who experienced the selected treatment at least once during their first four job assignments tended to be more successful years later than those who were never selected. This agrees with our theory investigation that early growth experiences are especially relevant to later career progress. These early job experiences may show at least a few of the ways that a leader's career investment can launch a subordinate onto the fast track to the inside.

Let's consider the seven helpful lifts up the organizational ladder:

Receive Career Investments from at Least One Immediate Superior

A single is the minimum required, but more is better. Without even one out of the four that was willing to invest, his or her odds for promotion were puny. Everyone who aspires to promotion beyond the routine should get at least one partnership. Don't be too fussy, the perfect leader doesn't exist. Take a work in progress if that's all that's available and make it work. This is good advice for both leaders and followers.

Career Influenced by Several Superiors

Seek out mentors whenever one travels inside and outside of the organization. Ask their advice and make them feel like real mentors. If you persuade them that you really value their accumulated knowledge and their insights, they will share gladly.

Gain Technical Expertise from Several Masters

Try to be a good student of the masters by asking good questions, doing your homework, and being grateful for any technical tidbits. Masters rarely have time to do technical training, but they can be convinced to do so for you by volunteering to do some of his/her scutwork. As any seducer knows, you can't get anything unless you ask nicely. So, ask and ask and ask again.

Learn How to Influence Others, Including Teams from Several Superiors

Giving orders and expecting people to carry them out with trust, respect, and commitment may be the Pygmalion theory of leadership (Eden, 1993), but also it requires partnership. Influence is built over time as part of leadership and cannot be ordered when needed. The true test of leadership is whether your followers are there when you need them the most. If they are not, it's a hell of a time to find out. When you look behind you and you are leading only your shadow, you've failed the test. No matter how you give orders unless you have built of partnership, your orders likely will go unfilled.

Career Development is Opportunistic and Assertive Regarding Specific Assignments

Make your assignment grow by actively seeking useful options. Take every opportunity to learn and perform. If your assignment takes you to strange and wonderful divisions and departments, build relationships by doing more than the minimum, ask questions, offer information, and seek to learn about the local competence network that you seek to join. Go beyond on each assignment and ask questions of local folks. This is a form of do-it-yourself (DIY) investment in your career.

Move to Different Job Assignments at Proper Times

This is somewhat manageable by a follower. If you are staying too long in the same job assignment, compared to your peers, you need to get your present and past leaders to help you move. You can do some of this yourself, but be careful that you aren't seen as asking too much and being too selfish. Clearly, one needs to keep moving up to even more challenging job assignments or one will be seen as plateauing.

Apply Education and Training to First Job

After coming out of the university, it is important to learn to use one's expertise right away. Because technical advantage will fade out in a short time, employ it while it's fresh. Next year's recruits may make your technical edge obsolete whether or not it's used this year.

WHAT LEADERS SEEK

Leaders seek to organize their team as quickly as feasible, but based on solid foundations of exchange. Thus, in the first wave of offers, they look for people who are the most ready to play key team roles for them. For the second wave, they seek the next most ready and so forth. Once these people are identified, they are made offers and courted to become key team players. However, what behaviors do leaders look for?

We performed a number of studies to investigate this question. In the first study, we asked managers from different manufacturing companies to describe the critical characteristics of their key players compared to their other players (Graen, 1989). Three summary characteristics, which were statistically significant, were as follows:

1. Given the same complex problem, this person and I will make the same decision independently. (68% key versus 25% others).

    This is part of the "*Respect*" dimension of the evaluation of followers. Leaders seek followers who can replicate their leaders' decision process when necessary, but can think independently when necessary. For example,
    - We have compared notes on previous complex problems, and I have developed confidence in the compatibility of our methods for solving problems.
    - We tend to think alike on important ethical issues.
    - We see the situation of the department within the company similarly.

- This follower can play "devils advocate" effectively and think creatively.
2. In an emergency, I can count on this person to complete an assignment I started. (85% versus 50%).

    This is part of the "*Trust*" dimension of the evaluations. Leader seeks followers that they trust. For example:
    - This follower has helped in a crisis in the past, and I have confidence that he or she would do so again when necessary.
    - This follower has the confidence to step into an emergency.
    - This follower is dependable and will not let me down when I really need him or her.
    - This, follower will protect my reputation.
3. My working relationship with this person is effective. (88% versus 65%).

    This is the part of "*Commitment*" dimension of the evaluations. Leaders seek followers that have committed. For example:
    - We have developed a mutually effective and rewarding working relationship.
    - We communicate effectively and coordinate our efforts efficiently.
    - We collaborate well in our work by exchanging required resources.
    - We are committed to similar ethical standards.

    This means that leaders tend to mold their key players into partners who have:
    a. the leader's respect that they will make the right decisions and do the right things,
    b. the leader's trust and confidence that they will complete the assignments successfully, and
    c. the leader's belief in their commitment to the partnership.

Clearly, this represents a most solid foundation for teams. These three characteristics: trust, respect, and commitment), are the dimensions assumed to underlie American workplace partnership. They also are the trilogy human relationships of the Hindu holy books and the Christian holy books.

We asked over one thousand managers in five leading manufacturing companies how they attempted to demonstrate their partnership potential to their leaders, (Graen 1989). Thirteen actions distinguished between key players and others.

1. Demonstrate initiative to get things moving
2. Attempt to exercise leadership to make the unit more effective
3. Show a willingness to take risks to accomplish assignments
4. Strive to add to the value of assignments
5. Actively seek out new job assignments for self-improvement
6. Persist on a valuable project after others give up
7. Build networks to extend capability
8. Influence others by doing something extra
9. Deal constructively to resolve ambiguity
10. Seek wider exposure to managers outside the home division
11. Apply technical training on the job, and build on that training to develop broader expertise
12. Work to build and maintain a close working relationship with the immediate supervisor
13. Work to get the immediate supervisor promoted

The following examples illustrate how each of these actions enabled these followers to become key players.

1. *Demonstrate Initiative.* By demonstrating initiative, followers make their boss aware that they are eager to outgrow their jobs. For example, they may demonstrate initiative by identifying problem areas in their jobs, and then act to correct the problems. Thus, when you see a problem with a customer order, and handle the problem the way you have seen your manager handle it before (even though this is not part of your job description), you are indicating to your boss that you are capable of and willing to take on added responsibilities.
2. *Exercise Leadership.* An important characteristic of key players is that they are able to exercise leadership when necessary. You show this by helping your co-workers perform their jobs more efficiently, and by providing direction when they are not certain as to the best method to use. In addition, you attempt to exercise leadership by offering to take charge of

special projects, such as interdepartmental task forces, which will help to develop leadership skills.

3. *Take Risks.* The need to take risks increases as managers reach higher levels in the organization. Similarly, those managers who are going to be successful in the organization are willing to take risks in their dealings with their boss and co-workers. One way managers may do this is by communicating to their supervisors the problems in the work unit, soliciting advice or added resources as needed even though pressure in the work group dictates that this is not done. Similarly, they may take risks by supporting issues that they believe are correct, even though others in the work unit may not support the issue. In addition, they are not afraid to talk about their mistakes. Rather, they use past follies to their advantage by indicating to others what they have learned from their mistakes.

4. *Add Value.* They are constantly looking for opportunities to grow in their jobs. They find that one of the best ways to do this is to make their work more challenging and meaningful. For example, in his job as a supervisor of a market research department, Bill Atsuta found that unless he added value to his work, his job became boring and repetitive and didn't allow him to develop his skills. Thus, rather than just monitoring the performance of the telephone interviewers, as his job description suggested, he added value to his job by offering his managers input as to how interviews could be conducted more effectively, and he wrote unsolicited reports to those in charge of the development of the interviews that identified problem areas and made suggestions for improvement. As a result of his extra effort, Bill found himself promoted to department head and on his way to the fast track.

5. *Self-improvement Assignment.* Rather than waiting for their bosses to offer them opportunities, followers seek opportunities on their own to make the most out of not only their jobs but also themselves. Thus, these managers look for opportunities that will allow them to develop their skills and to grow on the job. They may request special training or take on assignments that require them to use new skills.

6. *Persist on a Project.* If an assignment appears to be going nowhere, pause a moment in order to view the assignment in a new way. If this strategy leads to failure, which in some cases it does, assess the situation to find out what went wrong, and

use the mistake as an opportunity for learning. Perhaps most important, learn never to make the same mistake twice.
7. *Build Networks.* Getting ahead means making as many contacts as possible in your field, and, in particular, contacts with those in your competence network. Find out what was going on in the organization and who was responsible for getting work done. Then, initiate relationships with these people, which involved offering to do them favors or providing them with information that would help them in their positions. By building credits with the people in this network you are thus able to obtain resources that would not have been possible without the help of others.
8. *Influence Others.* Influencing others is not as easy as it may appear. It involves building credibility, as well as adjusting your interpersonal style to match those of others.
9. *Resolve Ambiguity.* One of the most difficult problems for managers in organizations is learning how to deal with ambiguity because ambiguity characterizes many of the difficult situations people face in the work place. Frequently, it's unclear what's not working, why it's not working, or what's needed in order to make things work. Also, people in the workplace may present ambiguous requests or offer ambiguous rationales. Those managers who learn how to handle these ambiguous situations most effectively find themselves on the fast track. When you find yourself working with a boss who was always very ambiguous in his requests, take several steps to deal with the ambiguity rather than simply becoming frustrated and not completing the assignments. Perhaps most importantly, take the initiative to gather as much information as possible from his supervisors, peers, and others. When necessary, make educated assumptions that allow you to continue the task. Throughout the process, approach your boss for brief feedback on whether you are performing the assignment properly. By using his knowledge and best judgment, completes ambiguous tasks while requiring very little of his supervisor's time.
10. *Seek Wider Exposure.* Because information is such a powerful resource in organizations, managers who aspire to get ahead actively seek ways to gather more information. One way to do this is by associating with managers outside the home division. By interacting with outside managers, they gain a better

understanding of their organization and its operations, as well as the different problems faced by members of other departments.
11. *Build on Existing Skills.* When new managers enter organizations, they have a certain amount of knowledge and technical skills that make them desirable to the organization. Often, however, this technical training is limited, and within a relatively short period of time, it may become obsolete. Thus, managers must continually work to keep their technical skills current.
12. *Develop a Good Working Relationship with your Boss.* One of the most powerful influences on your career progress is your boss. Your boss controls the types of opportunities and resources, as well as the types of rewards, you will receive from the organization. It is vital that you strive to develop the best working relationship possible with your boss.
13. *Promote your Boss.* One of the best ways to get to the fast track may be to work toward promoting your boss: Do your job the best you can so that you help make your boss look good. Then, when your boss advances through the organization, he or she may take you along.

These activities all require followers to grow out of the narrow confines of their job by assuming greater personal responsibility, by taking larger risks, and by growing more quickly professionally. Your boss notices these activities that make a difference to your career. Participation in these activities communicates readiness for career investment. Once noticed as a candidate for investment, additional opportunities to show your stuff likely will be forthcoming.

GETTING PICKED FIRST

Before you can hope to establish a partnership with your leader, you must pass his or her entrance test and convince him or her that you can be trusted to deliver on your promises and that you have something of value to offer. Convincing your potential partner of the former is more difficult than the latter; however, both require some thought. Even a great "pick up" line only gets momentary attention.

Some people believe that people trust you or not based on rumors about you. True, some basis for trust can be found in this way, although it is too unreliable. This is open to stereotyping and biases. What is recommended is a more direct approach called the "growth need interview." This interview is designed to suggest to leaders that you are interested in furthering your career by describing your interests and ambitions. This attempt to show your growth needs as an individual can go a long way toward passing the entrance test. Through such conversations, which may stretch out over several weeks, you tell your leader what you want now and what you want long term. Also, you ask your leader to share the same information with you. It may be uncomfortable at first, but it becomes routine after a few interviews.

After this interview, the next step is to achieve an initial challenge to begin growing out of one's job in the form of some small request which is somewhat outside of the job expectations. This offer should make clear that this request is for the unit. If you require special information or other resources, ask for them. In addition, if you get into trouble, your leader will get you out. Once the request is fulfilled, you should receive both your leader's thanks and something that you value. The early "grabber" rewards are material and the later "sustaining" rewards are social and self-fulfilling.

If you pass this initial test, you seek another larger project. After a few of these exchanges, your leader will begin to trust your promises. Never make a promise that you cannot keep. When your leader offers the challenges, seek more and explain the developmental process in terms of growing out of your job. If your leader demurs, keep working until all hope is lost. If you reject your leader's offers, they will cease being offered. You cannot rightly complain after you reject an offer. You may opt back into the process later when they see the growth and achievements of your peers who completed the process from the first offer.

Though these episodes of seeking and achieving appropriate challenges based on current work flows and the developing needs, getting support through your project, and rewards after the project is completed, mutual trust, respect, and commitment grow. Over this process, the challenging projects become more responsible and the corresponding rewards become more significant. The process of building partnership flows smoothly once the initial tests are passed and both parties continue to construct ever-stronger bonds of mutual trust, respect, and commitment.

Our research investigations have shown that leaders and followers who complete this process gain the advantages of performance beyond expectations, satisfaction with their jobs and their careers, mutual trust, respect, and commitment, and optimism about the future. Over their careers, they consistently develop these agreements with their leaders, followers, and peers, as they move up the hierarchy of their companies until they find their dream job. Finally, they move up higher and faster than their peers do over their careers and arrive home earlier.

WHAT IS THE ADVANTAGE?

From the leader's viewpoint, because a potential partner grows from a supporter to a partner through the process, he or she and the leader have created strategic human assets (Uhl-Bien, Graen & Scandura, 2000). When one partner has a problem that he or she cannot solve, the other partner will help even though it may cost him or her personally or professionally. As one partner goes beyond his or her job, the other reciprocates in kind. Both partners share information openly and honestly, even when it may be painful. Both create their own dyadic language based upon shared experiences (Fairhurst, 1993). This language allows one partner to talk to the other partner in code in the presence of others without their comprehending.

Finally, it allows the multiplier to work. This multiplier is the peer analog of the leader and member process in which peers grow mutual trust, respect, and commitment. This is a multiplier of the power partnership because it completes the pyramid of leader to one follower, to the other follower and back to the leader. Three bonds locked together in a triangle. Each triangle added then contributes to the strength of the pyramid forming the team. As the triangles add, the human assets of the structure multiply. It becomes almost a mission of connecting the dots to form the team. Strategically, unconnected dots are weakness and connected dots are strengths. Clearly, continuous 360-degree partnership making is recommended.

Diversity in the work place generally complicates and enhances the LMX process. Building trust with someone who doesn't share one's socialization is more difficult due to values and communication differences. Because the costs are higher with diverse pairs, are the results worth the extra costs? If the answer is sometimes, the question becomes can one specify the conditions in which diversity becomes a net gain for a work-group? This is one of the questions about diversity in the workplace that this book explores.

ORGANIZATION OF THE BOOK

In the next chapter by Hiller and Day, the distinction between surface-level diversity and deep-level diversity is integrated with LMX and teamwork. They speculate that the maturing LMX process is more about deep-level diversity than surface-level diversity. Strong and mature LMX bonds require the uncovering of these deep-level traits. Once uncovered by the parties involved, the transformation from economic-based to social-based LMX can proceed.

In support of this is a series of three studies focusing on LMX project team development and performance from strangers to teammates. Graen, Hui, and Phillips (2000) found that LMX based on early surface-level characteristics was transformed by the later discovery of deep-level traits. Moreover, this transformation held for leaders, members, and coworkers. Hiller and Day speculate that with strangers forming a work team, LMX is tentatively estimated employing surface-level characteristics which suggested the deep-level trait of dependability, but later information about deep-level traits transform the nature of the LMX bond. Moreover, one test of team LMX is whether or not former teammates on project teams would volunteer for another project with the same team members. For teammates with deep-level based dependability experience, the answers likely would be definitely yes or no.

The longitudinal effect of surface-level diversity and deep-level diversity suggest that surface-level weakens over time while deep-level becomes stronger over team member interactions as documented by Hiller and Day (2003). The question becomes what are the longitudinal effects of surface-level and deep-level diversity on coworker exchange (CWX) and team exchange (TMX)? This has implications for shared leadership in teams as discussed by Hiller and Day. Finally, Hiller and Day offer benefits of diversity for teams, and conclude with suggestions for LMX development initiatives for teams dealing with diversity.

In the next chapter, Douglas, Ferris, Buckley, and Gundlach (2003) discuss the organizational and social influences on LMX processes regarding the management of diversity. They focus on managing the "political environment" as the most critical role for leadership as diversity become ever more pervasive in organizations. They speculate on leader style involving political skills and emotional intelligence needed to create LMX relationships that can support diversity management programs. They hypothesize that key components of these LMX relationships are self-concepts of leaders and members, mentoring, social exchange, social networks, and organization values focusing on proper conduct and goals. They propose that organizations that implement diversity management programs featuring the above components of LMX relationships can get beyond surface-level diversity and utilize all of their human resources.

Baugh, Scandura, and Cogliser (2003) follow the mentoring route to LMX relationships and diversity. They discuss the contribution of relational demography to mentoring programs and developing LMX relationships. They hypothesize that mentoring may cease at the level of the executive suite, but LMX relationships may continue inside. Clearly, LMX and mentoring theories are overlapping yet distinct. Mentoring relationships can occur inside an LMX leadership relationship and outside of leadership.

Fairhurst and Hamlett (2003) next challenge the strict adherence to the quantitative approach to LMX leadership with the need for deep-level diversity through LMX narratives. They make their case for narrative and discourse, and sketch three narrative research agendas for LMX:

1. "Narrative reflection" and the "uniqueness paradox" in LMX stories,
2. "Stories lived together" as LMX making, and
3. Stories as "discursive formations".

These three research agendas should be fruitful in probing the boundaries of the ups and downs of LMX relationships. They present, as an exemplar from Fairhurst's groundbreaking multi-method investigation of strategic ways in which narrative may be used to build and validate LMX relationships in situ (see Graen & Wakabayashi, 1994). Combining the narrative (qualitative) with the LMX leadership evaluation (quantitative) permits the boundaries to be probed more completely.

Graen (2003) next explores the questions that arise from the crossroads of interpersonal workplace theory. Employing a comparative approach, LMX theory is contrasted with traditional leadership theory (Bass, 1990). The differences and similarities between the two theories suggest LMX is associated with followers possessing strong self-concepts, and traditional (charismatic) leadership is associated with followers with weaker self-concepts (Shamir & Howell 2000).

Sullivan, Mitchell, and Uhl-Bien (2003) discuss the new conduct of business in terms of capitalizing on deep-level cultural diversity. The values of LMX involving uncertainty, power, individualism, and gender are discussed in terms of the LMX processes of reciprocity (i.e., fair exchange) and LMX currencies of exchange (i.e., what gets transacted). They also propose new deep-level diversity research and practice. Finally, they suggest numerous hypotheses to be tested by future research.

Finally, Hackett, Farh, Song, and Lapierre (2003) perform a meta-analysis on LMX and organizational citizenship behavior (OCB) for both Western and Chinese samples. They document that LMX players tend to be better organizational citizens. They speculate that the relationship between LMX and OCB for both Western and Chinese samples is probably reciprocal. Better citizenship may help one get picked as a potential player and stronger LMX may motivate one to become a better citizen. They suggest a new bonding between LMX and OCB

Collectively, the chapters in Volume 1 of *Dealing With Diversity, LMX Leadership: The Series* contribute meaningfully to the development of a more informed understanding of the roles diversity plays in LMX processes. It is our fond hope that our attempts to "think outside of the box" will be fruitful and multiplies into new thinking and research about diversity and LMX development and employment.

REFERENCES

Bass, B. M. (1990). *Bass & Stogdill's Handbook of Leadership* (3rd Ed.). New York: Free Press.

Baugh, G., Scandura, T., & Cogliser, C. (2003). Leadership development in the context of diversity. In G. B. Graen (Ed.), *Dealing with diversity, LMX leadership: The series* (Vol. 1). Greenwich, CT: Information Age Publishing.

Douglas, C., Ferris, G. R., Buckley, M. R., & Gundlach, M. J. (2003). Organizational and social influences on leader-member exchange processes: Implications for the management of diversity. In G. B. Graen (Ed.), *Dealing with diversity, LMX leadership: The series* (Vol. 1). Greenwich, CT: Information Age Publishing.

Eden, D. (1993). Leadership and expectations: Pygmalion effects and self-fulfilling prophecies in organizations. *Leadership Quarterly, 56*, 215-239.

Fairhurst, G. T. (1993). The leader-member exchange patterns of women leaders in industry: A discourse analysis. *Communication Monographs, 60*, 322-351.

Fairhurst, G. T., & Hamlett, S. R., (2003). The narrative basis of leader-member exchange. In G. B. Graen (Ed.), *Dealing with diversity, LMX leadership: The series* (Vol. 1). Greenwich, CT: Information Age Publishing.

Graen, G. B. (1976). Role making processes within complex organizations. In M. D. Dunnette (Ed.), *Handbook of Industrial and Organizational Psychology*. (pp. 1201-1245), Chicago: Rand-McNally.

Graen, G. B. (1989). *Unwritten rules for your career: 15 secrets for fast-track success*. New York: John Wiley & Sons.

Graen, G. B. (2003). Interpersonal workplace theory at the crossroads: LMX and transformational theory as special cases of role making in work organizations. In G. B. Graen (Ed.), *Dealing with diversity, LMX leadership: The series* (Vol. 1). Greenwich, CT: Information Age Publishing.

Graen, G. B., & Cashman, J. (1975). A role-making model of leadership in formal organizations: A developmental approach. In J. G. Hunt & L. L. Larson (Eds.), *Leadership Frontiers* (pp. 143-166). Kent, OH: Kent State University Press.

Graen, G. B., Dharwadkar, R., Grewal, R., Wakabayashi, M., & Hui, C. (2003). Japanese career progress over the long haul: An empirical examination. *Journal of International Business Studies*. In Press.

Graen, G.B., Hui, C., & Phillips, E. (2000). *A dyadic approach to finding answers on engineering project teams: Dyadic leadership and friendship as predictors of team effectiveness and team success*. Unpublished paper, University of Cincinnati.

Graen, G. B., & Uhl-Bien, M. (1995). Development of leader-member exchange (LMX) theory of leadership over 25 years: Applying a multi-level multi-domain perspective. *Leadership Quarterly, 6*(2), 219-247.

Graen, G. B., & Wakabayashi, M., (1994), Cross-cultural leadership-making: Bridging American and Japanese diversity for team advantage. In H. C. Triandis, M. D. Dunnette, & L. M. Hough (Eds.), *Handbook of Industrial and Organizational Psychology* (2nd Ed., Vol. 4, pp. 415-446), New York: Consulting Psychologists Press.

Hackett, R. D., Farh, J. L., Song, L. J., & Lapierre. L. M. (2003). LMX and organizational citizenship behaviour: Examining the links within *and* across Western and Chinese samples. In G. B. Graen (Ed.), *Dealing with diversity, LMX leadership: The series* (Vol. 1), Greenwich, CT: Information Age Publishing.

Hiller N. J., & Day, D. V. (2003). LMX and teamwork: the challenges and opportunities of diversity. In G. B. Graen (Ed.), *Dealing with diversity, LMX leadership: The series* (Vol. 1), Greenwich, CT: Information Age Publishing.

Pfeffer, J., & Fong, C. T., (2002). The end of business schools? Less success than meets the eye". *Academy of Management Learning and Education, 1*, 78-95.

Phillips, E. (1996). Life cycle of project team effectiveness, from creation to conclusion, as a function of dyadic team composition: A naturally occurring field simulation. Unpublished doctoral dissertation, University of Cincinnati.

Shamir, B., & Howell, J. M., (2000). The role of followers in the charismatic leadership process: susceptibility, social construction, and leader empowerment. Paper presented at the Annual Meeting of the Academy of Management, Toronto.

Sullivan, D. M., Mitchell, M. S., & Uhl-Bien, M. (2003). The new conduct of business: How LMX can help capitalize on cultural diversity. In G. B. Graen (Ed.), *Dealing with diversity, LMX leadership: The series* (Vol. 1), Greenwich, CT: Information Age Publishing.

Uhl-Bien, M., Graen, G. B., Scandura, T. A. (2000). Implications of leader-member exchange (LMX) for strategic human resource management systems: Relationships as social capital for competitive advantage. In G. Ferris (Ed.), *Research in Personnel and Human Resources Management,* (Vol. 18, pp. 137-185), Elsevier Science Press. Oxford, UK: JAI Press/Elsevier Science.

George B. Graen began his career at the University of Minnesota (Minneapolis), where he received his PhD in Organizational Psychology. In 1967 Graen joined the Psychology and Industrial Relations Faculty of the University of Illinois (Champaign). During his tenure at Illinois, he received a Distinguished International Exchange Professorship and spent 1972 at Keio University in Tokyo. He left the University of Illinois in 1977 to found the University of Cincinnati Center, continuing his research in Japan after receiving the first Johnson's Wax Fulbright Research Fellowship in 1984. For the last eight years he and his cross-cultural research and consulting team have been engaged in projects to understand joint venture businesses in China, Hong Kong and Taiwan and to help them build effective local "Third Cultures" to enhance their competitiveness. In

1997 he was named the Gene Brauns Endowed Chair Professor of International Management at the University of Louisiana.

He is a Fellow of the American Psychological Society and enjoys membership in other professional societies including the Academy of Management, the International Association of Applied Psychology, the American Association for the Advancement of Science, the Society of Organizational Behavior, and the Association of Japanese Business Studies (President, 1992-1995).

CHAPTER 2

LMX AND TEAMWORK
The Challenges and Opportunities of Diversity

Nathan J. Hiller and David V. Day

This chapter explores the effects of diversity on relationships between leaders and team members over time. At early stages of relationship development, surface-level similarities such as race, gender, and age, are particularly influential in setting the stage for high quality relationships. As leaders and team members spend more time in interaction, perceived similarity in personality, values, and attitudes (deep-level variables) become more important to the maintenance and development of mature exchange relationships. Yet while similarity produces cohesion, diversity is more often the norm in modern work teams. Implications for dealing with and extracting value from both surface- and deep-level diversity are considered in the context of both leader-member (LMX) and member-member (CWX, TMX) relationships.

A recent advertisement for a popular sports magazine (*Sports Illustrated*) pictured a football player sitting on the bench with the hands of two other players on each shoulder, comforting him. The man sitting on the bench was white, while the hands placed on each shoulder were dark. The caption read, "What counts most in creating a successful team is not how compatible its players are, but how they deal with incompatibility." Although the ad was primarily targeted to potential readers of the sports magazine, it was curiously placed within the pages of a respected business publication, and was probably also intended to be a broader commentary about the requirements for success of organizational teams with diverse members in any environment.

In the present chapter we explore the issues of teamwork and team performance in the face of diversity with a particular focus on the leader's role in the relationship-making process. We argue that diversity presents both challenges and opportunities. The ability of a leader to deal appropriately and successfully with diversity can affect the quality of relationships among team members, and has important implications for team processes and performance, as well as the ability of team members to successfully work together in the future.

DIVERSITY, DEMOGRAPHY, AND TEAMWORK

Before further exploration of diversity in the context of teams and teamwork, we first need to consider the question: "What is diversity?" It may seem initially somewhat banal to pose such a purportedly simple question; however, a closer examination reveals that a common definition or framework for answering this question is not so simple. There are countless ways in which individuals can differ from each other, though not all differences are equally relevant or important in all circumstances. In this chapter, we have chosen to characterize diversity according to a basic taxonomy consisting of two broad types: (a) surface-level, and (b) deep-level. *Surface-level diversity* denotes the existence of differences in readily observable characteristics such as race, gender, or age (Jackson, May, & Whitney, 1995). In common usage, the term diversity most often refers to differences in these readily observable characteristics; as such, it is superficial or surface-level focused. But individuals may also differ in important but less readily transparent ways such as in personality, values, and attitudes. These underlying differences can be classified as *deep-level diversity* (Jackson et al., 1995). Conceptualizing diversity according to these two broad types provides a potentially useful framework for understanding differences and their consequences.

Regardless of the type of diversity being considered, it should be recognized that diversity is an inherently relational term. Implicit in the study of diversity is the notion that there are referents from which people diverge. In most organizations in the United States, the de facto surface-level referent has been the Caucasian male (Nkomo, 1992). Thus, when an organization attempts to promote diversity, it usually takes the form of encouraging inclusion—or assimilation—of traditionally underrepresented groups (i.e., those other than white males). In other words, diversity can only be understood in relation to differences, rather than in absolute terms.

This relational demography approach is central to our discussion of diversity because it takes the focus off demography in isolation and focuses on the effects of demography in the context of an interpersonal system. We would thus expect that the effects of being Hispanic and female would vary depending on the gender and racial makeup of the rest of the group. Furthermore, the way that her African American male boss relates to her will also depend on the extent and ways in which she is seen as different from the rest of the group. This approach is particularly important for understanding the relationships between individuals in work teams. In the context of LMX, diversity, and teamwork, a relational demography approach to diversity would propose that the effects of gender diversity on leader-member exchange in work teams is likely to depend on the gender of the leader and the gender of the subordinate within the context of the gender of the rest of the team, rather than the "average" gender of the team (Tsui, Xin, & Egan, 1995). Indeed, an average approach is nonsensical when categories of diversity are discrete.

THE CHANGING WORKFORCE AND CHANGING NATURE OF WORK

The surface-level approach to diversity and, in particular the focus on relational demography, has been predominant in the organizational sciences. This research focus on surface-level diversity is not unexpected, because organizations are confronted with understanding the challenges and benefits of a demographically diverse workforce—a trend that is likely to continue. For example, it is projected that the Asian, Hispanic, and African American labor forces will grow by 44, 36, and 21 percent, respectively, in the period 2000-2010 (Bureau of Labor Statistics, 2001). These figures are much greater than the projected nine-percent growth for Caucasian workers. The workforce will also continue to comprise more women and older workers.

At the same time that demographic diversity is increasing in organizations, the workplace has been redesigned in ways that more fully use teams to accomplish core tasks. As opposed to a more rigid and hierarchical form of organizing, the growing use of teams requires individuals to be in close contact with one another and to work interdependently. To be successful, teams must do such things as integrate their skills and knowledge and coordinate activities and resources. Many of these tasks, however, seem to face additional psychological obstacles and become increasingly difficult when attempted in the context of diversity.

Surface-Level Diversity Effects

Although there is some variation in research results and interpretation, the general finding and collective wisdom among those who study intact organizational teams is that surface-level diversity negatively impacts team process and performance (e.g., Bettenhausen, 1991; Tsui & Gutek, 1999; Williams & O'Reilly, 1998). Milliken and Martins (1996) concluded that demographic diversity produces lowered identification with the team, lowered satisfaction, more formal communication, and less communication frequency within the group. In addition, they also suggested that demographic diversity produces lower social cohesion, which has been found to have a significant negative impact on team performance across a wide variety of settings (Gully, Devine, & Whitney, 1995). Those who are demographically different are also more likely to leave the team.

A logical question to be posed by a manager is whether anything can be done to mitigate these negative outcomes. One approach would be to actively control or limit diversity. Surprisingly, much of the research in team diversity has emphasized the impact of surface-level diversity, seemingly under the assumption that organizations could somehow manage demographic diversity within their teams. In certain situations, organizations may attempt to construct teams according to outward demographics, but this strategy is fraught with problems. In addition to ethical concerns, potential legal problems await organizations that attempt to construct and manage teams by controlling outward demographic characteristics.

A more fruitful (yet difficult) approach to preventing the negative consequences of surface-level diversity concerns how best to deal with existing diversity. In other words, if we start from the perspective that diversity is a fact of life in North American society, our focus begins to center more on ways in which leaders and team members can effectively "lead diversity" as opposed to merely managing it. Part of an increased understanding of effectively leading diversity may come through a better understanding of the underlying mechanisms of surface-level diversity. In other words, we need to move beyond the "black box" of demography (Lawrence, 1997) in order to understand the mechanisms of team and dyad processes and interactions.

One presumed mechanism through which surface-level diversity affects teams is the operation of similarity-attraction processes (Byrne, 1971) or homophily biases (McPherson & Smith-Lovin, 1987). Based on the fundamental principles from the social identity literature (Tajfel, 1982), people are attracted to and prefer to affiliate with members of their own identity groups—those with similar values, attitudes, and personality—than with members of other groups. Similar people reinforce core values as well as a sense of identity in ourselves, and as such, we prefer to affiliate with them. Taking the similarity-attraction paradigm into the context of teams, members will generally affiliate with each other and as a group to the extent that they perceive themselves to be similar. When teams are in early stages of formation, however, members don't have accurate knowledge of other members' underlying values, attitudes, and personality, so they use surface-level variables as proxies for the underlying differences.

Certainly, surface-level variables are associated with some underlying differences. For example, much of the data supporting the Upper Echelons Perspective of strategic management has successfully relied on these proxies (see Hambrick & Mason, 1984 for a primer on this perspective). However, the link between surface-level diversity (race, gender, and age) and deep-level diversity (values, attitudes, and personality) is undoubtedly less than perfect and can lead to unfair treatment, miscommunication, and negative team-level outcomes.

THE IMPORTANCE OF DEEP-LEVEL DIVERSITY

As mentioned earlier in this chapter, deep-level diversity denotes the presence of differences in values, personalities, and attitudes between individuals or within a team. Although surface-level diversity has received considerably more attention in both academic and non-academic circles, the importance of *deep-level diversity* is beginning to be explored (e.g., Harrison, Price, & Bell, 1998). Evidence suggests that surface-level diversity matters less, whereas deep-level diversity matters more, as team members have greater opportunities to interact. Thus, there is a demonstrated longitudinal effect such that time interacts with diversity type in predicting group process and performance outcomes.

The diminishing effects of surface-level diversity on teamwork have been demonstrated in several recent studies. In a study of 45 teams from electronics divisions of three major corporations, Pelled, Eisenhardt, and Xin (1999) found that the effects of surface-level diversity (age) on emotional conflict diminished as a function of team longevity. Similarly, Chatman and Flynn (2001) found that demographic homogeneity (race and gender) was less predictive of team cooperation as team members interacted with each other. At the same time that the effects of surface-level diversity diminish over time, the effects of deep-level diversity appear to become more potent. In a study of 144 student project teams, Harrison, Price, Gavin, and Florey (2002) found that surface-level diversity negatively affected early cohesion in the team. Over the course of a semester working together, surface-level diversity became less predictive, whereas *actual* deep-level diversity (measured by conscientiousness, task meaningfulness, and outcome importance) and *perceptions* of deep-level diversity became increasingly important to team social cohesion and performance. This suggests that as team members interact, attributions about underlying differences based on race, gender, and age are likely to be minimized; however, the underlying differences in terms of personality, values, and attitudes are likely to have an increasingly negative effect on team cohesion and performance. Similarly, Harrison et al. (1998) found that the effects of surface-level diversity on group cohesion decreased in importance as group members engaged in meaningful interactions across time. In comparison, the effects of deep-level diversity were strengthened over time.

We feel that the basic processes that underlie the effects of diversity over time may also apply to LMX. Surface-level diversity is likely to be more important in the early stages of relationship development and become decreasingly important over time, while deep-level diversity is likely to become increasingly important to the relationship. But the effects of diversity are not deterministic; the leader, as a powerful actor in the relationship-making process, can act in deliberate ways to ensure that team functioning is maximized in the face of diversity, especially deep-level diversity.

LEADER-MEMBER EXCHANGE (LMX)

A primary focus of LMX is on the dyadic exchange that occurs between a leader and a follower. These relationships have generally been found to develop over time after a series of relationship assessments, offers, and tests. The relationship-making approach that is adopted by LMX researchers suggests that a high-quality relationship develops across three distinct stages (Graen & Uhl-Bien, 1995). At any point during this progression, if either the leader or the follower fail to meet certain conditions (described below), the relationship will be unlikely to mature.

The first of these stages is the *stranger* stage. At this stage, the relationship is characterized by contractual transactions; the leader generally tells the subordinate the tasks they want accomplished, and subordinates generally meet the minimum requirements of their job. In this stage, the leader and follower are "sizing each other up" to determine whether it is worth the risk to attempt to establish an improved working relationship.

In order for the relationship to progress to the *acquaintance* stage, a symbolic or literal offer to move the leadership-making relationship to the next level must be made. Whereas either the leader or the subordinate may make an offer, it is typically a leader's role to initiate such an offer (Graen & Uhl-Bien, 1995). Once the relationship has progressed to this stage, leaders and followers may begin to share greater information and resources on a personal and professional level (Graen & Wakabayashi, 1994). At this second stage, the process is not entirely transactional, but an equitable exchange is expected within a reasonable time frame. Polite disagreement is allowed, and roles become more widely negotiated (Fairhurst, 1993). At this point, trust is being tested.

If that trust develops, the relationship may progress to the *mature partnership* stage. In this stage, simple management is now totally replaced by a transformational relationship between the follower and the leader. The relationship includes both behavioral and emotional exchanges and is characterized by loyalty, support, mutual obligation, and respect (Graen & Uhl-Bien, 1995). At this third stage, both the leader and follower share similar mental models and vocabulary (Fairhurst, 1993), nonroutine problem solving, and often convergence of values. In a meta-analysis of the empirical LMX literature, Gerstner and Day (1997) found support for many of these descriptions surrounding high quality exchanges. They reported significant effect sizes between relationship quality and satisfaction, commitment, role conflict, role clarity, and turnover intentions. Given the description of high quality leader-member exchanges, it is probably also not surprising that relationship quality as measured from both the leaders' and the followers' perspectives were significantly related to job performance.

Surface- and Deep-Level Diversity in LMX Relationships

In order for mature relationships to develop, the preliminary perceptions and testing that occurs in the initial stages of the relationship must be successful. An offer must be made by one of the parties to move the relationship to a higher level of maturity. Although there is no evidence that leader or member demographic characteristics show any consistent patterns with LMX when considered alone, Gerstner and Day (1997) pointed out that relational demography might yield larger effects. Based on results from the teams literature, as well as social categorization processes, it seems likely that relational demography influences leader-member exchange relationships, particularly early in the relationship. In other words, at the initial appraisal stage of LMX development, when the dyad members are strangers, the influence of surface-level diversity is likely to be of increased importance. Both the leader and the member are likely to make rough appraisals of underlying similarity. Given that members do not have the underlying information about values, attitude, and belief congruence at this stage, they are likely to infer these characteristics based on similarity in observable, or surface-level characteristics. If there is perceived congruence, the leader and member will then experience mutual liking (based on the similarity-attraction paradigm), allowing the relationship to move forward (e.g., Liden, Wayne, & Stillwell, 1993; Phillips & Bedeian, 1994) to the acquaintance stage, where a better idea of personality, values, and attitudes (deep-level diversity) develops. If there is perceived deep-level congruence at the acquaintance stage, then the relationship is more likely to develop into the mature stage.

Based on the notion of time as an important consideration in the relationship between diversity (surface- and deep-level) and team outcomes, we would expect surface-level diversity to become decreasingly important in the LMX relationship as time passes. Leaders and followers can get beyond demographic differences, as long as there is congruence in basic values and beliefs. As the leader and follower collaborate, an initially low-quality exchange relationship has the potential to turn into a high-quality relationship when there is values congruence. In the long-term, it would therefore be expected that LMX relationship quality would be best predicted by underlying personality, values, and belief similarity. However, a low-quality relationship early on may have long-term effects. Research is needed to better understand the timing of these proposed effects (Mitchell & James, 2001), especially with regard to the effects of leader-member diversity and changes in relationship quality over time.

If members of the dyad do not initially perceive congruence, the offer to move the relationship to a more developed stage will not be made or readily accepted. This suggests, then, that surface-level diversity in the dyad may have a dangerous consequence in LMX relationships by preventing the relationship from moving forward because of perceived deep-level dissimilarity. If the relationship stalls, and true attitude, belief, and value congruence is not fully explored, then a potentially high-quality exchange relationship may be lost based on perceived incongruence. This may be why expectations formed in the first five days of leader-member relationships predicted LMX after six weeks (Liden et al., 1993). If a demographically different team member withdraws as she sees the leader developing mature or high-quality relationships with other team members, engagement with the group as well as her individual performance are likely to be negatively affected. In turn, this deterioration in relationships and performance lends credence to the perception of lower competence, thus further decreasing the likelihood of being able to negotiate a high quality relationship with the leader. Although collaboration and contact can decrease the importance of surface-level diversity, if a given individual withdraws and the interdependence of the team is low, collaboration (which mitigates the negative effects of surface-level diversity) may not occur.

The benefits of high quality LMX suggests that managers should strive to provide all employees with the opportunity to construct high quality LMX exchanges by offering to develop partnerships with each subordinate (Graen & Uhl-Bien, 1995). Without a concerted effort, however, surface-level diversity may present a psychological obstacle to an offer being made. As a result, high-quality LMX relationships might not develop and it is likely that individual, team, and even organizational performance will suffer.

COWORKER EXCHANGE (CWX)

Although LMX is often considered a theory of the relationships between leader and subordinate, it also holds implications for the relationship-making processes that can occur between peers (Graen & Uhl-Bien, 1995). In organizational environments where individuals work together closely (such as teams), peer exchanges may be particularly important to team functioning and perhaps even for formal leadership effectiveness. In a study of 110 coworker dyads, Sherony and Green (2002) found that relationship quality between two coworkers (CWX) was predicted by their LMX quality. In other words, when two peers have good relationships with their appointed leader (LMX), they are likely to have good relationships with each other (CWX). A correlational design prevented directionality from being assessed, though it is probably fair to say that there are reciprocal relationships between LMX and CWX. If so, then there are several potentially important implications from this study.

Given that coworker relationship quality is predicted by the quality of the team members' relationship with their leader (Sherony & Green, 2002), an important role for the formal leader is to promote team integration through fostering high quality CWX. If an individual member does not have a high-quality LMX, then he is more likely to be socially isolated (i.e., relegated to the out-group) among his or her peers. If those members who have high quality LMX integrate successfully, but those who have low quality LMX do not, then team cohesion and performance are likely to suffer. Thus, not only are there performance implications at the individual level when there are low quality LMX relationships (as indicated by much of the extant LMX literature), these impoverished relationships are likely to also affect coworker exchanges, team integration, and ultimately, team performance. This provides yet another reason for leaders to promote high quality LMX relationships with all team members (e.g., Graen, Novak, & Sommerkamp, 1982).

There may also be an effect in which CWX affects LMX. For example, if an individual member has low quality LMX but has a high quality CWX with a member who is in the in-group, a state of tension will exist in the relationship network until the relationships become balanced (Heider, 1958). One way this imbalance can be reduced is through the high quality LMX member acting as an advocate for the low quality LMX member. For example, either through verbal persuasion or through observation of the low quality LMX members' successful interactions with peers, the leader may come to trust and accept a member who previously had a low-quality exchange. This leads to the second implication. It might be possible for coworkers to build a more cohesive and high quality exchange team by promoting high quality LMX with out-group members. A third implication was offered by Sherony and Green (2002), who suggested that the leader may be able to promote high quality LMX with all members by promoting strong CWX relationships. Clearly, more empirical work needs to be done to determine the most effective ways in which both CWX and LMX can be enhanced and what the implications of each are for team functioning and performance. Nonetheless, the possibilities are intriguing.

One of the advantages of further examining the relationship between CWX and LMX may be in better understanding shared leadership, or the extent to which team members share in leadership roles and tasks (Pearce & Conger, 2003). A major expectation of work teams in organizations, particularly those that are semiautonomous or self-managing, is that team members engage in tasks and roles that had previously been considered the sole territory of a formal leader. For example, mentoring and development, as well as planning and organizing, may be activities that are expected of regular team members based on an assumption that widely engaging in these shared leadership tasks is related to enhanced team performance. But are teams that engage in shared leadership more effective? Early evidence suggests that this is the case. In a recent study, Hiller, Day, and Vance (2003) found that the extent to which team members engage in the sharing of leadership tasks is an important predictor of supervisor ratings of team effectiveness. The sharing of leadership roles, however, is not likely to automatically occur. In order for individuals to engage in coordinating leadership tasks, it is likely that team members need a sense of mutual trust, cooperation, and cohesion that characterize high quality exchanges. In this way, shared leadership is almost certain to require high quality exchanges between team members (CWX) in order for shared leadership to be possible. The implications of formal leader-member exchanges (LMX) to the sharing of leadership tasks between team members is also likely to be highly important, and the interaction of LMX and CWX in producing shared leadership is an interesting avenue for future research.

TEAM-MEMBER EXCHANGE (TMX)

In addition to leader-member (LMX) and member-member (CWX) relationships, an individual's perception of the team's relationship as a whole is also important. The measure of team-member exchange (TMX) quality, developed by Seers (1989), consists of 34 items with team-level referents. The items are organized into three subscales:

a. quality of working relationships,
b. effectiveness of team meetings, and
c. team cohesiveness.

In the original study, data from a sample of blue-collar industrial workers indicated that TMX was related to individual job satisfaction incremental to what was predicted by LMX. TMX was also directly related to supervisor ratings of individual job performance and as an interaction with peer motivation. In short, Seer's work demonstrates that a member's exchange quality with the aggregate peer group is a viable construct in studying work teams.

Dose (1999) extended the initial work of Seers (1989) in examining the effects of work values similarity on TMX and LMX. Her results indicated that perceived values similarity was related to LMX in the expected (positive) direction, although actual values similarity was unrelated to LMX. Conversely, actual similarity was positively related to TMX (team cohesiveness and meeting effectiveness subscales) but perceived values similarity was unrelated to TMX. Although these results are far from conclusive, they suggest that actual deep-level diversity (i.e., differences in work values) is related to TMX quality. In the only published study of the effects of surface-level factors on TMX, Baugh and Graen (1997) hypothesized that sex and race differences would result in lower TMX perceptions in cross-functional teams; however, this hypothesis was not supported.

The relationship quality that one has with the team as a whole appears to be a legitimate and important concern. In addition, TMX appears to be different from relationships negotiated with individual co-workers (CWX) or the formal leader (LMX). It is a reasonable conclusion that diversity factors likely will affect the quality of TMX, but the timing of measurement remains a critical and largely unexamined concern. Extrapolating from research conducted by Harrison and colleagues (Harrison et al., 1998, 2002), as well as the findings of Dose (1999), it would be expected that surface-level diversity would pose more of an obstacle to developing high-quality TMX early in a group's history, but deep-level diversity would become a greater concern over time.

A relevant issue that has not been investigated to date concerns whether those team members who are diverse in terms of demography (surface) or values (deep) perceive TMX quality to be poorer than those who are similar to the rest of the team. It is possible that having a diverse team member has a greater effect on others' ratings of TMX than it has on the TMX ratings of the different member. Previous research on relational demography demonstrated that women and minorities were generally unaffected by their demographic status in their work units, but whites and men showed larger negative effects for increased unit diversity (Tsui, Egan, & O'Reilly, 1992). From these results, it would be a mistake to assume that the member who is different always feels the effects of diversity in a team.

TEAMWORK BENEFITS OF DIVERSITY

Up to this point, we have focused on the negative implications of diversity in LMX and teamwork. However, in certain cases, diversity may be beneficial. In the context of teamwork, researchers have noted that when a team task is heavily dependent on information-processing and decision-making, diversity in knowledge, skills, and abilities may be beneficial (Williams & O'Reilly, 1998). To the extent that low-quality LMX (or CWX) is a reflection of heterogeneity in team members' knowledge, information, networks, skills, and abilities, then, low quality exchanges may have some specific benefits. As a notable example, the existence of a few out-group members may encourage a wider network of loose affiliations outside the team that may be absent in high quality exchanges. Members engaged in high quality exchanges (particularly in the mature relationship stage) are potentially more likely to have a limited number of strong relationships with other in-group members. But a wide network of affiliations may be beneficial.

In his groundbreaking research on social networks, Grannovetter (1973) assessed the importance of loose relationships, or weak ties, in helping people find jobs. Surprisingly, it was these loose relationships and affiliations that were more predictive of success in a job search than were strong ties with a few individuals. An extension to this idea was provided by Burt's (1992) structural hole hypothesis. He explicated the importance of non-redundant relationships in creating unique opportunities for access to timely information.

In the domain of teamwork, diverse members (both surface- and deep-level) would be expected to have different social networks as a function of being less likely to be in the leader's in-group. One of the few benefits of being in the out-group may be that it forces members to forge relationships with others in the organization. Thus, they would likely have access to information and network contacts that other team members do not have. In other words, individual diversity may promote diverse networks at an aggregate level. These networks and information sources may be of considerable value to the team in better understanding team threats and opportunities because they provide for "fresh" or non-redundant information. Access to outside information and networks may be a partial explanation why a number of studies have found positive outcomes as the result of functional background and team tenure diversity within a team (e.g., Hambrick, Cho, & Chen, 1996; Pelled, Eisenhardt, & Xin, 1997). However, a challenge still remains as to how the rest of the team would access the information gathered by an out-group member. One possibility might be through high-quality CWX with at least one member of the leader's in-group.

It was recently proposed that individuals who are different in terms of self-monitoring personality might have unique network advantages by virtue of the different kinds of resources that each personality type brings to a relationship (Day & Kilduff, 2003).

Self-monitoring refers to individual differences in the extent that people monitor the public appearances of self that the display in social settings, and in creating and managing their interpersonal relationships (Snyder, 1987). At the core of the construct are motive differences in how and why high and low self-monitors create and manage their relationships. By extension, social networks may vary systematically between high and low self-monitoring individuals. High self-monitors are expected to have greater access to informational resources through their tendency to occupy more advantageous positions in social networks (Mehra, Kilduff, & Brass, 2001), which provides them with novel, divergent, and nonredundant information (Brass & Krackhardt, 1999). Despite the informational advantages of their networks, high self-monitors are more likely to form low-commitment ties. As a result, their respective levels of psychosocial support are not as strong as low self-monitors. Day and Kilduff (2003) argued that the best type of network tie in terms of enhancing both the quality of information as well as psychological and emotional support might be between a high and low self-monitor. In this manner, those dyads or broader social networks with diverse ties (e.g., high and low self-monitor) might be more adaptive than ties among homogenous individuals in terms of self-monitoring.

Ironically, at the same time that diverse members (who are likely in the out-group) provide a potential benefit to teams, their information and resources are more difficult for the team to extract and utilize because there is less communication and trust between out-group members and the core in-group of the team. This suggests that there is likely to be a delicate balance for the leader and team members—stay cohesive enough and engage in high quality exchanges, but keep enough distance so that information and social networks are not totally overlapping. Exactly where the optimal balance lies is an important topic for future research consideration.

TACKLING DEEP-LEVEL DIVERSITY

Deep-level diversity is important in predicting team cohesion and LMX relationships in the longer term, but practitioners are confronted with devising immediate prescriptions for successfully dealing with existing deep-level diversity in teams. One option is to do nothing. The long-term implication of this non-action would be that high quality LMX relationships would more likely develop with similar members, whereas low-quality relationships would characterize those who are different from the leader in personality, values, and attitudes. This may have the benefit of reducing some of the burden that a leader would feel if they were expected to develop high-quality relationships with all team members (Liden, Sparrowe, & Wayne, 1997).

Another option, which is a variation of the first, recognizes that creating and maintaining high quality relationships with all team members is impractical because a leader's personal resources are too scarce. This second possibility goes further in suggesting that the formal leader should select the most competent and trustworthy subordinates and develop high quality relationships with them. In this way the leader could maximize the relational and social capital benefits within the constraints of limited personal resources. In this view, maximal team performance could be achieved when the leader uses deliberate discretion in choosing to construct high quality relationships. However, when team members are engaged in moderately or highly interdependent tasks that require the contribution of all members, this strategy is likely to fail. That is, if a leader purposefully selects some people to be in the in-group and lets others be in the out-group, this would likely cause poor team cohesion. As a result of poor cohesion, the team would be less effective. Related to this is the idea that out-group members are not likely to perform as well as in-group members (Gersnter & Day, 1997) and if the task is interdependent such that the team must rely on all members—including out-group members—to do a good job, then the strategy of purposefully allowing some people to be in the out-group is not likely to be effective.

Although both surface- and deep-level diversity often lead to process loss and difficulties in terms of team integration and cohesion, both types of diversity need to be acknowledged and formally encouraged. Organizations and teams have a tendency to drive out diversity over time (Schneider, Goldstein, & Smith, 1995), which is a tendency that needs to be explicitly counteracted. A first step might be in acknowledging that surface-level diversity can be a distinct competitive advantage to teams and organizations (Cox, 1993), and more should be done to leverage the advantages that have been associated with diversity. For example, Cox proposed five areas in which diversity can enhance organizational performance, including:

a. attracting and retaining talent,
b. enhanced marketing efforts,
c. better creativity and innovation,
d. superior problem solving, and
e. greater organizational flexibility.

Effective team performance requires effective team processes (e.g., communication, cohesion, and trust), which is enhanced when members are fully developed in mature relationships. But getting to this mature stage is difficult when a team is diverse. The leader, as a key mechanism in team functioning, must seek to develop high-quality exchanges with all team members, and particularly those who are most diverse. By developing high-quality exchanges, the leader and team can tap into a wider array of ideas, backgrounds, personalities, and relationships with outside members without the team becoming conflicted or otherwise falling apart. Leveraging the competitive advantages associated with diversity can enhance team functioning, but it will not necessarily be easy.

At the same time that the development of leader-member relationships are important, teamwork will be enhanced when exchanges among team members develop into partnerships. The role of the leader is fundamental in ensuring that conditions encourage the development of effective team and co-workers exchange relationships. However, this task is difficult given the psychological challenges associated with both surface- and deep-level diversity.

LMX DEVELOPMENT INITIATIVES FOR TEAMS

A successful approach to developing high quality leader-member, coworker, and team-member exchanges should consider multiple levels of analysis. Dyadic relationships and teams do not exist in a vacuum, and an appropriate consideration of ways that LMX and teamwork can be enhanced in the face of diversity should be approached systemically. What can organizations, leaders and team members do to enhance the advantages and minimize the disadvantages of diversity? The following are specific recommendations for how leaders, team members, and organizations can act to promote the development of high quality exchanges with leaders, coworkers, and teams.

Leader

- Seek to develop high quality LMX with all members while also extracting value from diverse perspectives, networks, information, and expertise. There are demonstrated benefits of high quality exchanges at the individual level (Gerstner & Day, 1997), but there are typically members within a team who do not have a fully developed exchange relationship with the leader (e.g., Graen, et al., 1982; Rosse & Kraut, 1983). This suggests that the leader has a significant opportunity to encourage more mature relationships with some team members, particularly those who are different from the leader. One way this can occur is through the display of respectful behaviors, which will foster a relationship of low immediacy, low equivalence, and low self-interest (Liden et al., 1997).

    Another way to encourage supportive, trusting, and challenging relationships is through a common approach toward handling diversity issues. Thomas (1993), in a study of 22 cross-race mentor-protégé relationships, found that higher-quality relationships developed when both members of the dyad agreed on an approach to deal with racial issues at work, regardless of whether the approach was one of open discussion or suppression. In other words, an open discussion of racial diversity (or other surface-level diversity issues) is not a prerequisite for high-quality relationships in diverse dyads, but agreement about preferences to discuss racial issues is. The leader, as the more powerful actor in the relationship, needs to delicately explore the preferences of the subordinate. Developing high quality relationships will make it easier for the leader and team member to extract value from divergent perspectives, networks, information, and expertise.
- Promote high-quality CWX by creating an open and non-hostile atmosphere where team members can be free to ask for help and admit mistakes. This type of open atmosphere, in which group members feel safe to take interpersonal risks with each other, has been termed psychological safety (Edmondson, 1999). In early stages of team development, promote interaction and cooperation so that team members

can move beyond the restraining effects of surface-level diversity (Williams & O'Reilly, 1998).
- Allow task conflict, but deal quickly in managing relationship conflict that is the result of surface- or deep-level diversity. Task conflict is a perception of disagreement among group members about the content of their decisions and involves differences in viewpoints, ideas, and opinions, while relationship conflict is a perception of interpersonal incompatibility and includes tension, annoyance, and animosity (Jehn, 1995). Research has shown that task conflict can lead to benefits such as better decision-making; however, relationship conflict has primarily negative effects such as lowered group satisfaction and commitment, reduced information processing abilities, and antagonistic attributions about team members' behaviors (Simons & Peterson, 2000). One of the dangers of task conflict, however, is that it could be misinterpreted as relationship conflict (see Simons & Peterson, 2000).
- Regardless of the type of conflict, encourage a cooperative approach to conflict that emphasizes trust. Seeing conflict as a win-lose situation can be debilitating for a team, but approaching conflict with a collaborative and trusting approach may allow conflict to be beneficial (Alper, Tjosvold, & Law, 2000; Jehn & Mannix, 2001; Lovelace, Shapiro, & Weingart, 2001; Simons & Peterson, 2000). A team-level cooperative approach to conflict depends largely on the example that the leader sets in dealing with conflict. All of the kinds of exchange relationships (LMX, CWX, and TMX) should be enhanced when the team environment is characterized by mutual trust and respect, and if the goal of the leader and members is to find mutually beneficial solutions to problems and conflict.
- Be patient. High-quality relationships in the face of diversity will take more time than under conditions of homogeneity. In specific situations where there is more likely to be endemic *a priori* mistrust based on history (such as may be the case with a lone African-American employee in a team of white employees), the relationship may have an even longer and rockier developmental trajectory. Leaders may need to vary the way in which they offer a developmental relationship and may need to engage in repeated attempts in order to establish trust that goes along with a high-quality relationship.

Team Members

- Strive for high quality relationships among all members of the team. This is especially important when LMX quality is low. In-group team members who perceive that another team member is in the out-group should purposefully and intentionally seek to develop a high quality member-member exchange relationship with the out-group member. In addition to enhancing team effectiveness by developing a mature relationship with another team member, this may have the added benefit of promoting a better relationship with the leader and the out-group member. Promoting high quality coworker exchanges may be particularly beneficial in cases where the member does not accept an offer of a mature relationship from the leader.

Unit or Organization Level

- Ensure that the challenges associated with diversity are acknowledged by having explicit policies about behavior toward demographically diverse others. More important is to initiate dialogue around these diversity challenges. Although overt racism has decreased over the last number of decades, the bias toward similar others can be a strong factor in decisions and actions, even among individuals who do not report or believe they hold racist views. In other words, race-based decisions are widespread. This form of racism, termed aversive racism (part of modern racism theory, Gaertner & Dovidio, 1986) is particularly problematic because it is not easily detected or remedied (Dovidio, 2001). The effects of aversive racism are most likely to be present in ambiguous situations where there are several reasonable factors involved in the decision (other than race), which allows the actor to attribute their action to something other than race. For example, a leader may attribute their failure to develop a high quality relationship with a subordinate to differences in work ethic, work performance, or personality differences, but in actuality race may have been a critical factor. This creeping form of racism is perhaps the biggest challenge to organizations and individuals,

because the actors are often unaware of the extent of their bias.
- Although organizations may often be tempted to believe that mere contact with those of other races may reduce prejudice, there is a small body of literature in the organizational context that suggests contact alone is not likely to improve attitudes toward those of a different race. Indeed, increased contact may promote increasingly negative attitudes (Brief, Burrows, Dietz, Umphress, Butz, & Scholten, 2003). This suggests that organizations will need to be proactive in attempting to deal with racist attitudes and that high quality LMX relationships will require active management beyond the simple passage of time.
- Organizations need to minimize negative exchanges based on race and may consider developing training programs to help leaders and followers monitor their beliefs and actions (see Brief & Barsky, 2000), and strive to promote an inclusive culture rather than one based on highly defined in- and out-groups (Williams & O'Reilly, 1998). In addition, the organization may promote strong employee identification with the organization (Tushman & O'Reilly, 1996) by having a superordinate culture. A strong example of this can be found in the US Army, where members often state, "there is no color but green," indicating that racial differences are irrelevant in the strong Army culture. A more moderate approach may seek to acknowledge and deal constructively with differences by accepting and respecting differences, while at the same time creating a third culture for leadership-making (Graen & Wakabayashi, 1994).
- Train leaders on how to develop high-quality exchanges with all team members. In a rare longitudinal field experiment that trained supervisors in the underlying skills needed to develop high-quality exchanges with followers, it was found that LMX training was associated with significant gains in the satisfaction and productivity of followers (Graen et al., 1982). The training in that study consisted of an overview of the LMX model, active listening skill training, exchanging mutual expectations, exchanging resources, and practicing one-on-one sessions. More research is needed to evaluate the beneficial effects of LMX training, but the preliminary evidence suggests that this is a process that could improve work relationships between leaders and followers, while also building team satisfaction and

productivity. Further, training of team members to have high-quality relationships with each other may be an additional avenue for promoting CWX and TMX in the context of diversity.

CONCLUSIONS AND IMPLICATIONS

The primary purpose of the present chapter was to explore the intersection of three substantial topics that have collided in modern-day work teams: LMX, diversity, and teamwork. In undertaking this task, some of the nuances of each of the separate literatures may have been omitted primarily because we wanted to bring the overlap among these areas to the foreground. What we chose to focus on were the main findings of each of the literatures, particularly as they relate to the conceptual whole of LMX in diverse work teams. There is undoubtedly value added in applying LMX to understanding diverse work teams, both practically and academically, yet there remain some significant unanswered questions.

First, the benefit of a convergence of values that occurs in mature LMX relationships is unknown when applied to the team setting. Graen and Uhl-Bien (1995), for example, note that leader and member values tend to converge in mature relationships, which has been supported in recent studies (e.g., Ashkanasy & O'Connor, 1997; Dose, 1999). But is values congruence a necessary (but insufficient) condition for a mature relationship to develop? Conversely, is it possible to have a mature, high-quality exchange when the values of a leader and follower are not aligned? Dose (1999) found that perceived similarity in the Protestant work ethic between leaders and members was predictive of LMX quality, but actual values similarity was unrelated to LMX. Research is needed to determine the importance of value diversity and how differences can be overcome to create mature LMX relationships.

Second, while there is an increased level of interest in co-worker and team-member exchanges, there is still much to be understood about the dynamics and how they relate to leader-member exchanges. The interactions are likely to be complex and not easily studied, though a better understanding of the dynamics of the entire team is important in developing actionable suggestions.

Third, the framework of surface- and deep-level diversity should be subject to additional scrutiny. We could begin by paying particular attention to deep-level variables such as work and non-work values, personality variables such as core self-evaluations, self-monitoring, and the Big Five, as well as attitudes such as importance of success or task meaningfulness. But we should also consider other variables that may not easily fit into the surface/deep distinction. Although the surface/deep framework is beneficial in its simplicity, we are confronted with the difficulty of categorizing all sorts of possible differences that may be important to understanding LMX and teamwork. Some research has examined team diversity from a framework of differences in knowledge, skills, and abilities (KSA) (e.g., O'Connell, Doverspike, Cober, & Philips, 2001), or has used proxies for KSA diversity such as organizational tenure and functional background diversity (e.g., Hambrick, Cho, & Chen, 1996; Goodman & Garber, 1988). A question to consider is whether KSA diversity operates at a deep or surface level? In some senses, KSA diversity could be considered as a type of deep-level diversity in that it is not immediately salient and does not invoke strong stereotypes such as differences in race, gender, and age. At the same time, however, KSA diversity is focused on differences in what members know and can do, rather than who they are as people, and is thus not synonymous with common conceptualizations of deep-level diversity. Perhaps KSA diversity is neither at the surface nor deep-level, but rather of an intermediate type between the surface and deep poles of a diversity continuum. If so, this holds implications for the temporal effects of diversity on LMX, CWX, and TMX processes and outcomes that were discussed in this chapter. Specifically, the negative effects of KSA diversity should be most potent at intermediate time periods in the relationship process.

The effect of KSA diversity is also likely to be much more task-dependent than surface- or deep-level diversity. In complex problem solving teams, KSA diversity is likely to be beneficial, but most teams operate under less cognitively complex conditions and thus the effects of KSA diversity may be of reduced importance. In other cases, KSA variables may be very salient and may act almost like surface-level variables. For example, a team consisting of accredited financial analysts may be slow to develop a high-quality relationship with a team member who brings needed expertise but is not an accredited analyst. Research is needed that examines these propositions empirically.

A careful examination of potential interactions between surface-, deep-, and intermediate- level diversity variables would also contribute to a more complete understanding of the relationship development process over time. For example, a lone woman in a team of men might be more wary of forming trusting, high-quality relationships early on with coworkers and her supervisor; and the other group members may similarly be wary of forming a trusting, high-quality relationship. The extent to which she engages in high-quality exchanges, however, may be moderated by functional background similarity (an intermediate-level variable). If she and several other team members are electricians, the gender effects may be significantly muted. Progress toward understanding the intricacies of the relationship-making process will significantly enhance our ability to intervene and create conditions for high-quality relationships.

In conclusion, we have attempted to summarize a simple organizing framework for addressing the effects of diversity on LMX and teamwork by borrowing the concepts of surface- and deep-level diversity. Although the effects of individual differences on LMX process are poorly understood (Liden et al., 1997), we argue that surface-level similarity is particularly important in the formation of high quality relationships early on. As team members have a chance to interact, deep-level similarity becomes increasingly important in predicting relationship quality and, ultimately, team performance. Very few teams select individuals based on their similarity (surface- or deep-level), and there are good reasons for this (e.g., legal, ethical, social). Nonetheless, given the realities of increasing diversity in modern organizations as well as the potential benefits of diversity that were summarized in the present chapter, a proactive approach to harnessing and leading differences needs to be established. Organizations, leaders, and team members need to actively engage in the promotion of high quality relationships between leaders and members, coworkers, and teams while recognizing the additional challenges that are presented by surface- and deep-level diversity factors.

REFERENCES

Alper, S., Tjosvold, D., & Law, K. S. (2000). Conflict management, efficacy, and performance in organizational teams. *Personnel Psychology, 53,* 625-642.

Ashkanasy, N. M., & O'Connor, C. (1997). Value congruence in leader-member exchange. *Journal of Social Psychology, 137,* 647-662.

Baugh, S. G., & Graen, G. B. (1997). Effects of team gender and racial composition on perceptions of team performance in cross-functional teams. *Group and Organization Management, 22,* 366-383.

Bettenhausen, K. L. (1991). Five years of group research: What we have learned and what needs to be addressed. *Journal of Management, 17,* 345-381.

Brass, D. J., & Krackhardt, D. (1999). The social capital of twenty-first century leaders. In J. G. Hunt, G. E. Dodge, & L. Wong (Eds.), *Out-of-the-box leadership: Transforming the twenty-first-century army and other top-performing organizations* (pp. 179-194). Stamford, CT: JAI.

Brief, A. P., & Barsky, A. (2000). Establishing a climate for diversity: The inhibition of prejudiced reactions in the workplace. *Research in Personnel and Human Resources Management, 19,* 91-129.

Brief, A. P., Burrows, J. W., Dietz, J., Umphress, E., Butz, R. M., & Scholten, L. (2003). Communities matter: The impact of racial demographics in organizations. Unpublished manuscript.

Bureau of Labor Statistics (2001). ftp://ftp.bls.gov/pub/news.release/History/ecopro.12032001.news

Burt, R. S. (1992). *Structural holes: The social structure of competition.* Cambridge, MA: Harvard.

Byrne, D. (1971). *The attraction paradigm.* New York: Academic Press.

Chatman, J. A., & Flynn, F. J. (2001). The influence of demographic heterogeneity on the emergence and consequences of cooperative norms in work teams. *Academy of Management Journal, 44,* 956-974.

Cox, T. (1993). *Cultural diversity in organizations: Theory, research, & practice.* San Francisco, CA: Berrett-Koehler.

Day, D. V., & Kilduff, M. (2003). Self-monitoring personality and work relationships: Individual differences in social networks. In M. R. Barrick & A. M. Ryan (Eds.), *Personality and work: Reconsidering the role of personality in organizations* (pp. 205-228). San Francisco: Jossey-Bass.

Dose, J. (1999). The relationship between work values similarity and team-member and leader-member exchange relationships. *Group Dynamics: Theory, Research, and Practice, 3,* 20-32.

Dovidio, J. F. (2001). On the nature of contemporary prejudice: The third wave. *Journal of Social Issues, 57,* 829-849.

Edmondson, A. (1999). Psychological safety and learning behavior in work teams. *Administrative Science Quarterly, 44,* 350-383.

Fairhurst, G. T. (1993). The leader-member exchange patterns of women leaders in industry: A discourse analysis. *Communication Monograph, 60,* 321-351.

Gaertner, S. L., & Dovidio, J. F. (1986). The aversive form of racism. In J. F. Dovidio & S. L. Gaertner (Eds.), *Prejudice, discrimination, and racism* (pp. 61-89). San Diego, CA: Academic Press.

Gerstner, C. R. & Day, D. V. (1997). Meta-analytic review of leader-member exchange theory: Correlates and construct issues. *Journal of Applied Psychology, 82*, 827-844.

Goodman, P., & Garber, S. (1988). Absenteeism and accidents in a dangerous environment: Empirical analysis of underground coal mines. *Journal of Applied Psychology, 73*, 81-86.

Graen, G. B., Novak, M., & Sommerkamp, P. (1982). The effects of leader-member exchange and job design on productivity and satisfaction: Testing a dual attachment model. *Organizational Behavior and Human Performance, 30,* 109-131.

Graen, G. B., & Uhl-Bien, M. (1995). Relationship-based approach to leadership: Development of leader-member exchange (LMX) theory of leadership over 25 years: Applying a multi-level multi-domain perspective. *Leadership Quarterly, 6*, 219-247.

Graen, G. B., & Wakabayashi, M. (1994). Cross-cultural leadership making: Bridging American and Japanese diversity for team advantage. In H. C. Triandis, M. D. Dunnette, & L. M. Hough (Eds.), *Handbook of industrial and organizational psychology* (Vol. 4, pp. 415-446). Palo Alto, CA: Consulting Psychologists Press.

Grannovetter, M. S. (1973). The strength of weak ties. *American Journal of Sociology, 78,* 1360-1380.

Gully, S. M., Devine, D. J., & Whitney, D. J. (1995). A meta-analysis of cohesion and performance: Effects of level of analysis and task interdependence. *Small Group Research, 26,* 497-520.

Hambrick, D. C., Cho, T., & Chen, M. (1996). The influence of top management team heterogeneity on firms' competitive moves. *Administrative Science Quarterly, 41,* 659-684.

Hambrick, D. C., & Mason, P. A. (1984). Upper echelons: The organization as a reflection of its top managers. *Academy of Management Review, 9,* 193-206.

Harrison, D. A., Price, K. H., & Bell, M. P. (1998). Beyond relational demography: Time and the effects of surface- and deep-level diversity on work group cohesion. *Academy of Management Journal, 41,* 96-107.

Harrison, D. A., Price, K. H., Gavin, J. H., & Florey, A. T. (2002). Time, teams, and task performance: Changing effects of surface- and deep-level diversity on group functioning. *Academy of Management Journal, 45,* 1029-1045.

Heider, F. (1958). *The psychology of interpersonal relations.* New York: Wiley.

Hiller, N. J., Day, D. V., & Vance, R. J. (2003). Understanding and measuring shared leadership in work teams. Unpublished manuscript.

Jackson, S. E., May, D. E., & Whitney, K. (1995). Understanding the dynamics of diversity in decision-making teams. In R. A. Guzzo & E. Salas (Eds.), *Team decision-making effectiveness in organizations* (pp. 204-261). San Francisco: Jossey-Bass.

Jehn, K. A. (1995). A multimethod examination of the benefits and detriments of intragroup conflict. *Administrative Science Quarterly, 40,* 256-282.

Jehn, K. A., & Mannix, E. A. (2001). The dynamic nature of conflict: A longitudinal study of intragroup conflict and group performance. *Academy of Management Journal, 44,* 238-251.

Lawrence, B. S. (1997). The black box of organizational demography. *Organization Science, 8,* 1-22.

Liden, R. C., Sparrowe, R. T., & Wayne, S. J. (1997). Leader-member exchange theory: The past and potential for the future. In G. R. Ferris (Ed.), *Research in personnel and human resources management* (Vol. 15, pp. 47-119). Greenwich, CT: JAI Press.

Liden, R. C., Wayne, S. J., & Stilwell, D. (1993). A longitudinal study on the early development of leader-member exchanges. *Journal of Applied Psychology, 78,* 662-674.

Lovelace, K., Shapiro, D. L., & Weingart, L. R. (2001). Maximizing cross-functional new produce teams' innovativeness and constraint adherence: A conflict communications perspective. *Academy of Management Journal, 44,* 779-793.

McPerson, J. M., & Smith-Lovin, L. (1987). Homophily in voluntary organizations: Status distance and the composition of face-to-face groups. *American Sociological Review, 52,* 370-379.

Mehra, A., Kilduff, M., & Brass, D. J. (2001). The social networks of high and low self-monitors: Implications for workplace performance. *Administrative Science Quarterly, 46,* 121-146.

Milliken, F. J., & Martins, L. L. (1996). Searching for common threads: Understanding the multiple effects of diversity in organizational groups. *Academy of Management Review, 21,* 402-433.

Mitchell, T. R., & James, L. R. (2001). Building better theory: Time and the specification of when things happen. *Academy of Management Review, 26,* 530-547.

Nkomo, S. M. (1992). The emperor has no clothes: Rewriting "race in organizations". *Academy of Management Review, 17,* 487-513.

O'Connell, M. S., Doverspike, D., Cober, A. B., & Philips, J. L. (2001). Forging work-teams: Effects of the distribution of cognitive ability on team performance. *Applied HRM Research, 6,* 115-128.

Pearce, C. L., & Conger, J. A. (Eds.). (2003). *Shared leadership: Reframing the hows and whys of leadership.* Thousand Oaks, CA: SAGE.

Pelled, L. H., Eisenhardt, K. M., & Xin, K. R. (1999). Exploring the black box: An analysis of work group diversity, conflict, and performance. *Administrative Science Quarterly, 44,* 1-28

Phillips, A. S., & Bedeian, A. G. (1994). Leader-follower exchange quality: The role of personal and interpersonal attributes. *Academy of Management Journal, 37,* 990-1001.

Rosse, J. G., & Kraut, A. I. (1983). Reconsidering the vertical dyad linkage model of leadership. *Journal of Occupational Psychology, 56,* 63-71.

Schneider, B., Goldstein, H. W., & Smith, B. D. (1995). The ASA framework: An update. *Personnel Psychology, 48,* 747-773.

Seers, A. (1989). Team-member exchange quality: A new construct for role making research. *Organizational Behavior and Human Decision Processes, 43,* 118-135.

Sherony, K. M., & Green, S. G. (2002). Coworker exchange: Relationships between coworkers, leader-member exchange, and work attitudes. *Journal of Applied Psychology, 87,* 542-548.

Simons, T. L., & Peterson, R. S. (2000). Task conflict and relationship conflict in top management teams: The pivotal role of intragroup trust. *Journal of Applied Psychology, 85,* 102-111.

Snyder, M. (1987). *Public appearances, private realities: The psychology of self-monitoring.* New York: W.H. Freeman.

Tajfel, H. (1982). *Social identity and intergroup relations.* Cambridge: Cambridge University.

Thomas, D. A. (1993). Racial dynamics in cross-race developmental relationships. Administrative Science Quarterly, 38, 169-194.

Tsui, A. S., Egan, T. D., & O'Reilly, C. A., III. (1992). Being different: Relational demography and organizational attachment. *Administrative Science Quarterly, 37,* 549-579.

Tsui, A. S., & Gutek, B. A. (1999). *Demographic differences in organizations: Current research and future directions.* Lanham, MD: Lexington.

Tsui, A. S., Xin, K. R., & Egan, T. D. (1995). Relational demography: The missing link in vertical dyad linkage. In S. E. Jackson & M. N. Ruderman (Eds.), *Diversity in work teams: Research paradigms for a changing workplace (pp. 97-129).* Washington, DC: American Psychological Association.

Tushman, M., & O'Reilly, C. (1996). The ambidextrous organization. Managing evolutionary and revolutionary change. *California Management Review, 38,* 1-23.

Williams, K., & O'Reilly, C. (1998). Demography and diversity in organizations: A review of 40 years of research. *Research in Organizational Behavior, 20,* 77-140.

Nathan J. Hiller is a PhD candidate in Industrial-Organizational Psychology at The Pennsylvania State University. He received a BA degree from the University of Calgary and a Master of Science from Penn State, and has also studied at the University of Cape Town, South Africa. He recently received the Kenneth E. Clark Leadership Research Award, sponsored by the Center for Creative Leadership, for work exploring collective leadership in work teams. Current research interests are in the areas of team leadership and leadership development, as well as bridging psychology and strategy research. Hiller has published in several journals including the *Journal of Applied Psychology*, and has been involved in a variety of consulting projects with the Pennsylvania Department of Transportation, the U.S. Marine Corps, Northwest Airlines, and the Center for Creative Leadership.

David V. Day is Professor of Psychology and Director of Graduate Training at the Pennsylvania State University (University Park). He is also a Fellow of the American Psychological Association. He received a BA degree in psychology from Baldwin-Wallace College, and MA and PhD degrees in industrial-organizational psychology from the University of Akron. Day has published more than 40 journal articles and book chapters, many pertaining to the topics of personality, leadership, and leadership development. Journals that have published his work include: *Academy of Management Journal, Journal of Applied Psychology, Journal of Management, Leadership Quarterly, Organizational Behavior and Human Decision Processes,* and *Personnel Psychology*. He serves on the editorial board of the *Journal of Management* and is an Associate Editor of *Leadership Quarterly*, and is lead editor of a recent book titled *Leader Development for Transforming Organizations* (Erlbaum, 2004). He is also an Adjunct Research Scientist with the Center for Creative Leadership and has recently served as a civilian member of the U.S. Army Panels for Training and Leader Development (Officer, NCO, and Army Civilian panels) that reported to the Army Chief of Staff on the state of the Army's practices in the areas of training and leader development.

CHAPTER 3

ORGANIZATIONAL AND SOCIAL INFLUENCES ON LEADER-MEMBER EXCHANGE PROCESSES
Implications for the Management of Diversity

Ceasar Douglas, Gerald R. Ferris,
M. Ronald Buckley, and Michael J. Gundlach

The need for managing diversity has never been stronger. Changing workforce demographics and organizational context has placed organizations in transition, increasing the importance of social and political skill in managing the new environment. In this article, we assert that leadership, and more directly, LMX relationships, are vital to this transition. By integrating conceptual foundations and concepts from role theory, social exchange, and self-concept, we examine the role of LMX in the process of incorporating diverse group members into organizations, and facilitating their work effectiveness. We argue that when leaders develop LMX relationships based on work-group values, this will lead to more high-quality relationships and greater success with diversity initiatives. Finally, we discuss the implications of this conceptualization, as well as directions for future research.

Several distinct trends document the increased importance of managing diversity. First, the demographic profile of the US workforce has changed; there are greater numbers of women and minorities in the workplace. For example, Mische (2000) projected that early in the 21st century, the majority of first-time job seekers will be minorities, and the percentage of married women entering the workforce will surpass 70 percent up from 35 percent in 1966. Another clear trend is that organizations are positioned to do more with fewer staff members. With fewer employees, because of downsizing and staff reductions, all employees now face a growing workload. The goal of managing diversity is to allow all employees to contribute to the organization unhindered by group identities (Cox, 1993), and with staff reductions, this becomes a requirement. Johnson (1991) has viewed the inclusion of more minorities and women in the workplace as the greatest challenge facing managers today.

Managing diversity represents a great transition for many organizations. In times of transition, leadership becomes increasingly important to provide direction through challenging times (Joplin & Daus, 1997). Leadership is not only important to give purpose and direction for organizational members, but also to proactively address how members' interact in achieving organizational goals. More directly, leadership at the individual level, through leader-member exchange (LMX) relationships, can play a vital role in the success of diversity management initiatives. LMX has been theorized as dyadic, interdependent patterns of behavior (Scandura, Graen, & Novak, 1986), a social exchange relationship (Deluga & Perry, 1991), and as individualized leadership (Dansereau et al., 1995), all of which have implications for managing diversity within organizations.

In this article, a number of issues related to managing diversity and the development of LMX relationships are discussed. First, we examine managing diversity in the changing organizational context. Next, we focus on the role of leadership and leader-member relations in managing diversity. Finally, the specific implications of LMX relationships and managing diversity are presented.

DIVERSITY MANAGEMENT WITHIN THE CHANGING ORGANIZATIONAL CONTEXT

Managing Diversity

The conceptualization of diversity management within organizations is approached in either narrow or broad terms. In the narrow view, managing diversity stems from affirmative action programs, with the goal of correcting past racial and gender discrimination (Jackson, Stone, & Alverez, 1992). Initial attempts with this perspective involved steps to insure that the organization had adequate representation from under-represented groups.

From a broader perspective, managing diversity means managing a heterogeneous workforce in ways that guarantee the same productivity, commitment, and profit achieved from the former homogenous workforce (Thomas, 1990[**AU: pls cite in refs.**]). With this approach, organizations are implementing systems and practices designed to affect: (1) how people feel about their work and employer; and (2) job performance and career outcomes (Cox, 1993). Indeed, whereas diversity has been actively discussed for some time predominantly at the more micro or individual level, the implicit assumption has always been that more effective diversity management will lead to organizations performing more effectively. However, until recently, this assumption has been largely untested empirically. In a recent large-scale study of two different samples of organizations, it was reported that the highest level of organization profitability was associated with workforce gender composition of nearly 50-50 for males and females (Frink, Robinson, Reithel, Arthur, Ammeter, Ferris, & Kaplan, in press). Also from this organization-level perspective, Ferris, Arthur, Berkson, Kaplan, Harrell-Cook, and Frink (1998) proposed a social context theory that specified a mediated model whereby human resources policies, such as workforce diversity, contribute to organizational effectiveness.

The value gained with the broad approach is increased human resource utilization and improved productivity. Arguably, these items are vital to the success of all organizations in today's competitive environment. However, movement from the narrow to the broad approach is not without complications. As organizations design systems to benefit from diversity, they must recognize the challenges associated with the cognitive and behavioral implications of managing diversity.

Changing Internal Contexts of Organizations

Widespread changes in the way organizations are designed and operate have contributed to quite different types of organizational contexts within which people must operate. Downsizing, restructuring, and the increased use of team-based work structures have altered traditional structures, interaction patterns, and social dynamics through modified roles of leaders and managers and increased distance and spans of control. With respect to such changes is the view that the fixed, static sets of duties and responsibilities that we have referred to as "jobs" are giving way to more dynamic, fluid, and constantly changing sets of roles needed to adapt to turbulent contexts (Cascio, 1995).

Such job and organizational changes have promoted the importance of social skill at work. Contemporary work on interpersonal or social skill has noted its distinctiveness from personality traits, and its importance in understanding job performance (Hogan & Shelton, 1998). Further, recent research suggests that social skill is becoming an even more critical set of characteristics in contemporary dynamic organizational contexts (e.g., Cascio, 1995; Guion, 1998), as an essential quality leadership and managerial effectiveness (e.g., Van Velsor & Leslie, 1995).

Social ineffectiveness also can lead to reduced communication, resulting in less-perceived openness, and the increased perceptions of politics, which can generate lack of trust and increased cynicism in employees. Thus, we would expect that those perceiving a political climate would tend to view leaders with whom they most frequently interact as less trustworthy. Accordingly, Golembiewski and McConkie (1975, p. 13) suggested that trust "implies reliance on, or confidence in some event, process, or person."

Because unsanctioned, self-indulgent behaviors can adversely affect the social fabric at work, such perceived closed and political environments have the potential to minimize reliance and destroy integrity. Further, Zand (1972) noted that trust occurs when one person increases his or her vulnerability to another person, suggesting that trust is augmented when one feels comfortable that others control important outcomes and rewards. Because politicking frequently involves competition for scarce resources, often at the expense of others, it is unlikely that political environments foster a spirit of trust among individuals and work groups.

Interestingly, as redesign activities reshape the nature of work within organizations, the demographic profile of Workforce 2000 provides additional challenges. Pfeffer (1983) argued that the variance in the demographic profile is reflected in the range of employee attitudes and values. By and large, it is difficult to conceive a more complex dilemma, working with fewer people and requiring more social interaction, while the similarity among workforce participants is decreasing, thus requiring unique interactions by leaders tailored to the specific needs of diverse organizational members.

With the problem well established, the remainder of this article focuses on the influence of leadership, with specific reference to LMX, on managing diversity. We suggest that leadership, and more directly LMX relations, will shape the experiences of individuals working in contemporary organizational contexts. Although not specifically articulated in prior work, we argue that the LMX approach to leadership, because of its specialized dyadic relationship perspective, is well positioned to effectively address diversity management challenges in organizations today.

ROLE OF LEADERSHIP IN EFFECTIVE DIVERSITY MANAGEMENT

Cox (1993) argued that managing diversity is vital to leadership because leaders within organizations look to achieve economic performance, and this is best accomplished through maximizing contributions made by all employees. Leadership has a clear role in managing diversity at two levels: first, at the organizational level, through its effect on the social and political processes, and second, at the interpersonal level, through leader-member relationships. Much speculation surrounds the actual effect diversity has on group conflict and the role demands of leaders/managers, but it is possible that these effects are dampened when diverse group members have equal opportunity and a positive relationship with the organization (House & Aditya, 1997), both of which can be achieved through effective leadership. Clearly, more research is needed to determine diversity actual affect on interpersonal relations and leadership's affect on managing diversity.

Leadership as Social Influence

Leadership is a social influence process where leaders influence the thoughts, feelings, and actions of organizational members. Organizational leadership is the influential increment above compliance with the basic directives of the organization (Katz & Kahn, 1978). This suggests that leadership may serve a valuable purpose beyond management. At the organizational level, leadership influences policies and procedures that form the template for decisions made within the organization.

Organizational leadership contributes to the development and achievement of organizational purpose through the use of non-routine influence designed to shape social and political processes (Zaccaro & Klimoski, 2001), all of which impacts diversity management initiatives. For example, consider a decision to include the professional growth and development of direct reports as a measure of performance against which managers are evaluated. Such a position would imply the importance of training and mentoring activities, however the success of this initiative would depend upon its weight in the performance evaluation process for those managers.

Attitudes toward diversity vary within and across organizations. Joplin and Daus (1997) suggested that organizations exist on a continuum with three distinct stages (i.e., intolerance, tolerance, and appreciation), each representing the level of acceptance of diversity at the organization level, where appreciation is the highest level of acceptance. The goal of diversity management should be to improve the organization's position on this continuum, and leadership is essential to this process. Organizational leaders must be involved with the process and recognize the importance of communication, political intelligence, and conflict resolution (Joplin & Daus, 1997). Movement along this continuum frequently represents a shift in the balance of power, thus altering the political environment.

Leadership and the Political Environment

A contemporary perspective that has gained considerable support over the years is that organizations are inherently political arenas, and thus a political perspective on organizations is appropriate (e.g., Ferris & Judge, 1991; Mintzberg, 1983, 1985; Pfeffer, 1981). If we think of the organization as a structure designed to control resources and the behaviors of its members, where conflicting constituencies compete for scarce resources, then this position becomes clearer. Fairholm (1993) argued that political environments are based on the exchange of power, and management, because of its resource allocation activities, is a political activity. Within organizations, scarce resources and social structures are often the source of power struggles, but the diversity movement tends to increase tension (Joplin & Daus, 1997). Managing diversity is designed to restructure the power allocation process with organizations, and hence reshape the political environment.

To a great extent, it can be argued that politics has garnered an undesirable reputation over the course of the last twenty years (Gandz & Murray, 1980; Porter, Allen, & Angle, 1981). For example, Porter et al. (1981, p. 359) defined politics as "(s)ocial influence attempts that are discretionary, intended to promote or protect the self-interests of individuals and groups, and threaten the self-interests of others." Further, Kacmar and Baron (1999, p. 4) contended that "(a)ctions by individuals that are directed toward the goal of furthering their own self-interests without regard for the well-being of others within the organization" represent political behavior at work. Whereas this line of research represents the "dark side" of employee behavior, we see politics as an inherently necessary component of organizational functioning (Pfeffer, 1981). Further, we view political behavior as activity designed to minimize the vast amount of ambiguity that occurs in organizations (Bolman & Deal, 1991), and to give meaning to organizational phenomena where uncertainty exists (Ferris & Judge, 1991). Despite the good intentions, managing diversity adds a dimension of uncertainty and ambiguity to the workplace, which leadership at the organization level must reduce.

Managing the political environment is arguably the most critical role for organizational leadership as diversity increases. Uncertainty fosters political activity, but political activity is essential to the change process, and leaders must engage in political activity to facilitate change. An effective leader will first make an assessment of the organization's tolerance for diversity, and then use focused communication and conflict resolution to provide vision and maintain an objective orientation (Joplin & Daus, 1997). Leaders not only need political savvy, but also they need to understand its importance and be willing to actively engage in politics to move the organization forward in productive and goal-directed ways.

Leader Style

Leader style has been discussed as a potentially important factor in leader effectiveness, but it has not always been clear just what scholars were referring to when they used the term *leader style*. Early work in leadership seemed to use style to reflect particular patterns of or approaches to leadership. Fiedler (1967) included style as a central component of his theory of leadership effectiveness. He defined leadership style as: ". . . the underlying need structure of the individual which motivates his behavior in various leadership situations." Jackall (1988) used terms like articulateness, social poise, conversational ability, and engaging and friendly demeanor in reference to style, arguing that effective style necessitates self discipline and behavioral flexibility because individuals must adapt to the changing demands of different situations at work. Further, leader style has been regarded as the manner in which leaders express particular behaviors, which likely contributes to the target's interpretation of and subsequent effectiveness of such behaviors (House & Aditya, 1997).

At the interpersonal level, leader style is critical to the implementation of any organizational change initiative. As diversity initiatives are introduced, leaders will need to proactively address issues and openly communicate with individuals about changes taking place (Joplin & Daus, 1997). Here the leader's communication style may be more important than the actual message content (Gardner & Avolio, 1998). Leaders must discover ways to deliver the same message to diverse and majority group members; identifying with the challenge that each group faces.

Workplace change is difficult, but it is even more challenging when it involves social change, such as increasing diversity. Leader style must show empathy while providing direction and vision. More specifically, leaders need a high level of political skill to effectively promote social change within organizations, and political skill is suggested to be a critical manifestation of leader style that is important for the effective execution of leader behavior.

Political Skill

Political skill is one of the few constructs that has emerged which was developed to explicitly address social influence and effectiveness skills in work settings (e.g., Ferris, Perrewé, & Douglas, in press; Ferris, Perrewé, Anthony, & Gilmore, 2000; Perrewé, Ferris, Frink, & Anthony, 2000), and perhaps most effectively embodies the very essence of leader style. Indeed, Mintzberg (1983) was perhaps the first to coin the term "political skill," and he referred to it as exercising influence effectively through persuasion, manipulation, and negotiation.

Attempting to identify strategies of effective managers/organizational politicians, Jackall (1988) reported the following actor characteristics:

1. mastery of public faces; enabling situationally-appropriate behavior;
2. ability to read and conform to social situations; enabling self and social adaptation; and
3. self control of emotion, expression, etc. to convey proper image (pp. 46-47).

Thus, we view political skill as an interpersonal style construct, which combines interpersonal perceptiveness or social astuteness with the capacity to adjust one's behavior to different and changing situational demands in a manner that inspires trust, confidence, genuineness, and effectively influences and controls the responses of others.

Typically, diversity initiatives are designed to affect the overall employment profile, the level of total representation within the organization, and heterogeneity in the organization's power structure (Cox, 1993). Making changes in either area requires political skill on the leaders' part because of the consequences of the changing power dynamics. Leaders must use political savvy to build alliances and momentum to facilitate change. However, without the requisite political skill, leaders and organizations will face formidable impediments.

Leadership and Emotional Intelligence

To implement diversity management initiatives, leaders must be able to assess subordinate reactions to these initiatives, and employ leadership styles that develop LMX relationships supportive of these initiatives and cognizant of subordinate concerns. Some subordinates may be supportive of diversity initiatives whereas others may resist such change. Effective leaders have the capacity to identify varying subordinate reactions, and adapt their style to develop LMX relationships with subordinates in ways designed to maintain their support of diversity management initiatives.

In order to accomplish this, leaders not only need to assess and influence subordinates' emotional reactions to diversity management initiatives, they also need to understand and control their own. This ability is captured by the concept of leader emotional intelligence. By using emotional intelligence to interpret subordinate behavior and control their own, leaders will be able to exhibit leadership styles that develop LMX relationships which are most supportive of diversity management initiatives.

Before discussing how emotional intelligence can serve leaders managing workforce diversity initiatives, some background on emotional intelligence and how it relates to leadership is presented. With the exception of work on charisma (e.g., Conger & Kanungo, 1998; Lindholm, 1990), how emotions influence the process of leadership has rarely been highlighted (George, 2000). This is not unexpected, given the cognitive perspective that has driven the preponderance of research in the organizational literature (Fineman, 1996; Ilgen & Klein, 1989). Even though leadership research has largely neglected consideration of how emotions influence the leadership process, some studies have begun to indicate the importance of emotions in this process (e.g., George, 1995, 2000; George & Bettenhausen, 1990; Megerian & Sosik, 1996). Some leaders may be more effective than others in achieving organizational goals because their levels of emotional intelligence contribute to the social influence processes necessary to, for example, successfully manage diversity initiatives.

Emotional intelligence describes a capacity by which individuals are able to sense, interpret, regulate, and utilize their own emotional experiences as well as understand and influence others' emotions, to achieve desired outcomes (e.g., Caruso, Mayer, & Salovey, 2002; Goleman, 1995, 1998; Mayer & Salovey, 1993, 1997). Even though the term "emotional intelligence" has appeared only recently, it is similar to and somewhat overlaps with earlier constructs such as social intelligence (Sternberg & Smith, 1985; Thorndike, 1920; Vernon, 1933). Also, Rafaeli and Sutton's (1989) work, examining how displayed emotions can be used as a means of social influence, highlights how emotional insights can lead to success in social exchanges. In fact, Salovey and Mayer (1990) originally defined emotional intelligence as a subset of social intelligence indicating that individuals need emotional intelligence to negotiate social interactions and to predict others' emotional reactions.

The social influence needed to successfully manage diversity initiatives falls on the shoulders of organizational leaders, and their emotional intelligence and political skill levels will encourage the success of this process through the LMX relationships they develop with subordinates. As George (2000, p. 1040) stated:

> By accurately appraising how their followers currently feel, relying on their knowledge of emotions to understand why they feel this way, and influencing followers' emotions so that they are receptive to and supportive of the leader's goals or objectives for the organizational and proposed ways to achieve them, leaders may help to ensure that their vision is shared or collective.

With respect to managing diversity initiatives, trust and support from followers is absolutely critical to the success of such initiatives. Indeed, if followers do not support the vision of the diversity initiative, or if this support is not collective and a lack of trust exists between leaders and followers, the initiative may fail. Thus, leaders must use their emotional intelligence and political skill to tailor their styles to create LMX relationships that have the quality to support diversity management initiatives.

This may involve developing high-quality LMX relationships with subordinates of diverse backgrounds via styles in the execution of behaviors that are unique to those relationships. Leader emotional intelligence and political skill will assist in guiding this process, and in creating social interactions that encourage trust and support of the initiative. Although little empirical research has been conducted to date on emotional intelligence or political skill, some validation of these notions has been found recently. Douglas, Hochwarter, Kacmar, and Ferris (2002) reported a significant positive relationship between leader political skill and employee/follower trust.

This monitoring and shaping of emotions through social influence should not be viewed as a manipulative process, but rather as a crucial aspect of achieving success in managing diversity initiatives. Because the implementation of diversity initiatives involves working with subordinates who are of diverse backgrounds, leaders must be prepared and equipped to interpret the emotional reactions of these individuals and other subordinates in light of changes brought on by such initiatives. Deficits in such may jeopardize the success of diversity initiatives because not relating to the self-concept of subordinates and their emotions may result in a lack of trust between these subordinates and their leaders. For example, subordinates who were present before a diversity initiative was instituted may feel threatened by it, or the political realities associated with such change implementation may upset some followers. A leader's lack of sensitivity to these reactions, and inability to manage them effectively through social influence, may result in the failure of diversity initiatives.

By adapting their exchanges with organizational members through their leadership styles based on assessing emotional reactions to diversity initiatives, leaders will be better able to develop high-quality and specially-tailored LMX relationships that foster the success of these initiatives so that, in turn, the organizational advantages of the initiatives can be realized. If they are unable to appraise how their followers feel about a diversity initiative and influence these feelings, leaders will be at a loss to develop LMX relationships that will contribute to the initiative's success. High-quality relationships between leaders and their subordinates have been shown to be advantageous to leaders, subordinates, and organizations (e.g., Gerstner & Day, 1997; Graen & Uhl-Bien, 1995).

Understanding and effectively responding to subordinate emotions is crucial for leaders to build high-quality relationships with their subordinates (Carusco et al., 2002). By developing high-quality relationships with subordinates, due to their capability of interpreting and influencing subordinate emotions via their leadership styles, leaders high in emotional intelligence will be able to generate enthusiasm and optimism regarding diversity initiatives, develop a climate of cooperation and trust, and rally for support and manage negative reactions when subordinates are resistant to diversity initiatives.

In summary, because of the changing workforce demographics and organizational alignments that require increased social interaction, organizations are undertaking major changes. "In times of great transition, leadership becomes critically important. Leaders, in essence, offer us a pathway of confidence and direction as we move through the seeming chaos" (Conger, 1993, p. 46). Managing diversity presents a challenge for all organizational members, but especially for leaders within the organization. To achieve success within the dynamic realities of contemporary organizational environments, leaders must actively influence others to facilitate change. In the next section, we expand our examination of leadership and workforce diversity by examining leadership at the dyadic level through LMX.

LMX AND DIVERSITY MANAGEMENT

Leader-member exchange (LMX) theory has become one of the most significant advancements in leadership in the past three decades (e.g., Graen, 2003; Graen & Uhl-Bien, 1995; Liden, Sparrowe, & Wayne, 1997). Focusing on how leaders develop unique relationships with each of their subordinates, LMX challenged the traditional assumption that leaders treat all subordinates in a uniform manner. Thus, LMX, by its very nature, appears to fit well with contemporary organizational environments characterized by workforce diversity, downsizing and restructuring, resulting in increased manager spans of control, yet the need to craft individual (not collective) employment relationships and psychological contracts with each employee.

Although LMX theory has been tested empirically in numerous studies and refined over the years, there has been little examination of LMX relative to workforce diversity. There has been some work that has investigated LMX relative to gender similarity (Green, Anderson, & Shivers, 1996; Liden, Wayne, & Stilwell, 1993; McClane, 1991), more extensive indices of relational demography (Epitropaki & Martin, 1999), and employee disability (Colella & Varma, 2001). However, few if any systematic efforts have been made to investigate the broader considerations of workforce diversity initiatives as they relate to LMX leadership. Plainly stated, we feel that LMX relationships are at the core of a successful diversity management initiative.

LMX interactions develop and reflect interpersonal relationships. A leader-member exchange represents a relationship involving both members of a dyad involved in interdependent patterns of behavior, sharing outcomes and perceptions (Scandura, Graen, & Novak, 1986). Critical to the effectiveness of diversity initiatives is how LMX relationships develop. Dienesch and Liden (1986) attributed LMX development to the interaction between leader and member characteristics, performance attributions, role theory, and organizational context issues, whereas Graen and Scandura (1987) linked development to the role-making process model. Each model offers a somewhat different view of LMX development, however both models deem role theory, social exchange, and organizational context as important to the development process, and each has implications for managing diversity.

Role Theory

Since early in its development, LMX theory has utilized role theory as an integral part of the development process. Graen (1976) suggested that the member's direct supervisor is dominant in the role-making process, and, further, Graen and Scandura (1987) argued that this occurs as a three-step process; role-taking, role-making, and role routinization. The role-making process is at the core of the LMX development process, but as this process begins, the role sender or leader has expectations for the relationship, which are important for the management of diversity.

Leader Expectations

Perceptions of performance are critical to newcomer development, and leader expectations factor into this process. Leaders' high expectations lead to internal attributions of performance, leader support, training, and feedback (Wayne, Shore, & Liden, 1997). Leader expectations are guided by past personal experiences, newcomer characteristics, and relevant organizational experience. If the leader and or organization has had limited experience with members of diverse groups, then the leader may have no foundation on which to formulate high performance expectations. In a worst case scenario, the leader and/or organization has had a negative experience with members of a diverse group, then based on that experience, it is likely that the leader's initial expectation will be reduced. In this situation, the leader may withhold full support and resources, reducing the chance of success.

Organizational Context

In the role theory framework, organizational context represents the interrelated conditions within organizations that may affect individual behavior. Dienesch and Liden (1986) indicated a number of factors that contribute to LMX development, but organizational culture and policies are most important to the interaction between LMX and managing diversity.

Through the context created by the policies and culture of organizations, firms can shape leader behavior, and frame social interaction dynamics (Ferris et al., 1998). Policies represent a direct approach to achieving organizational goals and objectives. Nahapiet and Ghosal (1998) linked the development of social capital to organizational advantage. High-quality LMX relationships aid in developing social capital. However, organization policies may be necessary to insure that leaders create high-quality relationships with members of diverse groups. If the management of diversity is important to organizations, then such organizations should be prepared to reward appropriate behavior and reprimand inappropriate behavior (Brief et al., 1997).

Culture drives actions and relationships, and creates a broad set of organizational cues that form the bases for rules, procedures, and communications that constrain leadership (Waldman, 1993). Leaders will establish LMX relationships that align with established norms. If the culture values diversity and provides cues to the organization, managers will initiate actions in accordance with the culture, including developing high-quality LMX relationships with diverse group members. Organizational policies and culture must be examined early in any diversity initiative because of their shaping influence on leader behavior. Leaders will use these organizational cues to guide member development activities.

Social Exchange

A key component of the LMX relationship is the social exchange process whereby leaders and members are expected to contribute valued resources to the exchange. Because of their resource position, leaders have far more than members to offer. Members, especially newcomers, have only their trust, loyalty and commitment to exchange.

As newcomers, employee options are limited because they are positioned in a dyadic relationship that is their primary social exchange. Clearly, if this exchange process does not develop, other opportunities may exist within the organization. However, there may be fewer opportunities for diverse group members. Research indicates that, initially, the relationships within superior-subordinate dyads are more likely affective rather than cognitively based (Lord, Brown, & Freiberg, 1999), develop early and predict LMX quality (Liden et al., 1993). Members of diverse groups may have fewer opportunities based on the current level of diversity within the organization, and the stigma associated with having failed to develop a successful relationship. This represents a challenge for diverse group members who often view skills and abilities as their primary means for success.

Incumbent Attributes

Within role theory, individual behavior is the product of forces from different levels including the social level, where targets (i.e., members) and senders (i.e., leaders) are involved in multiple relationships with others in the work environment. The dyadic development process is influenced by the attributes and characteristics of other incumbents. Issues such as incumbent tenure and knowledge, skill, abilities are typical factors in LMX development. Because we are concerned with managing diversity, we must consider members' demographic differences, which will affect the similarity-attraction phenomenon and influence work-group cohesiveness (Jackson et al., 1992). Leaders working with homogenous work groups will find that increasing diversity generates tension among incumbents, and may question leader status among incumbents.

LMX Relationships

Although LMX research has focused on the effects of the relationships between leader behavior and follower outcomes, we believe that in the context of managing diversity, a more balanced approach is needed. That is, followers will respond to leader behaviors and leaders will approach and respond to the relationship differently based on the nature of diversity within the relationship. From this, we believe that the diversity within these dyadic relationships also will impact social network development and mentoring, both of which are important to high-quality LMX relationships.

Social Networks

Social networks represent patterns of social relationships that provide access to information and other resources, and it has been argued to be integral to leadership processes (Brass, 2001). As a vehicle for utilizing human capital, social networks allow individuals the opportunity to leverage their skills and ability through personal relationships (Ulh-Bien, Graen, & Scandura, 2000). For example, Seibert, Kraimer, and Liden (2001) found social networks, as measured by access to information, resources, and career sponsorship, to be positively related to the number of promotions received and career satisfaction. These findings indicate the importance of social networks to career development and thus, highlight the value of LMX relationships.

Initially, LMX research focused on explaining why newcomers were placed on either the assimilation or termination paths (Cashman, Dansereau, Graen, & Haga, 1976). LMX relationship quality is pivotal to accessing the assimilation path, which leads to the leader's inner circle and legitimacy within other social networks within the organization (Sparrowe & Liden, 1997).

Although grounded at the dyadic level, the network of relationships within the organization affects LMX development. Sparrowe and Liden (1997) asserted that LMX quality legitimizes members and allows them to compete for resources and status within the leaders network of contacts. As diversity increases, doubts may emerge among incumbents about power sharing and their position within the leader's network. Further, leaders may become hesitant to establish high-quality relationships with dissimilar individuals for fear of disrupting existing incumbent relationships. However, the exclusion of diverse group members from the leader's network essentially serves to position such employees for personal failure (Cashman et al., 1976), thereby contributing to the collective demise of the diversity initiative.

Mentoring

Mentoring is an extensive form of networking that involves a mentor providing a protégé with information and support aimed at career development. Focused on similar issues such as good working relationships, and sharing knowledge, and experience; LMX and mentoring are viewed as related constructs. Scandura and Schriesheim (1994) demonstrated the perception of similarity between LMX and mentoring, in that leaders (supervisors) were able to distinguish between mentoring and LMX, however subordinates failed to do the same. Subordinates' response to mentoring and LMX are similar because they both express acceptance by the leader. This form of affective feedback conveys dignity and respect and creates a basis for subordinates to identify with the leader (Lord et al., 1999), and underscores the value of LMX relationships.

It could be argued that mentoring is the key component to a successful diversity initiative. Diversified mentoring relationships (i.e., mentoring relationships that cross gender and racial boundaries) are unique due to the power and group membership differences that contradict the typical mentor/protégé relationship (Ragins, 1997). For example, Thomas (1993) revealed the importance of mentor/protégé agreement on the strategy selected for managing racial differences within cross-race developmental relationships, but also revealed that senior party preferences dictate strategy selection. This gives the mentor, typically a senior majority-group member, control over the way racial differences are approached, which ultimately affects the success of the mentoring relationship.

As previously mentioned, mentoring relationships are typically based on similarities between the mentor and protégé, where the mentor sees him or herself in the protégé. In the absence of this form of self-reflection, mentoring may take place to enhance one's power within the organization (Ragins, 1997). Accordingly, diversity must be important to the organization, if not, diversified mentoring relationships may not develop.

The importance of LMX relationships is that they are entrenched in networks of exchange relationships (Liden, Sparrowe, & Wayne, 1997), which serve as the foundation for mentoring activities. Newcomers depend on the leader's contacts to establish relationships with connected others, and these contacts are based on leader expectations of high performance (Sparrowe & Liden, 1997). As mentioned earlier, leader expectations are often driven by the perception of similarity, which creates problems for diverse group members.

Prospective mentors may be inclined to choose individuals who are similarly based with respect to demographic variables (Cox, 1993), but this can be problematic for both parties in the mentoring process. In most organizations, the demographic profile of the lower hierarchical level differs greatly from the profile of the middle and upper layers. Kanter (1977) argued that a homogenization effect (i.e., she called "homosocial reproduction") takes place in most organizations as employees filter upward to higher ranks through promotion and mobility systems. So, there tends to be limited diversity as you move up the organization hierarchy, and fewer opportunities for diverse group members to be mentored.

LMX development is vital to the mentoring process because it provides each member an opportunity to develop other important relationships through the leader's social network, and to be the recipient of critically important information and other resources which are typically transmitted from mentor to protégé. Potential mentors may not initially seek out members of diverse groups, but if they gain access to potential mentors through the leader's network, a mentoring relationship may develop. This suggests that initiation of a mentoring relationship can be introduced by either leader (i.e., mentor) or employee (i.e., protégé), and whereas we encourage leaders to be more receptive to mentoring members of diverse groups, we also suggest that diverse group members be proactive in creating and orchestrating their own mentorship opportunities by actively initiating contact with leader/mentors.

Self-Concept and LMX

Self-concept is the view that a person has of him/herself, which greatly influences behaviors in and reactions to social situations (Kihlstrom & Klein, 1994). An understanding of self-concept gives another perspective on interpersonal interactions that may aid in better understanding LMX relationships and management of diversity.

Self-concept is comprised of personal and social identities (Banjati & Prentice, 1994). Personal identity is self-categorization based on perceived similarity and differences among individuals (Lord et al., 1999), and social identity involves the processes of social categorization that segment the world into in-groups and out-groups based on group prototypes (Hogg, 2001). In an organizational context, an individual's self-concept is affected by the socialization process (Ashforth & Mael, 1989) and leadership (Lord et al., 1999). LMX and diversity management are affected by dyadic interactions, and how leaders and members view and define themselves impacts both processes.

Turner (1987) believed that social perception operates on a continuum between two opposite views of the self; that is, self as a unique being and self as a group member. The importance of this is that when leaders and members see themselves as group members, a greater opportunity exists for high-quality LMX relationships. However, as either leaders or members view themselves as unique, they look for ways to differentiate themselves from others, thereby reducing the likelihood of high-quality LMX relationships.

Leadership is most effective when it is matched to the predominant identity level of subordinates (Lord et al., 1999). The goal is to establish a level of congruence between leaders and subordinates. That is, if the leader is operating at the personal level, where individual characteristics and traits are most important, it is helpful if the subordinates are also operating at this level because they will then work to distinguish themselves from their peer group via personal traits. However, if the leader is operating at the social level and subordinates are working from the personal level, the leader will make evaluations based on contributions to the group's success, not on individual achievement.

Interestingly, the leaders have the greatest influence in this process because individuals very often view themselves somewhere near the mid-point of the self-perception spectrum (Turner, 1987), and newcomers rely heavily on their supervisors/ leaders for information on role expectations (Sparrowe & Liden, 1997). If most subordinates begin the work experience with little indifference to self-concept level, then leader actions will be pivotal in subordinates' self-definitions.

Commonly, we think of leaders influencing the self-concept of followers, but followers also can impact the leaders' self-identity level. One's self-concept is anchored by the self/other contrasts, and these contrasts then determine the salience of the self-concept level which is based on the need to identify with a positive reference group (Jackson et. al., 1992). In organizations today, terms like empowerment, value-added employee, and knowledge worker are frequently used. A highly empowered work group leads to a strong group identity among group members, and leadership that emphasizes individual-level identities may interfere with the development of group identity (Organ, 1988).

Leaders, in this context, may either view the work group as a positive reference group, or recognize the importance of the group-level identity for continued group success and adopt this position. As the leader adheres to the social identity position, this may become salient because individuals have difficulty activating more that one identity level at a time (Lord et. al., 1999). This relationship cannot be taken as an absolute, but we can recognize that the quality of worker and the cohesiveness among workers will influence the leader's self-identity level.

The value of self-concept to the development of high-quality LMX relationships lies in the interaction of congruence between leaders' and followers' self-concept and the work context. We assert that leaders are more likely to develop high-quality LMX relationships when working from the social-identity level, viewing themselves in relation to others. At the social level, the leader's self-identity is largely based on follower reactions to leader behavior (Lord et al., 1999), making leaders cognizant of the actions necessary to maintain a positive self-identity, and contributing to high-quality LMX relationships.

Because follower self-identity level is based largely on the cues received from the leader, when working from the social identity level, leaders will engage followers by focusing on similarities, which should improve overall LMX relations. Also, working with highly interdependent, empowered, and/or cohesive followers gives the leader an incentive to use the social-identity level, as opposed to limited skilled and or independent followers. In the later instance, the context warrants leaders viewing themselves as different from most followers, and using affect and individual traits as the foundation for LMX relationships.

Diversity, Self-concept, and LMX

LMX relationships affect self-concept and impact the success of diversity initiatives. An individual's self-concept is partly defined by group affiliations (Ashforth & Mael, 1989), and when these affiliations are based on visual differences they have added implications for developing LMX relationships with members of diverse groups. One's social identity contains numerous dimensions and the dimension that becomes salient depends largely on situational context (Jackson, et al., 1992). Diverse group members may see themselves as a member of a diverse group (e.g., race or gender), as a work group or organization member, depending on the situational cues. Peers and co-workers can influence one's social identity, however leadership is more influential.

At the work group level, leaders may establish high-quality LMX relationships with diverse group members, but this may serve to alienate them further if the relationship is solely based on their diversity. LMX relationships are associated with social network development and mentoring, which are vital to the success of diverse group members, however, inclusion into the leader's inner circle can be counterproductive and disruptive to other relationships if it is based primarily on race or gender. Leaders must develop a process to establish LMX relationships that is beneficial to and understood by all group members.

Organizational and work unit values that focus on activities (modes of conduct) and outcomes (goals or objectives) are good criteria for developing high-quality LMX relationships. Values provide a sense of purpose for behavior that aids individuals in conforming to the needs of their work group or organization (Schartz, 1992), and will improve the LMX development process. More importantly, as leaders exhibit or support a coherent pattern of values they can influence subordinate social identity (Lord & Brown, 2001).

Organization or work unit values are influenced by leader actions. Leaders explicitly shape values through communication or indirectly through behaviors that support, group values and membership, and group acceptance to group members (Lord & Brown, 2001). Moreover, when leaders use adherence to group values as the basis for developing high-quality LMX relationships, the social identity for all group members then becomes that of group member. This represents an important step for diverse group members by having a degree of transparency in the LMX development process. Thus, when leaders focus on accepted modes of conduct and group goals and objectives as metrics for developing high-quality relations, *all* work group members will be positioned to develop high-quality LMX relationships.

SUMMARY AND INTEGRATION

The position we have taken in this article is that LMX leadership is uniquely well positioned to effectively address the challenges of workforce diversity management as such processes operate within the context of organizational environmental and social influence and effectiveness dynamics. LMX leaders have the potential to address the unmet need that currently exists in organizations concerning how and where members of diverse groups can obtain the necessary resources, information, access to influential others and opportunities, and anecdotal education in the "rules of the game" that are all so critical for success in organizations today.

Whether ethnic/racial minorities and women have suffered from blatant discriminatory treatment or simply benign neglect, whereas the processes may be somewhat different, the outcomes are similar. That is, success in organizations is believed to be a result of individual skills, talents, and motivation, coupled with "positioning;" that is, learning what needs to be known to gain access to how to get ahead through the sponsorship of influential others who promote your case. Privileged insiders who are able to form high-quality LMX relationships and thus be the recipient of valued mentoring and social capital building from one's mentor are well positioned to be successful if they apply themselves appropriately.

However, those who do not gain or acquire such access find themselves "out of position," and thus being forced to compete in the "organization success game" without a rule book (i.e., inside information about how things really operate, etc.), and on a field that is far from level. Indeed, this has been characterized as the "political skill deficiency" explanation for the lack of progress of diversity initiatives (Ferris, Frink, & Galang, 1993; Ferris, Bhawuk, Frink, Keiser, Gilmore, & Canton, 1996). Perrewé, Young, and Blass (2002) discussed the importance of mentoring in organizations as largely focused on teaching employees the informal aspects of how things get done, and in building political knowledge and skill aimed at helping people to be positioned well to be successful.

Leaders can address this situation by recognizing the importance of self-concept, and leaders' ability to affect subordinate self-concept. As leaders view themselves as group members and evaluate subordinate performance in terms of contributions made to the group's success, this will lead to a group level identity among group members. A strong group identity leads to organizational citizenship behaviors (Organ, 1988), which are vital to organization success.

LMX and self-concept are important to the success of diversity initiatives. The goal is to create a situational context that allows diverse group members to move beyond a social identity that is linked to racial or gender characteristics, and toward a social identity linked to group values. Developing high-quality LMX relationships centered on accepted modes of conduct and group outcomes gives all group members a fair chance at establishing high-quality LMX relationships, as opposed to high-quality LMX relationships based on leader-similarity (Lord et al., 1999) and liking (Wayne et al., 1997).

The US Armed Services are often applauded for achieving diversity across all ranks, and that accomplishment is closely tied to their value system. Granted, the Armed Services may not be the ideal model for civilian organizations because they do not manage under military conditions, however, a widely understood value system may improve diversity management in civilian organizations.

High-quality LMX relationships are essential to the success of diverse group members and diversity programs. By actively including diverse group members in the development of high-quality LMX relationships, based on adherence to group values, whereby they receive the resources and support, and develop the trust and confidence necessary to be effective in their jobs and careers.

IMPLICATIONS AND DIRECTIONS FOR FUTURE RESEARCH

We have suggested that LMX can facilitate the management of diversity in organizations. We suggest that there are a number of issues for researchers to consider in examining LMX and the management of diversity that can serve as potentially productive directions for future work aimed at developing a more informed understanding of workforce diversity as well as adding to the growing knowledge base in LMX theory and research.

First, we believe that there is a need for empirical work that examines how the LMX process influences the attainment of diversity needs in an organization. We have made the case that LMX may facilitate diversity management in organizations from a number of different perspectives. Second, there is a need to evaluate whether the LMX process positively influences the work-related effectiveness of members of diverse groups. Outcomes such as job performance, job satisfaction, and career progress (among others) would be interesting variables to investigate in this context. This type of research approach further reinforces the need for longitudinal studies in this area, as opposed to the cross-sectional approach that has been taken in many of the available diversity research efforts.

Third, the next logical step, given the availability of longitudinal data, is the evaluation and determination of optimal LMX dyad composition using demographic variables. Research in mentoring

(Alleman, Newman, Huggins, & Carr, 1987) has been equivocal on this issue. The identification of more effective dyad combinations, and their relationships with important job and career outcomes, would facilitate the success of LMX in the management of diversity. The fourth important issue that follows from this paper is the recognition that there are a number of control variables (i.e., rank in an organization, political skill of dyad members, ability to develop idiosyncratic credit in organizations, the nature of the focal position, etc.) that must be included in research studies evaluating the effectiveness of LMX as a facilitator of diversity in an organization. A number of these variables may be found to be important considerations for the successful implementation of LMX-facilitated diversity programs in organizations.

CONCLUSION

The effective management of diversity is a critically important topic today in organizations, particularly in light of the demographic changes projected in workforce composition. The fact of the matter is that organizations simply must find a way to effectively manage and utilize *all* their human resources, or find themselves unable to compete. We have argued that diversity is fundamentally an organizational and social relationship issue, and as such, should be approached that way in organizations if we expect to see progress. Leader-Member Exchange (LMX) theory focuses on the unique relationships leaders form with each of their members, and therefore, it provides a useful opportunity to examine how LMX leaders might be well positioned to effectively address diversity issues. Hopefully, the perspective presented in this article will stimulate further work in this very important area.

REFERENCES

Alleman, E., Newman, I, Huggins, H., & Carr, L. (1987). The impact of race on mentoring relationships. *International Journal of Mentoring*, *1*(2), 20-23.

Ashforth, B. E., & Mael, F. (1989). Social identity theory and the organization. *Academy of Management Review*, *14*, 20-39.

Banaji, M. R., & Prentice, D. A. (1994). The self in social context. *Annual Review of Psychology, 45,* 297-332.

Bolman, L. G., & Deal, T. E. (1991). *Reframing organizations: Artistry, choice, and leadership.* San Francisco: Jossey-Bass.

Brass, D.J. (2001). Social capital and leadership. In S. J. Zaccaro & R. J. Klimoski (Eds.), *The nature of organizational leadership* (pp. 132-152). San Francisco: Jossey-Bass.

Brief, A. P., Buttram, R. T., Reizenstein, R. M., Pugh, S. D., Callahan, J. D., McClure, R. L., & Vaslow, J. B. (1997). Beyond good intentions: The next steps toward racial equality in the American workplace. *Academy of Management Executive, 11,* 59-72.

Caruso, D. R., Mayer, J. D., & Salovey, P. (2002). Emotional intelligence and emotional leadership. In R. E. Riggio, S. E. Murphy, & F. J. Pirozzolo (Eds.), *Multiple intelligences and leadership* (pp. 55-74). Mahwah, NJ: Lawrence Erlbaum.

Cascio, W. F. (1995). Whither industrial and organizational psychology in a changing world of work. *American Psychologist, 50,* 928-939.

Cashman, J., Dansereau, F., Graen, G., & Haga, W. J. (1976). Organizational understructure and leadership: A longitudinal investigation of managerial role-making process. *Organizational Behavior and Human Decision Processes, 15,* 278-296.

Colella, A., & Varma, A. (2001). The impact of subordinate disability on leader-member exchange relationships. *Academy of Management Journal, 44,* 304-315.

Conger, J. (1993). The brave new world of leadership training. *Organization Dynamics, 21,* 46-57.

Conger, J. A., & Kanungo, R. N. (1998). *Charismatic leadership in organizations.* Thousand Oaks, CA: Sage.

Cox, T. (1993). *Cultural diversity in organizations: Theory, research, & practice.* San Francisco: Berrett-Koehler.

Dansereau, F., Yammarino, F. J., Markham, S. E., Alutto, J. A., Newman, J., Dumas, M., Nachman, S. A., Naughton, T. J., Kim, K., Al-Kelabi, S. A., Lee, S., & Keller, T (1995). Individualized leadership: A new multiple-level approach. *Leadership Quarterly, 6,* 413-450.

Deluga, R. J. & Perry, T. J. (1991). The relationship of subordinate upward influencing behaviour, satisfaction and perceived superior effectiveness with leader-member exchanges. *Journal of Occupational Psychology, 64,* 239-252.

Dienesch, R. M., & Liden, R. C. (1986). Leader-member exchange model of leadership: A critique and further development. *Academy of Management Review, 11,* 618-634.

Douglas, C., Hochwarter, W. A., Kacmar, C., & Ferris, G. R. (2002). *Leader political skill and employee reactions.* Research in progress.

Epitropaki, O., & Martin, R. (1999). The impact of relational demography on the quality of leader-member exchanges and employees' work attitudes and well-being. *Journal of Occupational and Organizational Psychology, 72,* 237-240.

Fairholm, G. W. (1993). *Organizational power and politics: Tactics in organizational leadership.* Westport, CT: Praeger.

Ferris, G. R., Arthur, M. M., Berkson, H. M., Kaplan, D. M., Harrell-Cook, G., & Frink, D. D. (1998). Toward a social context theory of the human resources management–organization effectiveness relationship. *Human Resource Management Review, 8,* 235-264.

Ferris, G. R., Bhawuk, D. P. S., Frink, D. D., Keiser, J., Gilmore, D. C., & Canton, R. (1996). The paradox of diversity in organizations. In A. Gutschelhofer & J. Scheff (Eds.), *Paradoxical management: Contradictions in management—A management of contradictions* (pp. 203-229). Vienna: Linde Verlag.

Ferris, G. R., Frink, D. D., & Galang, M. C. (1993). Diversity in the workplace: The human resources management challenges. *Human Resource Planning, 16,* 41-51.

Ferris, G. R., & Judge, T. A. (1991). Personnel/human resources management: A political influence perspective. *Journal of Management, 17,* 447-488.

Ferris, G. R., Perrewé, P. L., & Douglas, C. (in press). Social effectiveness in organizations: Construct validity and research directions. *Journal of Leadership and Organization Studies.*

Ferris, G. R., Perrewé, P. L., Anthony, W. P., & Gilmore, D. C. (2000). Political skill at work. Organizational Dynamics, 28, 25-37.

Fiedler, F. E. (1967). *A theory of leadership effectiveness.* New York: McGraw-Hill.

Fineman, S. (1996). Emotion and organizing. In S. R. Clegg & C. Hardy (Eds.), *Studying organization* (pp. 289-310). Thousand Oaks, CA: Sage Publications.

Frink, D. D., Robinson, R. K., Reithel, B., Arthur, M. M., Ammeter, A. P., Ferris, G. R., & Kaplan, D. M. (in press). Gender demography and organization performance: A two-study investigation with convergence. *Group and Organization Management.*

Gandz, J., & Murray, V. (1980). The experience of workplace politics. *Academy of Management Journal, 23,* 237-251.

Gardner, W. L., & Avolio, B. J. (1998). The charismatic relationship: A dramaturgical perspective. *Academy of Management Review, 23,* 32-58.

George, J. M. (1995). Leader positive mood and group performance: The case of customer service. *Journal of Applied Social Psychology, 25,* 778-794.

George, J. M. (2000). Emotions and leadership: The role of emotional intelligence. *Human Relations, 53,* 1027-1056.

George, J. M., & Bettenhausen, K. (1990). Understanding pro-social behavior, sales performance, and turnover: A group-level analysis in a service context. *Journal of Applied Psychology, 75,* 698-709.

Gerstner, C. R., & Day, D. V. (1997). Meta-analytic review of leader-member exchange theory: Correlates and construct issues. *Journal of Applied Psychology, 82,* 827-844.

Golembiewski, R., & McConkie, M. (1975). The centrality of interpersonal trust in group processes. In C. Cooper (Ed.), *Theories of group processes* (pp. 131-185). New York: Wiley.

Goleman, D. (1995). *Emotional intelligence.* New York: Bantam Books.

Goleman, D. (1998). *Working with emotional intelligence.* New York: Basic Books.

Graen, G. B. (1976). Role-making processes within complex organizations. In M. D. Dunnette (Ed.), *Handbook of industrial and organizational psychology* (pp.1201-1245). Chicago: Rand McNally.

Graen, G. B. (2003). Interpersonal Workplace Theory at the Crossroads: LMX and Transformational Theory as Special Cases of Role Making in Work Organizations. In G. B. Graen (Ed.), *Dealing with diversity, LMX leadership: The series* (Vol. 1). Greenwich, CT: Information Age Publishing.

Graen, G. B., & Scandura, T. A. (1987). Toward a psychology of dyadic organizing. In L. L. Cummings & B. M. Staw (Eds.), *Research in organizational behavior* (Vol. 9, pp. 175-208). Greenwich, CT: JAI Press.

Graen, G. B., & Uhl-Bien, M. (1995). Relationship-based approach to leadership: Development of leader-member exchange (LMX) theory of leadership over 25 years: Applying a multi-level multi-domain perspective. *Leadership Quarterly, 6,* 219-247.

Green, S. G., Anderson, S. E., & Shivers, S. L. (1996). Demographic and organizational influences on leader-member exchange and related work attitudes. *Organizational Behavior and Human Decision Processes, 66,* 203-215.

Guion, R. M. (1998). Some virtues of dissatisfaction in the science and practice of personnel selection. *Human Resource Management Review, 8,* 351-365.

Hogan, R., & Shelton, D. (1998). A socioanalytic perspective on job performance. *Human Performance, 11,* 129-144.

Hogg, M. A. (2001). A social identity theory of leadership. *Personality and Social Psychology Review, 5,* 184-200.

House, R. J., & Aditya, R. N. (1997). The social scientific study of leadership: Quo vadis? *Journal of Management, 23,* 409-473.

Ilgen, D. R., & Klein, H. J. (1989). Organizational behavior. In M. R. Rosenzwieg & L. W. Porter (Eds.), *Annual review of psychology* (Vol. 40, pp. 327-351). Palo Alto, CA: Annual Reviews.

Jackall, R. (1988). *Moral mazes: The world of corporate managers.* New York: Oxford University Press.

Jackson, S. E., Stone, V. K., & Alverez, E. B. (1992). Socialization amidst diversity: The impact of demographics on work team old-timers and newcomers. In L. L. Cummings & B. M. Staw (Eds.), *Research in organizational behavior* (Vol. 15, pp. 45-109). Greenwich, CT: JAI Press.

Joplin, J. R. W., & Daus, C. S. (1997). Challenges of leading a diverse workforce. *Academy of Management Executive, 11,* 32-47.

Johnson, W. (1991). Global work force 2000: The new world labor market. *Harvard Business Review, 69,* 115-127.

Kacmar, K. M., & Baron, R. A. (1999). Organizational politics: The state of the field, links to related processes, and an agenda for future research. In G. R. Ferris (Ed.), *Research in personnel and human resources management* (Vol. 17, pp. 1-39). Stamford, CT: JAI Press.

Kanter, R. M. (1977). *Men and women of the corporation.* New York: Basic Books.

Katz, D., & Kahn, R. L. (1978). *The social psychology of organizations* (2nd Ed.). New York: John Wiley.

Kihlstrom, J. F., & Klein, S. B. (1994). The self as a knowledge structure. In T. K. Srull & L. S. Wyer (Eds), *Handbook of social cognitions, Vol 1: Basic processes* (pp. 153-208) Hillsdale, NJ: Erlbaum.

Liden, R. C., Sparrowe, R. T., & Wayne, S. J. (1997). Leader-member exchange theory: The past and potential for the future. In G. R. Ferris (Ed.), *Research in personnel and human resources management* (Vol. 15, pp. 47-119). Greenwich, CT: JAI Press.

Liden, R. C., Wayne, S. J., & Stilwell, D. (1993). A longitudinal study of the early development of leader-member exchanges. *Journal of Applied Psychology, 78,* 662-674.

Lindholm, C. (1990). *Charisma.* Cambridge, MA: Basil Blackwell.

Lord, R. G., & Brown, D. J. (2001). Leadership, values, and subordinate self-concepts. *Leadership Quarterly, 12,* 133-152.

Lord, R. G., Brown, D. J, & Freiberg, S. J. (1999). Understanding the dynamics of leadership: The role of follower self-concepts in the leader/follower relationship. *Organizational Behavior and Human Decision Processes, 78,* 167-203.

Mayer, J. D., & Salovey, P. (1993). The intelligence of emotional intelligence. *Intelligence, 17,* 443-450.

Mayer J. D., & Salovey, P. (1997). What is emotional intelligence? In P. Salovey & D. Sluyter (Eds.), *Emotional development and emotional intelligence: Implications for educators* (pp. 3-31). New York: Basic Books.

McClane, W. E. (1991). The interaction of leader and member characteristics in the leader-member exchange (LMX) model of leadership. *Small Group Research, 22,* 283-300.

Megerian, L. E., & Sosik, J. J. (1996). An affair of the heart: Emotional intelligence and transformational leadership. *Journal of Leadership Studies, 3*(3), 31-48.

Mintzberg, H. (1983). *Power in and around organizations.* Englewood Cliffs, NJ: Prentice-Hall.

Mintzberg, H. (1985). The organization as political arena. *Journal of Management Studies, 22,* 133-154.

Mische, M. A. (2000). *Strategic renewal: Becoming a high performance organization.* Upper Saddle River, NJ: Prentice Hall.

Nahapiet, J., & Ghoshal, S. (1998). Social capital, intellectual capital, and the organizational advantage. *Academy of Management Review, 23,* 242-266.

Organ, D. W. (1988). *Organizational citizenship behavior: The good soldier syndrome.* Lexington, MA: Lexington Books.

Pfeffer, J. (1981). *Power in organizations.* Boston: Pitman.

Pfeffer, J. (1983). Organizational demography. In L. L. Cummings & B. M. Staw (Eds.), *Research in organizational behavior* (Vol. 5, pp. 299-357). Greenwich, CT: JAI Press.

Perrewé, P. L., Ferris, G. R., Frink, D. D., & Anthony, W. P. (2000). Political skill: An antidote for workplace stressors. *Academy of Management Executive, 14,* 115-123.

Perrewé, P. L., Young, A. M., & Blass, F. R. (2002). Mentoring within the political arena. In G. R. Ferris, M. R. Buckley, & D. B. Fedor (Eds.), *Human resources management: Perspectives, context, functions, and outcomes* (4th Ed., pp. 343-355). Upper Saddle River, NJ: Prentice-Hall.

Porter, L. W., Allen, R. W., & Angle, H. L. (1981). The politics of upward influence in organizations. In L. L. Cummings & B. M. Staw (Eds.), *Research in organizational behavior* (Vol. 3, pp.109-149). Greenwich, CT: JAI Press.

Rafaeli, A., & Sutton, R. I. (1989). The expression of emotion in organizational life. In L. L. Cummings & B. M. Staw (Eds.), *Research in organizational behavior* (Vol. 11, pp. 1-42). Greenwich, CT: JAI Press.

Ragins, B. R. (1997). Diversified mentoring relationships in organizations: A power perspective. *Academy of Management Review, 22,* 482-521.

Salovey, P., & Mayer, J. D. (1990). Emotional intelligence. *Imagination, Cognition, and Personality, 9,* 185-211.

Scandura, T. A., Graen, G. B., & Novak, M. A. (1986). When managers decide not to decide autocratically: An investigation of leader-member exchange and decision influence. *Journal of Applied Psychology, 71,* 579-584.

Scandura, T. A., & Schriesheim, C. A. (1994). Leader-member exchange and supervisor career mentoring as complementary constructs in leadership research. *Academy of Management Journal, 37,* 1588-1602.

Schwartz, S. H. (1992). Universals in the content and structure of values: theoretical advances and empirical tests in 20 countries. In M. P. Zanna (Ed.), *Advances in experimental social psychology* (Vol. 25, pp. 1-65) San Diego, CA: Academic Press.

Siebert, S. E., Kraimer, M. L., & Liden, R. C. (2001). A social capital theory of career success. *Academy of Management Journal, 44,* 219-237.

Sparrowe, R. T., & Liden, R. C. (1997). Process and structure in leader-member exchange. *Academy of Management Review, 22,* 522-552.

Sternberg, R. L., & Smith, C. (1985). Social intelligence and decoding skills in nonverbal communication. *Social Cognition, 3,* 168-192.

Thomas, D. A. (1993). Racial dynamics in cross-race developmental relationships. *Administrative Science Quarterly, 38,* 169-194.

Thomas, R. R. (1990). From affirmative action to affirming diversity. *Harvard Business Review, 68,* 107-117.

Thorndike, E. L. (1920). Intelligence and its uses. *Harper's Magazine, 140,* 227-235.

Turner, J. C. (1987). *Rediscovering the social group: A self-categorization theory.* New York: Basil Blackwell.

Uhl-Bien, M., Graen, G. B., & Scandura, T. A. (2000). Implications of leader-member exchange (LMX) for strategic human resource management systems: Relationships as social capital for competitive advantage. In G. R. Ferris (Ed.), *Research in personnel and human resources management* (Vol. 18, pp. 137-185). Stamford, CT: JAI Press.

Van Velsor, E., & Leslie, J. B. (1995). Why executives derail: Perspectives across time and cultures. *Academy of Management Executive, 9,* 62-72.

Vernon, P. E. (1933). Some characteristics of the good judge of personality. *Journal of Social Psychology, 4,* 42-51.

Waldman, D. A. (1993). A theoretical consideration of leadership and TQM. *Leadership Quarterly, 4,* 65-79.

Wayne, S. J., Shore, L. M., & Liden, R. C. (1997). Perceived organizational support and leader-member exchange: A social exchange perspective. *Academy of Management Journal, 40,* 82-111.

Zaccaro, S. J., & Klimoski, R. J. (2001). The nature of organizational leadership: An introduction. In S. J. Zaccaro & R. J. Klimoski (Eds.), *The nature of organizational leadership: Understanding the performance imperatives confronting today's leaders.* San Francisco, CA: Jossey-Bass.

Zand, D. (1972). Trust and managerial problem solving. *Administrative Science Quarterly, 17,* 229-239.

Ceasar Douglas (PhD) is an Assistant Professor of Management at Florida State University. He received his PhD in Management from the University of Mississippi. Prior to his academic career, Dr. Douglas worked 15 years as a manufacturing manager for Clorox Company, Sun Chemical, Hexcel Chemical, and Herman Miller. Dr. Douglas's research interests are in the areas of work team development, leadership, leader political skill, and temporary work force issues. He has published articles in *Leadership Quarterly, Journal of Managerial Psychology, Journal of Management,* and *Supervision.*

Gerald R. Ferris is the Francis Eppes Professor of Management and Professor of Psychology at Florida State University. Formerly, he held the Robert M. Hearin Chair of Business Administration, and was Professor of Management and Acting Associate Dean for Faculty and Research in the School of Business Administration at the University of Mississippi from 1999-2000. Before that, he served as Professor of Labor and Industrial Relations, of Business Administration, and of Psychology at the University of Illinois at Urbana-Champaign from 1989-1999, and as the Director of the Center for Human Resource Management at the University of Illinois from 1991-1996. Ferris received a Ph.D. in Business Administration from the University of Illinois at Urbana-Champaign. He has research interests in the areas of social influence processes in human resources systems, and the role of reputation in organizations. Ferris is the author of articles published in such journals as the *Journal of Applied Psychology, Organizational Behavior and Human Decision Processes, Personnel Psychology, Academy of Management Journal,* and *Academy of Management Review.* Ferris served as editor of the annual series, *Research in Personnel and Human Resources Management,* from 1981-2003.

M. Ronald Buckley (Professor of Management, Professor of Psychology) is the McCasland Foundation Professor of American Free Enterprise in the Michael F. Price College of Business at the University of Oklahoma. He received his PhD in Industrial/Organizational Psychology from Auburn University. He has published over 70 refereed scholarly journal articles on a wide variety of topics in human resources management, emphasizing performance evaluation, organizational socialization, and interview processes.

Michael J. Gundlach is an assistant professor of management in the School of Business at Bond University, Gold Coast, Queensland, Australia. He received his PhD in organizational behavior/human resources from Florida State University. His current research interests include whistle-blowing and counterproductive workplace behavior.

CHAPTER 4

LMX AND MENTORING DIVERSE FOLLOWERS
Finding the Competitive Advantage for Each

S. Gayle Baugh, Terri A. Scandura, and Claudia C. Cogliser

The increasing diversity in the composition of the workforce in the United States has led to greater attention toward the effects of relational demography on developmental relationships in the workplace. This chapter examines the effects of dyadic diversity on two such developmental relationships—leader-member exchange and mentoring. These relationships are described and evidence with respect to the effects of diversity within the dyad is summarized for each type of relationship. Dyadic diversity seems to have a greater influence on mentoring relationships than on leader-member exchange relationships. The two types of developmental relationships are compared in an attempt to uncover potential explanations for the differential effects of diversity. Suggestions are offered for organizations that wish to increase diversity within the workforce and enhance the quality of developmental relationships within demographically diverse dyads. Issues needing further empirical attention are identified.

Dealing with Diversity
A Volume in: LMX Leadership: The Series, pages 91–115.
Copyright © 2003 by Information Age Publishing, Inc.
All rights of reproduction in any form reserved.
ISBN: 1-930608-49-7 (hardcover), 1-930608-48-9 (paperback)

Organizations have experienced pressures from the external environment, including increasing competition from global competitors. At the same time, there have also been internal pressures from an increasingly diverse workforce. As a result, there has been a search for methods to develop leaders who can maintain competitiveness in the face of an increasingly diverse workforce. Developmental relationships such as the leader-member exchange and mentoring have been offered as potentially effective for developing the requisite skills. Thus, the effects of diversity on these developmental relationships will be explored.

The increasing diversity of the workforce was first noted in the landmark publication, *Workforce 2000* (Johnston & Packer, 1987). This document, produced by the Hudson Institute in conjunction with the Department of Labor, predicted economic and demographic shifts affecting American business in the year 2000 and beyond. Most notably, *Workforce 2000* predicted that the proportion of women and minorities entering the workforce would increase to the point where 85 percent of the new entrants to the workforce in 2000 would be identified as non-white or female (Johnston & Packer, 1987). This publication drew the attention of business to issues related to diversity within the workforce.

The millennial year has passed. However, businesses are still grappling with the concerns related to workforce diversity. The later publication, *Workforce 2020* (Judy & D'Amico, 1997), suggests that diversity will continue to increase into the foreseeable future. Several trends in workforce participation were identified which will affect management practices. These trends are briefly summarized in the following paragraphs.

TRENDS IN WORKFORCE PARTICIPATION

Women have gradually increased their presence in the workforce. Women were predicted to comprise 47 percent of the working population by 2000. This workforce percentage has been achieved, and the numbers are predicted to rise to the point where women and men will have equal representation by 2020. That figure hardly seems surprising until it is compared to the 38 percent share of the workforce that women comprised in 1970. Further, the greatest increase in workforce participation has come from women with children in the home, suggesting yet another facet to the increasing diversity of American workers (Johnston & Packer, 1987; Judy & D'Amico, 1997; Khojasteh, 1994).

The workforce will also become more ethnically diverse, as the participation of minority group members in the workforce steadily increases. A little over half of the new entrants to the workforce up to 2020 will be minority group members. Among the various ethnic groups, Hispanics are predicted to show the most rapid increase for participation in the labor force. The percentage of Hispanic workers will grow from 9 percent in the 1990s to 14 percent by 2020. Individuals of Asian descent comprised only a very small proportion of the workforce in the 1980s (about 3%), but that percentage is rising rapidly and is projected to reach 6 percent within the next twenty years. By contrast, the proportion of blacks in the workforce is projected to remain fairly steady at about 11 percent. Ethnic diversity will be increased even further by the large number of immigrants expected to enter the workforce in the future (Johnston & Packer, 1987; Judy & D'Amico, 1997; Khojasteh, 1994).

These projections all indicate that white males will comprise a smaller proportion of the working population in the future than is the case now. It is expected that in the next few years, 62 percent of workers will be identified as something other than white males (US Department of Labor, 1995). While the numerical dominance of white men in the workforce will diminish, it is unlikely that their dominance at the top levels of corporations will be seriously challenged in the near future (Federal Glass Ceiling Commission, 1997; Judy & D'Amico, 1997; Ragins, Townsend, & Mattis, 1998).

One other trend will significantly impact the demographic composition of the workforce in the future. The "baby boom" generation will be aging and a smaller number of younger workers will begin their working lives. Additionally, there is a tendency for workers to remain longer in the workforce, resulting in both a significant "aging" of the working population and a greater age range. This, too, will contribute to a more diverse workforce (D'Amico, 1997; Judy & D'Amico, 1997).

Statistics on diversity with respect to religious affiliation, disability status, and sexual orientation within the workforce are less available than information on age, gender, and ethnicity in the workforce. These characteristics can be less visible and immediately identifiable than age, race, and gender. These factors nonetheless contribute to the overall diversity of the workforce that managers face.

These projections suggest that individuals will be working with others who are unlike them with respect to one or more demographic characteristics (Ragins, 1997). Given this trend, it is important to focus empirical attention on relationship development between demographically dissimilar individuals in the workforce. In particular, leadership relationships have long been recognized as key relationships influencing organizational functioning (e.g., Chemers, 1993; Fiedler & House, 1988), and among leadership models, leader-member exchange theory is the most specifically focused on the dyadic relationship between superiors and subordinates (Graen & Uhl-Bien, 1995). The next section will briefly review the development of leader-member exchange theory.

LEADER-MEMBER EXCHANGE THEORY

Leader-member exchange (LMX) theory has been developing over the past 25 years, with empirical results informing conceptual development and the reverse (Graen & Uhl-Bien, 1995). The theory was originally suggested as an alternative to the view of leadership as an individual-to-group phenomenon, which was the more traditional model at the time (Bass, 1990; Katerberg & Hom, 1981). Leader-member exchange theory focused on the dyadic exchange between a leader and a subordinate, with much of the early research on LMX investigating the existence of differentiated exchanges within work units (Graen & Cashman, 1975; Katerberg & Hom, 1981; Vecchio, Griffeth, & Hom, 1986). The early research established that leaders simply did not exhibit the same behavioral style toward all subordinates, nor did subordinates all respond similarly to leader behavior (Dansereau, Cashman, & Graen, 1973).

The relationships investigated varied along a continuum that could be described as "low quality exchange" to "high quality exchange." The low quality relationships were predicated on the "contract" offered by the employing organization and enacted by the leader without much elaboration over a relatively limited time horizon. Low quality relationships encompassed low levels of trust, support, respect, and obligation between the two parties involved. High quality relationships were described in opposite terms: they were characterized by high levels of trust, support, respect, and mutual obligation, which extended over a long time period and involved an exchange of rewards that were unique to each relationship, rather than those which were organizationally-prescribed (Dienisch & Liden, 1986; Graen, 1976; Graen & Scandura, 1987; Zalesny & Graen, 1985). Not surprisingly, the quality of the exchange relationship had significant implications for the parties involved.

Subordinates in high-quality relationships reported generally more positive work experiences than those in low-quality relationships. A high-quality relationship was associated with greater trust within the dyad, more attention and support from the leader, higher levels of job satisfaction, greater organizational commitment, and fewer job problems (Gerstner & Day, 1997; Graen & Cashman, 1975; Graen, Liden, & Hoel, 1982; Seers & Graen, 1984; Vecchio & Gobdel, 1984). Quality of exchange was also positively related to job performance and organizational citizenship behavior, and negatively associated with turnover (Ferris, 1985; Graen et al., 1982; Scandura & Graen, 1984; Scandura, Graen, & Novak, 1986; Vecchio & Gobdel, 1984). Further investigation revealed long term effects on subordinates' career progress (Graen & Wakabayashi, 1994; Wakabayashi & Graen, 1984; Wakabayashi, Graen, Graen, & Graen, 1988).

The generally positive experiences of individuals in high quality relationships with their superior suggest that the predictors of relationship development are of great interest. In particular, given the increasing levels of diversity cited in the earlier section of this chapter, the effects of demographic differences between superior and subordinate on the development of the dyadic relationship should warrant a great deal of empirical attention. It is surprising, then, that so little LMX research has focused on the demography of the dyad.

DIVERSITY EFFECTS ON LEADER-MEMBER EXCHANGE

There are a number of reasons to believe that relational demography (Tsui, Xin, & Egan, 1994) should have an effect on the exchange relationship developed between leaders and subordinates (Kim & Organ, 1982). Most notably, trust and mutual respect are essential characteristics of high quality relationships (e.g., Graen & Scandura, 1987), but it may be more difficult to develop these qualities across demographic differences, especially gender or racial differences (Carver & Livers, 2002; Gudykunst, 1994; Morrison, White, & Van Velsor, 1992; Thomas, 2001). However, the limited empirical research that has been conducted on the effects of demographic characteristics on the development of exchange relationships suggests that the influence of relational demography on exchange quality is slight (Scandura & Lankau, 1996).

Among the demographic variables included in research on LMX, gender was most commonly studied. In a study using a student sample, Larwood and Blackmore (1978) found that same-sex acquaintances were solicited for voluntary participation in a leadership study more frequently than opposite sex acquaintances were. This result held for both men and women, but occurred only when asking for volunteers among acquaintances, not among strangers. The authors suggested that this preference for gender similarity when utilizing one's social network might lead to preference in favor of promoting members of one's own gender in the workplace. In addition, these results imply that there might be a preference for one's own gender in developing high-quality leadership relationships.

Liden (1985) conducted research on preferences among female bank employees for a male or a female manager when both were available. He found that, even controlling for the fact that men were in higher positions in the bank, women chose male managers as the superiors with whom they were most likely to develop a good quality relationship. The differences in preference may well have been attributable to the greater tenure in position and fewer restraints on actions reported by male than female managers, rather than simply a preference for a manager of the same gender.

Gender preferences were also found in a study of Junior Achievement working groups (Duchon, Green, & Taber, 1986). Most of the Junior Achievement company presidents were young women, and young men were more frequently nominated as having poor quality relationships with the company president than young women. These results suggest a preference for the same gender, which was also found in a sample of librarians (Green, Anderson, & Shivers, 1996). Gender dissimilarity was related to lower quality LMX in this sample. It is important to note, however, that both settings were unusual, in that women were dominant in upper-level positions.

One study reported effects for dissimilarity on a measure constructed from several demographic variables (gender, race, age, and education) (Liden, Wayne, & Stilwell, 1993). Dissimilarity on this complex measure was not related to quality of leader member exchange as reported by either the superior or the subordinate over a time span of 6 months. This report echoes an earlier study (Graen

& Cashman, 1975), in which gender, age, and education were found to be unrelated to relationship quality as reported by the subordinate. Dissimilarity on one or more demographic variables does not seem to be a strong predictor of the quality of LMX.

A study on leader-subordinate communication (Fairhurst, 1993) suggests that the effects of demographic diversity on exchange quality may be influenced by the organizational context. This study provides very rich data on the verbal exchanges within a small sample of leader-member dyads. The leaders were all women who were working in a non-traditional (i.e., predominantly blue-collar industrial) setting. The female leaders in this setting were struggling to establish credibility with their subordinates, who were predominantly male, older, with longer tenure in the organization. Analysis of the verbal exchanges between bosses and subordinates yielded the finding that the dyad with the greatest demographic dissimilarity (an older, white, male, less educated subordinate reporting to a younger, black, female, highly educated leader) produced the only low quality relationship identified. This relationship was remarkable in that the interactions of this dyad could be characterized as truly negative, whereas low-quality LMX relationships are usually indicated by the absence of positive interactions. These results highlight the influence that contextual factors may have on the nature of LMX development, as well as suggesting that status incongruence may amplify the effects of low-quality exchange. Further research into these issues is clearly needed.

While the quantity of research examining the relationship between demographic similarity and LMX quality is small, the available results indicate that the effects, when they appear, are also small. The relative absence of effects for relational demography on exchange quality is puzzling, given that such effects seem to be found in mentoring relationships. Mentoring relationships, like high quality leadership relationships, are developmental relationships that result in positive outcomes for the participants. Mentoring relationships will be described next, followed by an examination of demographic effects on those relationships.

MENTORING RELATIONSHIPS

Mentoring relationships have important implications for an individual's long-term professional and personal development. Mentoring relationships occur when an individual who is more advanced in his or her career and who has achieved some hierarchical success (the mentor) offers career-related support to an individual less experienced and less advanced in his or her career (the protégé) (Fagenson, 1994; Kram, 1985; Ragins, 1997). Mentoring relationships are typically intense and span a period of several years or more (Kram, 1983, 1985; Levinson, 1978). Unlike supervisory relationships, however, there is a greater degree of choice in mentoring relationships—that is, they are not organizationally mandated, although they may at times be organizationally facilitated (e.g., Fagenson-Eland, Marks, & Amendola, 1997; Noe, 1988; Scandura & Williams, 2001).

Mentors support protégés with respect to both professional and personal development. Thus, mentors provide both instrumental (or career-related) support and psychosocial support. Instrumental functions include sponsorship, coaching, exposure to higher levels of management, protection, and provision of challenging assignments. Psychosocial functions include acceptance, confirmation, counseling, and emotional support (Burke, 1984; Dreher & Ash, 1990; Kram, 1983). Role modeling may be included within the set of psychosocial functions or may be categorized as a third and separate mentoring function (Ragins & McFarlin, 1990; Scandura, 1992).

Mentoring relationships have a positive effect on the protégé's career. Protégés experience greater job and career satisfaction, have higher expectations for career success, perceive more employment alternatives, feel less role stress, and have more positive self-evaluations than non-protégés (Baugh, Lankau, & Scandura, 1996; Corzine, Buntzman, & Busch, 1994; Fagenson, 1989; Whitely & Coetsier, 1993). In addition to these more subjective benefits, protégés also receive higher salaries, more promotions, and exhibit better performance on the job than those who have not been mentored (Burke, 1984; Dreher & Ash, 1990; Fagenson, 1989; Scandura, 1992; Turban & Dougherty, 1994; Whitely, Dougherty, & Dreher, 1991).

Mentoring relationships are generally initiated by the hierarchical superior in the dyad (e.g., Kram, 1985; Levinson, 1978; Scandura & Schriesheim, 1994; Scandura & Williams, 2001), although the potential protégé may take a proactive approach, as well (Ragins & Cotton, 1991). One might speculate as to whether diversity influences the likelihood of developing mentoring relationships or the benefits of such relationships that are developed. Despite the absence of strong effects of relational demography on the quality of leader member exchange relationships, the evidence with respect to mentoring relationships presents a different picture.

DIVERSITY EFFECTS ON MENTORING RELATIONSHIPS

It is important first to establish whether individuals with diverse backgrounds are as likely to develop a mentoring relationship as individuals who are white and male. The evidence suggests that there are few gender differences in the availability of mentoring relationships (Dreher & Cox, 1996; Ragins & Cotton, 1991), although empirical evidence with respect to the availability of mentoring to racial minorities is scant (e.g., Dreher & Cox, 1996; Ragins, 1997; Thomas, 1990). Ragins (1997) has pointed out the importance of investigating the demographic composition of the mentoring dyad and the effects of that composition on mentoring outcomes.

As noted earlier, mentoring relationship are formed across hierarchical levels of the organization (e.g., Kram, 1985). As a result of the relative absence of women and minorities in the upper echelons of organizations (Judy & D'Amico, 1997; Morrison & Von Glinow, 1990; Morrison, White, & Van Velsor, 1992), it is much more likely that women and minorities will form diversified mentoring relationships than it is that white men will (Ragins, 1997). The evidence suggests that this is indeed the case. Thomas (1990) found that white men tended to develop mentoring relationships that were same-sex and same-race—only one white man out of 107 included in the study reported a developmental relationship with an individual of another race. By contrast, cross-race relationships were predominant among blacks, and women reported that the majority of their developmental relationships were cross-gender (Thomas, 1990). Other studies have found similar patterns with respect to the relational demography of mentoring dyads (e.g., Dreher & Cox, 1996; Ragins, 1989; Ragins & Cotton, 1991). The importance of identification in mentoring relationships (Kram, 1985; Levinson, 1978), coupled with the frequency of dissimilarity in those relationships for women and minorities, leads one to question whether women and minorities reap equivalent benefits from their mentoring experiences as those of white men.

There appear to be some effects of relational demography on the mentoring functions received by protégés, but they are not easily interpreted. Mentors indicate that they provide more psychosocial support to protégés of the same race as themselves, but not more career-related support. In addition, men suggest they are less likely to remain in contact with protégés who are of a different race than themselves (Ensher & Murphy, 1997). This last finding hints that perhaps the redefinition phase of the mentoring relationship may be more problematic when racial dynamics come into play (Ensher & Murphy, 1997; Kram, 1983). Protégé reports with respect to mentoring functions received are somewhat more difficult to interpret. In one study, protégés indicated more career support but not more psychosocial mentoring from same-race mentors (Ensher & Murphy, 1997), whereas the pattern was the opposite in another study (Thomas, 1990). Both career support and psychosocial mentoring were unaffected by the racial demography of the dyad in a third study (Turban, Dougherty, & Love-Stuart, 1997).

Gender effects are also difficult to interpret. In a study asking managers to respond to a written scenario, mentors showed a tendency to provide more career support to a protégé of the opposite gender, but no effect was found for psychosocial functions (Olian, Carroll, & Giannantonio, 1993). Protégé responses to actual mentoring relationships show a different pattern, however. Protégés of the same gender as their mentor reported more social activities with their mentor, and women were particularly likely to find a female mentor to be a role model (Ragins & McFarlin, 1990). In a different study, protégés reported receiving both more career and more psychosocial support from mentors of the same gender than from mentors of the opposite gender as themselves (Thomas, 1990), although another study suggested that there were no effects of gender differences on mentoring functions reported by protégés (Turban, Dougherty, & Love-Stuart, 1997). In addition, gender did not play a part in the separation or redefinition phases of the mentoring relationship, at least from the protégé's perspective (Ragins & Scandura, 1997).

It is possible that the mixed findings in these studies are the result of a lack of agreement between mentors and protégés on the nature of their relationship, with the disagreement being most pronounced when the mentor and protégé have differing demographic characteristics. The agreement between members of the mentoring dyad on the nature of their relationship is generally not strong, but relational demography does not seem to influence the level of congruence of perceptions (Ensher & Murphy, 1997; Fagenson-Eland, Baugh, & Lankau, 2001).

In addition to exploring the effects of relational demography on the nature of the mentoring relationship, there has been some limited attention to the effects of relational demography on the outcomes of the mentoring relationship. Female lawyers with male mentors reported higher earnings than those with female mentors, while female mentors were associated with higher career satisfaction and greater intent to stay in the profession (Wallace, 2001). While not directly tested, these findings were interpreted as the result of the provision of more career functions in the cross-gender relationships and greater attention to psychosocial functions in the same-gender relationships (due, perhaps, to higher levels of identification) (Wallace, 2001). The results also lend themselves to a different interpretation, however. That is, men are more able to provide career support than women due to their generally more advantageous position in the organization, whereas women provide support that is rooted in their personal skills (Ragins, 1997).

Men seemed to facilitate greater levels of instrumental, as opposed to affective, outcomes for their protégés. Having a white male mentor provided advantages in compensation regardless of the protégé's race or gender in one study (Dreher & Cox, 1996). Another investigation found that male protégés with male mentors received higher levels of compensation than protégés in any other dyadic pairing, and that the trend was similar for promotions. Women with male mentors also received benefits in terms of salary and promotion (Ragins & Cotton, 1999).

The evidence does not support clear statements about the effects of relational demography on either the quality of the mentoring relationship or the outcomes associated with mentoring. The research that has been conducted, however, has generally found some effects on both the quality of the relationship and the outcomes associated with the relationship based on racial or gender composition. These results stand in contrast to the general absence of effects of gender or race on leader-member exchange relationships. It seems that mentoring relationships are somewhat more complex with respect to the influence of demography on the interpersonal dynamics. There has as yet been no research that directly compares mentoring relationships to leader member exchange relationships, but there are some obvious differences between the two types of developmental relationships.

A COMPARISON OF MENTORING AND LMX RELATIONSHIPS

The definitions of both high quality leader member exchange relationships and mentoring relationships suggest some conceptual overlap between the two types of associations. Research suggests, also, that the two may not be empirically distinct (e.g., Scandura & Schriesheim, 1994; Thibodeaux & Lowe, 1996). Nonetheless, there are some differences between the two types of relationships that might lead to differential effects of demography.

The most obvious difference between the two types of relationships is volition. Mentoring relationships are voluntary, but leadership relationships are not. Even in established formal mentoring programs within organizations, there is still some component of volition. The mentors and/or the protégés may volunteer for the program, rather than being required to participate, and there may be some choice about the assignment of mentors and protégés (Murray, 1991; Ragins, Cotton, & Miller, 2000). Even in the cases that offer only limited discretion with respect to participation and partnering, the members of the dyad still have a great deal of control with respect to how frequently they interact. If the interactions are difficult or unpleasant, one or the other party may choose to severely restrict time and emotional commitment to the relationship.

The freedom of choice inherent in mentoring relationships, as opposed to leadership relationships, may allow for the operation of demographic effects. While mentors may be willing to enter into developmental relationships with protégés who are demographically dissimilar, they may find that there are unanticipated difficulties that arise as the relationship unfolds. A mentor may then choose to constrain involvement in the relationship in certain ways or simply to allow the relationship to disintegrate through lack of attention.

Leaders are in a somewhat different position. They do not have complete freedom of choice about the individuals within their work unit either because the subordinate entered the work unit prior to the leader or because of organizational rules or policies about internal mobility. Further, the leader's success depends to a much greater degree on the actions of subordinates than does a mentor's success. Mentors may seek out and develop relationships with protégés that they consider "the best and the brightest" while at the same time dissociating from other, less promising potential protégés (Ragins & Scandura, 1999), but leaders are not able to change the membership of work units quite so freely. It is certainly not without risk or cost to withdraw from a mentoring relationship. The risk of admitting to a failed mentoring relationship is somewhat less than that of admitting to a failed leadership relationship, however, because the mentoring relationship is not formally mandated. Leaders may be more dependent on the success of their subordinates, as the success of their work unit depends on the success of its members, but mentors do not depend on protégés to the same extent. Thus, leaders are motivated to overcome any interpersonal difficulties arising from demographic dissimilarity. The difference in degrees of freedom to choose and to change one's choices with respect to partners in developmental relationships may account for some of the differences in findings about the effects of relational demography in leader-member exchange and mentoring relationships.

There is an alternative explanation for the same result—that is, a lesser influence of demographic diversity on leader-member exchange than on mentoring relationships. Leaders and members may have less freedom on choice with respect to dyadic partners, but there is a great deal of freedom with respect to the quality of the relationship that they develop. Leaders and members will remain in relatively impoverished, low-quality exchanges unless both individuals choose to accept the risk (and potential reward) of a more enriched relationship. Nevertheless, even dyads involved in low-quality exchanges will have a reasonable amount of interaction, as accomplishing the assigned activities of the work unit will probably require the participation of all of the work unit members. As a result of this interaction, leaders and members may have more opportunity to see beyond the surface-level diversity and identify sources of deep-level similarity (see Hiller & Day, in this volume). As a result, surface-level diversity can be expected to have less effect on leader-member exchanges than on mentoring relationships.

The two types of relationships, leadership and mentoring, also differ with respect to their breadth. While some research on mentoring has examined only the career functions (e.g., Whitely,

Dougherty, & Dreher, 1991), for the most part mentors provide both career and psychosocial functions and are expected to support both professional and personal development (e.g., Chao, 1998; Kram, 1985; Levinson, 1978; Mullen, 1998). Leadership relationships within the LMX model are more explicitly work focused. LMX is defined as a working relationship, which develops within and remains focused on the work setting (Graen, 1989). Issues like personal development that are not related to work goals and work/life balance do not find their way into the LMX literature.

Mentoring relationships, then, are more comprehensive than leader-member exchange relationships. There is more opportunity for identity issues such as cultural background and other life situations to be expressed within mentoring relationships because mentoring relationships penetrate more deeply into the participants' non-work identity than leadership relationships do. The success of mentoring relationships between individuals who are demographically dissimilar may hinge upon their willingness to constructively confront identity issues, whereas it may be more possible in leadership relationships to leave such matters unexpressed (Thomas, 1993).

It is possible for the two types of relationships to overlap. In some cases, individuals report that their mentor is also their direct superior in the organizational hierarchy. In other cases, the mentor may be positioned higher in the same organizational chain of command, outside of the chain of command, or even outside of the organization entirely (Chao, 1998; Baugh & Fagenson-Eland, 2000). There has as yet been limited empirical attention on the effects of overlapping leadership and mentoring relationships, although it is certainly possible to speculate. Chao (1998) suggests that the closer the mentor is to the protégé's everyday experience of work, the more influence the mentor can have on the protégé's career outcomes. Protégés who are mentored by their hierarchical superior should experience the greatest level of career or instrumental support. There is some limited empirical evidence to support this suggestion (Baugh & Fagenson-Eland, 2000; Burke & McKeen, 1997). By the same token, protégés who are mentored by their hierarchical superior may be more reluctant to disclose anxiety, uncertainty, and insecurity about work and even non-work issues to their superior, who will eventually evaluate their performance. As a result of this diffidence, it has been suggested that protégés of boss-mentors may experience less psychosocial support than other protégés. Empirical evidence with regard to this prediction is still lacking. Speculating, however, one might suggest that if mentoring relationships overlap with high-quality LMX relationships, then the level of trust required to develop a high-quality exchange may overcome the hesitation to discuss such sensitive subjects.

There are several implications for developmental relationships that can be inferred from this discussion. The differences between formal (organizationally cultivated) and informal (naturally developed) mentoring relationships have been discussed in the mentoring literature, always with the implication that formal relationships are less likely to provide the full range of benefits to the involved parties (Ragins, Cotton, & Miller, 2000). Formal mentoring relationships may be beneficial, however, especially for women and minorities (e.g., Dreher & Cox, 1996). Formal mentoring relationships may be a "hybrid" of sorts between supervisory relationships (focused and organizationally prescribed) and informal mentoring relationships (comprehensive and voluntary). Women and minority group members may be able to attain many of the benefits of mentoring relationships in a context that is somewhat more like that of a high-quality leadership relationship.

There are two structural features that would have to be incorporated into formal mentoring programs in order to increase their similarity to leader member exchange. The first is a limitation on the focus of the relationship to work-related concerns. Unlike informal relationships, which include issues both within and outside of the workplace, formal mentoring relationships might be more effective if they are clearly directed toward professional development and workplace concerns. In addition, if ineffective formal mentoring relationships were subject to the same sort of informal sanctions that occur in ineffective leadership relationships, participants in formal mentoring relationships might be more motivated to invest in the success of the relationship. Some of the work directed toward enhancing leader member exchange (e.g., Graen, Novak, & Sommerkamp, 1982; Graen & Uhl-Bien, 1991) might prove useful for developing formal mentoring programs.

In order to offer sound prescriptive advice with regard to enhancing diversity within developmental relationships it is important to clarify the nature of the developmental relationships under discussion. A persistent question from both a theoretical and a practical perspective is the degree of overlap between enriched leadership relationships and mentoring relationships. The two relationships can occur simultaneously, as in the case of a mentor who is also the direct hierarchical superior, or may be far removed from one another, as in the case of an individual whose mentor works in a different organization than he or she does. Conceptually there is a great deal of overlap between the career and psychosocial functions provided in mentoring relationships and the developmental activities that occur within high-quality LMX relationships. It is not clear just how much the relationship development process differs between LMX and mentoring relationships or how much the relationships themselves really differ.

It is clear that trust, respect, and loyalty are crucial to the success of both types of relationships, but it is not clear that both types of relationships require these elements to the same degree. Perhaps these factors are less essential and less well developed in mentoring relationships than in LMX relationships because mentoring relationships can be terminated (or allowed to disappear through benign neglect) more easily, especially early in the relationship (Ragins & Scandura, 1997). A relationship with one's superior cannot easily be terminated, unless one of the partners is willing to leave the work unit, but damage to the relationship may result in a permanent change in the quality of the relationship. It is likely that as the partners begin to invest in a leadership relationship, they are aware of the long-term implications of such an investment. They may only be willing to do so if the levels of trust, respect, and loyalty are quite high.

Initially, surface-level diversity—diversity based on observable characteristics such as gender and race—may delay or even preclude the development of a high-quality leadership relationship because the parties may not believe that the appropriate levels of trust can be developed (e.g., Carver & Livers, 2002). As indicated earlier, however, the greater frequency of required interaction may allow the parties to see beyond the surface level diversity and develop high quality leadership relationships with dyadic partners unlike themselves.

Whenever dyadic partners, whether in a leadership or a mentoring relationship, are able to develop a strong bond despite surface-level differences, deep-level diversity—diversity based on personality, values, and attitudes—will become an issue. Speculating, one might suggest that deep-level diversity may be both more problematic and more beneficial in a high-quality LMX relationship than in a mentoring relationship. Deep-level diversity will make it more difficult for the parties to trust that each will behave in the expected manner, as expectations about appropriate behavior may differ with deep-level diversity. The consequences of failure to meet expectations may be greater in a leadership relationship, where the performance of the work unit depends on the willingness of each unit member to provide requisite levels of performance, than in a mentoring relationship, where the mentor's career success is less directly tied to the protégé's performance. However, deep-level diversity provides the superior with an alternative perspective on organizational activities that may prove to be quite beneficial to the superior in coordinating the work unit's performance with organizational expectations, thus suggesting that deep-level diversity may also be more beneficial to a direct superior than to a mentor. Clearly, questions about the effects of deep- and surface-level diversity within leadership and mentoring relationships are ripe for exploration.

FACILITATING DIVERSITY IN DEVELOPMENTAL RELATIONSHIPS

While organizations may be concerned about the success of developmental relationships that incorporate demographic dissimilarity, it is also important to encourage more of those relationships to be initiated. Individuals tend to form developmental relationships, particularly mentoring relationships, with others who are similar to themselves in terms of demography (Turban, Dougherty, & Love-Stuart, 1997). Organizations may wish to encourage the frequency of developmental relationships between demographically dissimilar individuals in order to reap the benefits in terms of understanding across demographic "barriers" that such relationships can provide. This may be a necessary first step in breaking the "glass ceiling" that appears to block the entrance of women and minorities to the highest managerial levels.

The research cited previously (Turban et al., 1997) provides a hint for organizations wishing to enhance the number of developmental relationships that incorporate demographic diversity. In this research, perceived similarity was strongly associated with protégé reports of career mentoring received, psychosocial support received, and the value of the relationship to the individual. Perceived similarity, as reported by the protégé, included similarity to the mentor with respect to values and attitudes, career aspirations, and work style. Similarity on these factors may be more important than dissimilarity on demographic characteristics for developmental relationships (see Hiller & Day, this volume).

Organizations with strong cultures, which emphasize values and attitudes that are organizationally sanctioned and important for membership in the organization, may find that the resulting similarity in attitudes works to their advantage. Members of organizations with strong cultures are likely to perceive themselves as similar with respect to many values and attitudes due to the powerful socialization processes in such organizations. Demographic differences may be less salient in organizations with strong rather than weak cultures, and the occurrence of developmental relationships between individuals who are demographically dissimilar may as a result be enhanced.

In addition, organizations that develop diversity programs emphasizing similarity, rather than dissimilarity, across subcultures may reap the benefits of cross-race and cross-gender developmental relationships. Diversity programs that encourage individuals to look for similarities in attitudes and values that lie beneath obvious differences in appearance, such as race and gender, may facilitate relationship development across demographic dissimilarity. Individuals may discover that despite demographic differences, there is enough similarity on which to base a relationship that will, in addition, allow for learning about the differences that exist. This learning, in turn, may cause individuals to be more confident in initiating additional developmental relationships with demographically dissimilar individuals.

Organizations will need to facilitate relationship development among dyads that are demographically dissimilar by whatever means possible in order to support professional growth within a diverse workforce. The continued existence of a glass ceiling for women and minorities despite increasing diversity in the workforce suggests that serious effort will be needed in order to offer truly equal opportunity. Developmental relationships that support women and minorities up through the point of entry to the executive suite are one mechanism to encourage equal opportunity. Given the dearth of women and minorities currently at executive levels to offer such support, it is clear that many if not most of these relationships at the upper levels of organizations must develop between demographically different individuals.

Leadership relationships along with mentoring relationships may be crucial for bringing diverse individuals into executive positions. Individuals under consideration for executive positions are likely to be at a point in their career when they are no longer considered a protégé. Protégé status tends to be associated with earlier stages in one's career and executive status with later stages. Leader-member relationships are a feature of one's career at all stages, however, so individuals are likely to have greater access to leader support at the later stages of their career. The value of high quality leader-member exchange relationships as a feature of a diverse workforce has yet to be discovered and utilized.

A CONCLUDING THOUGHT

The research on the relational demography of both LMX relationships and mentoring relationships was comprised of studies of the effects gender and race. Studies including race as a variable generally included only two sub-groups—whites and blacks. Diversity encompasses identity groups beyond just race and gender, including religion, disability status, ethnicity, age, and sexual orientation, as well as racial groups in addition to blacks and white (e.g., Goto, 1999). Attention to these demographic characteristics in LMX and mentoring research and theory has been virtually non-existent. Further, there are reasons to believe that the effects of demographic dissimilarity may differ depending on the particular characteristics under consideration. The relative visibility of demographic characteristics, for example, may lead to differential effects within developmental relationships. There is a great deal more to learn about the effects of relational demography on developmental relationships. Given the trends in the composition of the workforce, it is crucial that research begin now, lest we lose the untapped potential of the diverse participants in the workforce of the future.

REFERENCES

Bass, B. M. (1990). *Bass & Stogdill's handbook of leadership.* New York: The Free Press.

Baugh, S. G., & Fagenson-Eland, E. A. (2000). Different is not always better: A comparison of mentoring functions among intra- and extra-organizational mentors. In S. H. Barr (Ed.) *Proceedings of the Southern Management Association* (pp. 66-72).

Baugh, S. G., Lankau, M. J., & Scandura, T. A. (1996). An investigation of the effects of protégé gender on responses to mentoring. *Journal of Vocational Behavior, 49*, 309-323.

Burke, R. J. (1984). Mentors in organizations. *Group and Organization Studies, 9*, 353-372.

Burke, R. J., & McKeen, C. A. (1997). Benefits of mentoring relationships among managerial and professional women: A cautionary tale. *Journal of Vocational Behavior, 51*, 43-57.

Carver, K. A., & Livers, A. B. (2002, November). Dear white boss. *Harvard Business Review, 81*, 76-81.

Chao, G. T. (1998). Invited reaction: Challenging research in mentoring. *Human Resource Development Quarterly, 9*, 333-338.

Chemers, M. M. (1993). An integrative theory of leadership. In M. M. Chemers & R. Ayman (Eds.), *Leadership theories and research: Perspectives and directions* (pp. 293-319). San Diego, CA: Academic Press.

Corzine, J. B., Buntzman, G. F., & Busch, E. T. (1994). Mentoring, downsizing, gender, and career outcomes. *Journal of Social Behavior and Personality, 9*, 517-528.

D'Amico, C. D. (1997). Back to the future: A current view of Workforce 2000 and projections for 2020. *Employment Relations Today, 24*, 1-11.

Dansereau, F., Jr., Cashman, J., & Graen, G. (1973). Instrumentality theory and equity theory as complementary approaches in predicting the relationship of leadership and turnover among managers. *Organizational Behavior and Human Performance, 10*, 184-200.

Dienesch R. M., & Liden, R. C. (1986). Leader-member exchange model of leadership: A critique and further development. *Academy of Management Review, 11*, 618-634.

Dreher, G. F., & Ash, R. A. (1990). A comparative study of mentoring among men and women in managerial, professional, and technical positions. *Journal of Applied Psychology, 75*, 539-546.

Dreher, G. F., & Cox, T. H. (1996). Race, gender, and opportunity: A study of compensation attainment and the establishment of mentoring relationships. *Journal of Applied Psychology, 81*, 297-308.

Duchon, D., Green, S. G., & Taber, T. D. (1986). Vertical dyad linkage: A longitudinal assessment of antecedents, measures, and consequences. *Journal of Applied Psychology, 71*, 56-60.

Ensher, E. A., & Murphy, S. E. (1997). Effects of race, gender, perceived similarity, and contact on mentor relationships. *Journal of Vocational Behavior, 50*, 460-481.

Fagenson, E. A. (1989). The mentor advantage: Perceived career/job experiences of protégés vs. non-protégés. *Journal of Organizational Behavior, 10,* 309-320.

Fagenson, E. A. (1994). Perceptions of protégés' vs. non-protégés' relationships with their peers, superiors, and departments. *Journal of Vocational Behavior, 45,* 55-78.

Fagenson-Eland, E. A., Baugh, S. G., & Lankau, M. J. (2001). A dyadic Investigation of perceptions of mentoring and the influence of relational demography. Paper presented at the annual meeting of the Academy of Management, Washington, D.C.

Fagenson-Eland, E. A., Marks, M. A., & Amendola, K. L. (1997). Perceptions of mentoring relationships. *Journal of Vocational Behavior, 51,* 29-42.

Fairhurst, G. T. (1993). The leader-member exchange patterns of women leaders in industry: A discourse analysis. *Communication Monographs, 60,* 321-351.

Federal Glass Ceiling Commission. (1997). The glass ceiling. In D. Dunn (Ed.), *Workplace/women's place* (pp. 226-233). Los Angeles, CA: Roxbury.

Ferris, G. R. (1985). Role of leadership in the employee withdrawal process: A constructive replication. *Journal of Applied Psychology, 70,* 777-781.

Fiedler, F. E., & House, R. J. (1988). Leadership theory and research: A report of progress. In C. L. Cooper & I. Robertson (Eds.), *International review of industrial and organizational psychology* (pp. 73-92). London: Wiley.

Gerstner, C. R., & Day, D. V. (1997). Meta-analytic review of leader-member exchange theory: Correlates and construct issues. *Journal of Applied Psychology, 82,* 827-844.

Goto, S. (1999). Asian Americans and their developmental relationships. In A. J. Murrell, F. J. Crosby, & R. J. Ely (Eds.), *Mentoring dilemmas: Developmental relationships within multicultural organizations* (pp. 47-62). Mahwah, NJ: Lawrence Erlbaum Associates, Inc.

Graen, G. B. (1989). *Unwritten rules for your career: 15 secrets for fast-track success.* New York: John Wiley & Sons.

Graen, G. (1976). Role-making processes within complex organizations. In M. D. Dunnette (Ed.), *Handbook of industrial and organizational psychology.* Chicago, IL: Rand-McNally.

Graen, G., & Cashman, J. F. (1975). A role-making model of leadership in formal organizations: A developmental approach. In J. G. Hunt & L. L. Larsen (Eds.), *Leadership frontiers* (pp. 143-166). Kent, OH: Kent State University Press.

Graen, G., Liden, R., & Hoel, W. (1982). Role of leadership in the employee withdrawal process. *Journal of Applied Psychology, 67,* 868-872.

Graen, G., Novak, M., & Sommerkamp, P. (1982). A field experimental test of the moderating effects of growth need strength on productivity. *Journal of Applied Psychology, 71*, 109-131.

Graen, G., & Scandura, T. A. (1987). Toward a psychology of dyadic organizing. In B. Staw & L. L. Larsen, *Research in organizational behavior* (Vol. 9, pp. 175-208). Greenwich, CT: JAI Press.

Graen, G. B., & Uhl-Bien, M. (1995). Relationship-based approach to leadership: Development of leader-member exchange (LMX) theory of leadership over 25 years: Applying a multi-level multi-domain perspective. *Leadership Quarterly, 6*, 219-247.

Graen, G. B., & Uhl-Bien, M. (1991). The transformation of professionals into self-managing and partially self-designing contributors: Toward a theory of leader-making. *Journal of Management Systems, 3*, 33-48.

Graen, G. B., & Wakabayashi, M. (1994). Cross-cultural leadership-making: Bridging American and Japanese diversity for team advantage. In H. C. Triandis, M. D. Dunnette, & L. M. Hough (Eds.), *Handbook of industrial and organizational psychology* (Vol. 4, pp 415-446). New York: Consulting Psychologist Press.

Green, S. G., Anderson, S. E., & Shivers, S. L. (1996). Demographic and organizational influences on leader-member exchange and related work attitudes. *Organizational Behavior and Human Decision Processes, 66*, 203-214.

Gudykunst, W. B. (1994). *Bridging differences: Effective intergroup communication* (2nd Ed.). Thousand Oaks, CA: Sage Publications, Inc.

Johnston, W. B., & Packer, A. E. (1987). *Workforce 2000*. Indianapolis, IN: Hudson Institute.

Judy, R. W., & D'Amico, C. (1997). *Workforce 2020*. Indianapolis, IN: Hudson Institute.

Katerberg, R., & Hom, P. W. (1981). Effects of within-group and between-groups variation in leadership. *Journal of Applied Psychology, 66*, 281-233.

Khojasteh, M. (1994). Workforce 2000: Demographic changes and their impacts. *International Journal of Public Administration, 17*, 465-505.

Kim, K. I., & Organ, D. W. (1982). Determinants of leader-subordinate exchange relationships. *Group and Organization Studies, 7*, 77-84.

Kram, K. E. (1985). *Mentoring at work*. Glenview, IL: Scott Foresman.

Kram, K. E. (1983). Phases of the mentor relationship. *Academy of Management Journal, 26*, 608-625.

Larwood, L., & Blackmore, J. (1978). Sex discrimination in managerial selection: Testing predictions of the vertical dyad linkage model. *Sex Roles, 3*, 359-367.

Levinson, D. (1978). *The seasons of a man's life*. New York: Knopf.

Liden, R. C. (1985). Female perceptions of female and male managerial behavior. *Sex Roles, 12*, 421-432.

Liden, R. C., Wayne, S. J., & Stilwell, D. (1993). A longitudinal study on the early development of leader-member exchanges. *Journal of Applied Psychology, 78,* 662-674.

Morrison, A. M., & Von Glinow, M. A. (1990). Women and minorities in management. *American Psychologist, 45,* 200-208.

Morrison, A. M., White, R. P., & Van Velsor, E. (1992). *Breaking the glass ceiling.* Reading, MA: Addison-Wesley Publishing Company.

Murray, M. (1991). *Beyond the myths and magic of mentoring: How to facilitate an effective mentoring program.* San Francisco: Jossey-Bass.

Mullen, E. J. (1998). Vocational and psychosocial mentoring functions: Identifying mentors who serve both. *Human Resource Development Quarterly, 9,* 319-331.

Noe, R. A. (1988). An investigation of the determinants of successful assigned mentoring relationships. *Personnel Psychology, 41,* 457-479.

Olian, J. D., Carroll, S. J., & Giannantonio, C. M. (1993). Mentor reactions to protégés: An experiment with managers. *Journal of Vocational Behavior, 43,* 255-278.

Ragins, B. R. (1989). Barriers to mentoring: The female manager's dilemma. *Human Relations, 42,* 1-22.

Ragins, B. R. (1997). Diversified mentoring relationships in organizations: A power perspective. *Academy of Management Review, 22,* 482-521.

Ragins, B. R., & Cotton, J. L. (1999). Mentor functions and outcomes: A comparison of men and women in formal and informal mentoring relationships. *Journal of Applied Psychology, 84,* 529-550.

Ragins, B. R., & Cotton, J. L. (1991). Easier said than done: Gender differences in perceived barriers to gaining a mentor. *Academy of Management Journal, 34,* 939-951.

Ragins, B. R., Cotton, J. L., & Miller, J. S. (2000). Marginal mentoring: The effects of type of mentor, quality of relationships, and program design on work and career attitudes. *Academy of Management Journal, 43,* 1177-1194.

Ragins, B. R., & McFarlin, D. B. (1990). Perceptions of mentor roles in cross-gender mentor relationships. *Journal of Vocational Behavior, 37,* 321-339.

Ragins, B. R., & Scandura, T. A. (1999). Burden or blessing? Expected costs and benefits of being a mentor. *Journal of Organizational Behavior, 20,* 493-509.

Ragins, B. R., & Scandura, T. A. (1997). The way we were: Gender and the termination of mentoring relationships. *Journal of Applied Psychology, 82,* 945-953.

Ragins, B. R., Townsend, B., & Mattis, M. (1998). Gender gap in the executive suite. *Academy of Management Executive, 12,* 28-42.

Scandura, T. A. (1992). Mentorship and career mobility: An empirical investigation. *Journal of Organizational Behavior, 13,* 169-174.

Scandura, T. A., & Graen, G. B. (1984). Moderating effects of initial leader-member exchange status on the effects of a leadership intervention. *Journal of Applied Psychology, 69*, 428-436.

Scandura, T. A., Graen, G. B., & Novak, M. A. (1986). When manager decide not to decide autocratically. *Journal of Applied Psychology, 71*, 579-584.

Scandura, T. A., & Lankau, M. J. (1996). Developing diverse leaders: A leader-member exchange approach. *Leadership Quarterly, 7*, 243-263.

Scandura, T. A., & Schriesheim, C. A. (1994). Leader-member exchange and supervisor career mentoring as complementary constructs in leadership research. *Academy of Management Journal, 37*, 1588-1602.

Scandura, T. A., & Williams, E. A. (2001). An investigation of the moderating effects of gender on the relationships between mentorship initiation and protégé perceptions of mentoring functions. *Journal of Vocational Behavior, 59*, 342-363.

Seers, A., & Graen, G. (1984). The dual attachment concept: A longitudinal investigation of the combination of task characteristics and leader-member exchange. *Organizational Behavior and Human Performance, 33*, 283-306.

Thibodeaux, H. F., III, & Lowe, R. H. (1996). Convergence of leader-member exchange and mentoring: An investigation of social influence patterns. *Journal of Social Behavior and Personality, 11*, 97-114.

Thomas, D. A. (1993). Racial dynamics in cross-race developmental relationships. *Administrative Science Quarterly, 38*, 169-194.

Thomas, D. A. (1990). The impact of race on managers' experiences of developmental relationships (mentoring and sponsorship): An intra-organizational study. *Journal of Organizational Behavior, 11*, 479-492.

Thomas, D. A. (2001, April). Race matters: The truth about mentoring minorities. *Harvard Business Review, 80*, 98-107.

Tsui, A. S., Xin, K. R., & Egan, T. D. (1994). *Relational demography: The missing link vertical dyad linkage.* Greensboro, NC: American Psychological Association Conference on Diversity.

Turban, D. B., & Dougherty, T. W. (1994). Role of protégé personality in receipt of mentoring and career success. *Academy of Management Journal, 37*, 688-702.

Turban, D. B., Dougherty, T. W., & Love-Stuart, M. S. (1997, August). *Mentor demographic, relational demographic, and perceived similarity effects in developmental relationships.* Paper presented at the Academy of Management meetings, Boston, MA.

U.S. Department of Labor. (1995). Final report on the glass ceiling. Washington, DC: Government Printing Office.

Vecchio, R. P., & Gobdel, B. C. (1984). The vertical dyad linkage model of leadership: Problems and prospects. *Organizational Behavior and Human Performance, 34*, 5-20.

Vecchio, R. P., Griffeth, R. W., & Hom, P. W. (1986). The predictive utility of the vertical dyad linkage approach. *Journal of Social Psychology, 126,* 617-625.

Wakabayashi, M., & Graen, G. B. (1984). The Japanese career progress study: A 7-year follow-up. *Journal of Applied Psychology, 69,* 603-614.

Wakabayashi, M., Graen, G. B., Graen, M. R., & Graen, M. G. (1988). Japanese management progress; Mobility into middle management. *Journal of Applied Psychology, 73,* 217-227.

Wallace, J. E. (2001). The benefits of mentoring for female lawyers. *Journal of Vocational Behavior, 58,* 366-391.

Whitely, W. T., & Coetsier, P. (1993). The relationship of early career mentoring to early career outcomes. *Organization Studies, 14,* 419-441.

Whitely, W., Dougherty, T. W., & Dreher, G. F. (1991). Relationship of career mentoring and socioeconomic origin to managers' and professionals' early career progress. *Academy of Management Journal, 34,* 331-351.

Zalesny, M. D., & Graen, G. B. (1985). Exchange theory in leadership research. In A. Kieser, G. Reber, & R. Wanderer (Eds.), *Handbook of leadership* (pp. 714-727). Stuttgart, Germany: Verlag.

Gayle Baugh received her doctorate from the University of Cincinnati in 1992. She is currently employed at the University of West Florida as a full time faculty member teaching Organizational Behavior, Human Resource Management, and Quantitative Methods. Her research on mentoring, leadership, and diversity has been published in sources such as the *Journal of Vocational Behavior, Group and Organization Management,* and the *Journal of Applied Social Psychology.*

Terri A. Scandura is a Professor of Management at the University of Miami. Her work has appeared in *Journal of Applied Psychology, Academy of Management Journal, Leadership Quarterly,* and *Research in Organizational Behavior.* She serves on several editorial boards. Her research interests include mentoring, relational leadership, fairness, and diversity.

Claudia C. Cogliser, Assistant Professor of Management, Price College of Business, University of Oklahoma, PhD (University of Miami). Professor Cogliser's teaching interests are in organizational behavior, leadership, and research methods. Her research lies in the area of leader/follower relationships, leader-member exchange, leadership in virtual teams, psychometrics, and research methods.

CHAPTER 5

THE NARRATIVE BASIS OF LEADER-MEMBER EXCHANGE

Gail T. Fairhurst and Stephanie Rhea Hamlett

In this chapter, we argue that extant measurement of LMX force-fits judgments of relational quality into numerical scales in ways that obscure the experience of LMX. A discursive approach is required to reclaim this experience and the narrative basis for sensemaking in communication. We propose a narrative research agenda for LMX that suggests that: 1) the uniqueness paradox may apply to actors' sensemaking narratives suggesting some common scriptal elements over interpretation of high versus low quality LMX experiences, 2) the ways that narratives come to constitute, not merely reflect, LMX relationship quality will reveal itself in the actual dialogue of leaders and members, and 3) the character of certain stories told will be influenced by the Discourses of the corporate community and society, which serve as interpretive resources from which leaders and members draw to construct what is normal and reasonable as they set and solve problems in an LMX context.

One of the most enduring leadership theories of the past thirty years has been Leader-Member Exchange (LMX), which suggests that leaders exchange their personal and positional resources for a member's performance (Graen & Scandura, 1987). In high quality LMXs, leader and member exert high levels of mutual influence, trust, and support, an internalization of common goals, extra-contractual behavior, and an exchange of social resources. In low quality LMXs, there is formal authority, contractual behavior exchange, role-bound relations, low trust and support, and economic rewards. In an extensive review of LMX outcomes, Liden, Sparrowe, and Wayne (1997) document the differential impact of LMX quality on job satisfaction, performance, communication, turnover, productivity, and job problems, among others.

LMX research is voluminous (see reviews by Fairhurst, 2001; Gerstner & Day, 1997; Graen & Uhl-Bien, 1995; Liden et al., 1997; Schriesheim, Castro, & Cogliser, 1999), but not without controversy (Barge & Schleuter, 1991; Dansereau, Yammarino, & Markham, 1995; Dienesch & Liden, 1986; House & Aditya, 1997; Keller & Dansereau, 1995; Schriesheim et al. 1999; Schriesheim, Cogliser, & Neider, 1995; Yukl, 1994). Measurement has been a particularly difficult issue as LMX has been without a consistent operationalization and charges that many LMX studies contain psychometrically unsound and/or theoretically questionable measures have been raised (Dienesch & Liden, 1986; Schriesheim, Neider, Scandura, & Tepper, 1992; Vecchio & Gobdel, 1984).

Our aim in this chapter is not to address the psychometric issues surrounding LMX measurement, but to reconsider the force-fitting of judgments about LMX into scales of any kind as the exclusive means by which to study it. While a scaled judgment is one way to study LMX, it is not without limitations. Such a practice minimizes the experience of LMX and ignores narrative as an alternative means by which relationship sensemaking and construction occurs. To address this thesis, we examine the psychological, empiricist orientation of mainstream LMX researchers, the need to understand the narrative and discursive basis of LMX, and a research agenda for LMX narratives.

MAINSTREAM LMX RESEARCH

Recently, Gronn (2002) argued that the focus of mainstream leadership research on the ascending series of individual-dyad-group-organization as ontological units of study has been confounded with levels of analysis and overshadowed by the dominance of leader-centrism relative to other units. While the latter charge is hardly true of LMX research, its proponents nevertheless observe individuals and analyze their perceptions and summary judgments even though the ontological unit of study is the leader-member relationship. Such is the orientation of cognitive and social psychologists with an empiricist orientation, the background of many U.S. leadership scholars.

Cronen (1995) argues that scholars in this psychological tradition form and statistically analyze the cognitive, affective, and conative variables that they believe capture experience. However, such an orientation reduces behavior to statements of intention while losing all sense of coordinated action and any real sense of experience. This is not a problematic stance for the study of cognitive operations as they relate to leadership (e.g., implicit theories, schemas, etc.). However, it remains one for LMX and other contemporary leadership phenomena like distributed leadership, which place a premium on concertive action and conjoint agency (see also Fairhurst, in press; Gronn, 2002). In one way or another, these approaches assert that leadership is an inherently social phenomena and communication is the primary social process.

House and Aditya (1997) have taken Graen and Uhl-Bien (1995) to task for insufficient psychologizing of the LMX construct by marginalizing the role of the individual leader and member within operationalizations of LMX. However, Graen (personal communication, 1995) has consistently eschewed an individualistic focus calling the path of individualism "a failed paradigm" to draw attention to the inherently social nature of leadership. However, how can such a position be taken seriously when the social is *equated* with the study of individuals and their summary judgments of a relational history captured in seven point scales?[1] As described below, a discursive approach is required to reclaim the experience of LMX and the narrative basis for sensemaking within relationships.

THE CASE FOR NARRATIVE AND DISCOURSE

Mainstream LMX researchers treat leaders and members as information processors who gain perspective on their LMXs by calculating the resources one puts into a relationship as weighed against what one receives in return. According to the theory, the amount and type of resources exchanged differentiate high from low quality relationships (Graen & Scandura, 1987). While social exchange theories do not assume that people are always calculating or that they are necessarily aware of calculating, Roloff (1981) argued that "the description of decision-making certainly implies that people are both active and highly self-aware calculators" (p. 128). The calculation may be situational, gradual, post hoc, or an individualized tendency, but it remains more or less of a rational, resources in/resources out assessment (Roloff, 1981). LMX scale items are designed to elicit this calculation.

However, the information processing model of LMX calculation in the extant literature ignores another equally plausible means by which sense is made of the relationship through narrative. Bruner (1986, 1990) argues that there are two distinct modes of cognition: the *information processing mode* of rational analysis of data and paradigmatic thinking, and the *narrative mode* in which actors almost continuously narrate experience in order to restore order to a disorderly world. Without dismissing rational-analytic thought, Bruner (1990) argues for a narrative psychology in which "people organize their experience in, knowledge of, and transactions with the social world" (p. 35). He suggests that as humans we have an innate narrative capacity that is a basic means of understanding, the means by which we frame experience and our memory of it.

Drawing from Bruner (1990), Weick (1995) offers an especially good explanation of the sensemaking powers of narrative:

> The requirements necessary to produce a good narrative provide a plausible frame for sensemaking. Stories posit a history for an outcome. They gather the strands of experience into a plot that produces that outcome. The plot follows either the sequence beginning-middle-end or the sequence situation-transformation-situation. But sequence is the source of sense. (p. 128)

Thus, sequence is the source of sense by enabling actors to impose a coherent frame on equivocal events. However, Weick (1995) enumerates several other benefits to storytelling that make it such a powerful heuristic for sensemaking:

1. stories assist comprehension because they integrate the known and the speculative;
2. stories suggest a causal order for unorganized or unrelated events;

3. stories enable people to call forth the absent to talk about the present in order to construct meaning;
4. stories are mnemonics that help people to reconstruct prior complex events;
5. stories can guide action before routines are formed and can enhance routines after they are formed;
6. stories can enable people to build a data base of experience from which they can infer how the world works; and
7. stories can convey shared values and meaning (p. 129).

Scientists such as Czarniawska-Joerges (1997), Greimas (1983, 1987), and Weick (1995) suggest that narrating *is* organizing because of the causal link established between the general organization of events and signification or meaning. However, narrative psychology is not unlike the more literary narratology, the study of stories, in viewing language as transparent representation, focusing on narrative structure, and generally viewing the individual as a sensemaking perceiver (Edwards, 1997). The problem as Edwards (1997) explains is that:

> Studies of narrative, both in cognitive psychology and in the literary 'narratology,' have tended to pursue generalized types and categories of narrative *structure*, rather than dealing with how specific story content, produced on and for occasions of talk, may perform social actions in-the-telling (emphasis in the original, p. 266).

However, this imbalance is quickly correcting itself as the study of narrative as discourse has assumed many forms in the burgeoning literature on organizational discourse (for reviews see, Boje, 2001; Czarniawska-Joerges, 1997; Edwards, 1997; Putnam & Fairhurst, 2001). Several strands of narrative discourse research include:

1. the study of stories as cultural artifacts, a reflection of organizational culture (Ouchi & Wilkins, 1985; Schein, 1985);
2. narrative as storytelling performances as they occur in naturally occurring conversations (e.g., through turn-by-turn pacing [Jefferson, 1978] and joint construction and enactment [Boje, 1991]), which differentiate among organizational subgroups, signal turbulence and change, and aid in problem diagnosis (Boje, 1991; O'Connnor, 1997; Orr, 1990);

3. narrative talk as ideological control, which furthers the interests of dominant groups, instantiates values, reifies structures, and reproduces power (Helmer, 1993; Mumby, 1987, 1988); and
4. narrative as a form of organizing through the episodic ordering of speech acts and sentence grammars as found within texts operating as non-human agents (along with objects, technologies, architectural elements, etc.) within organizations (Cooren, 2001; Fairhurst & Cooren, in press; Taylor & Van Every, 2000).

As stories have evolved from cultural artifact to narrative modes of knowing and organizing (Boland & Tenkasi, 1995; Patriotta, 2003), its relevance to LMX becomes increasingly clear.

THE NARRATIVE BASIS FOR LMX

To their credit, LMX researchers theorize and study relationship development more than most leadership theories. However, the manner in which they theorize and study relationship development underplays the experience of LMX and its attendant sensemaking and communication processes (Fairhurst, 2001). We believe this minimizes opportunities to appreciate the power of narrative as interpretive devices (modes of knowing) and as a discursive form (modes of organizing). For example, the leadership making model describes a three stage process through which relationships may become high quality (Graen & Uhl-Bien, 1995; Uhl-Bien & Graen, 1992). The first phase, role finding, is an initial 'stranger' phase in which individuals relate mostly on a formal basis with a 'cash and carry' contractual economic exchange. If an implicit or explicit offer for an improved working relationship is made and accepted, dyads may mature into a second role-making or 'acquaintance' stage. Marked by testing within the relationship, individuals make both social and contractual exchanges in this phase. Finally, not all dyads reach the final stage of role implementation, which is a 'mature partnership' stage. In this stage, the exchanges are 'in kind,' highly developed, and marked by loyalty, support, and trust. Other researchers have added to LMX developmental theory by focusing on the role of trust (Bauer & Green, 1996), leader-member expectancies and member performance (Dienesch & Liden, 1986;

Liden, Wayne & Stilwell, 1993), social networks (Sparrowe & Liden, 1997), and friendship development (Zorn, 1995).

However, Fairhurst (2001) has argued that all of the models reflect an assumption that successful LMXs follow a unidirectional and cumulative path toward increasing levels of closeness or fusion, relational stability, and transformation beyond self-interests. Work in dialectical approaches to relationship development calls into question usual assumptions about relational stability, arguing that even healthy relationships are marked by dialectical oppositions that create simultaneous pulls to fuse with and differentiate from the other (Altman, Vinsel, & Brown, 1981; Baxter, 1988; 1992; Baxter & Montgomery, 1996; Montgomery, 1992; Rawlins, 1992). Relational bonding not only implies fusion, closeness, and interdependence, but also separation, distance and independence. Importantly, a dialectical perspective suggests that it is the strategic responses to contradiction in message behavior that forms the basis for understanding how relationships are forged (Baxter, 1988; 1990).[2]

Fairhurst's (2001) argument is that few LMX developmental studies question the assumption of relational stability (cf. Lee & Jablin, 1995). Moreover, few LMX studies in general focus on the discourse of LMX (cf. Fairhurst, 1993; Fairhurst & Chandler, 1989; Sias, 1996). It follows that if relational stability is assumed, there is scant attention to the tension, contradiction, dynamism, and flux in relationships-as-they-happen that serve as prompts for sensemaking. Narrative as a mode of knowing would be obscured because of a requested ratings judgment that takes a single snapshot of the relationship as effective or ineffective, trusting or untrusting, etc, the usual scale item indicators of high or low quality LMX. Just *what* is experienced as effective or ineffective, trustworthy or not, etc. is most likely to be narratively organized, but is not a subject of inquiry. Moreover, when the discursive basis of LMX is ignored, two situations may obtain. First, individuals are not given the opportunity to openly and discursively *reflect* upon their LMX experiences in a meaningful way, thus bypassing the ways that sensemaking and meaning gets worked out in communication. Second, ignoring the study of actual dialogue within the LMX relationship precludes an examination of the ways narratives are used to *construct* LMX. In the following section, these two observations are used to develop three research agendas for narrative study within LMX.

THREE NARRATIVE RESEARCH AGENDAS FOR LMX

Narrative Reflection and the Uniqueness Paradox in LMX Stories

The organizational culture literature has long studied stories as reflections or manifestations of culture (Ouchi & Wilkins, 1985; Schein, 1985). Schein (1985) distinguished at least three levels of culture: basic assumptions, values, and artifacts, the latter of which includes stories, special jargon, rituals, dress, and décor. Stories are important cultural artifacts because they powerfully illustrate the core values of a culture, and the story creation process is one means of expressing the alternative values of counter-cultures. Martin and Siehl's (1983) analysis of John Delorean's re-storying of 'the refrigerator story' in his attempts to transform General Motors is a case in point. Although the role of narrative in this genre as 'cultural object' is quite narrowly prescribed, there are at least two applications to LMX.

The first suggests that the stories leaders and members tell about their relationship should be reflective of the quality of their exchange. When actors are asked to reflect upon their relationships through in-depth interviews, the opportunity to reflect is more than just a sensegiving exercise in which actors share the meanings that they have already assigned to the relationship. Fundamentally, it is a sensemaking exercise where actors work out meanings for the relationship *in communication.* That is, they discover their meanings in the work of producing them (Boden, 1994; Cronen, 1995), an idea that forms the foundation for Weick's (1979) notion of retrospective sensemaking. To wit, how can I know what I think (about my LMX) until I see what I say? Similarly, Tsoukas and Hatch (2001) comment on the reflexivity of narrative discourse as they quote White (1987), "narrative discourse does not simply reflect or passively register a world already made; it works up the material in perception and reflection, fashions it, and creates something new" (p. 999).

Based on Patriotta's (2003) work on narratives of knowledge in organization, narratives will show how knowledge of LMX is mobilized through discourse, reflecting a distinctive mode of knowing related to the everyday coping with the world. Patriotta explains:

> In fact, the strength of narratives as interpretive devices stems precisely from their ability to link the present to the past and the future,

anticipation to retrospection and repetition . . . . Because of their connection to experience, narratives display common-sense wisdom—in the form of anecdotes, jokes, and war stories—in organizational discourse. Common sense is based on unspoken premises and therefore underscores the tacit aspects of knowledge in organizations. (p. 353)

It is our assertion that narratives are not just depositories of organizational culture and conventional wisdom, but will form a distinctive way of knowing and talking about LMX. The opportunity to reflect and work out the meanings for one's LMX in communication and through discourse will reveal experiential knowledge about the LMX relationship previously ignored in extant forms of measurement.

However, a second application of narrative in culture research for LMX concerns the uniqueness paradox. The uniqueness paradox suggests that a culture's claim to uniqueness, as expressed through cultural manifestations such as organizational stories and rituals, are not in fact unique (Martin, Feldman, Hatch, & Sitkin, 1983). Martin et al. (1983) found that seven common story types (e.g., 'The rule breaker,' 'Is the big boss human?' 'Can the little person rise to the top?' 'Will I get fired?' 'How will the boss react to mistakes?') had both positive and negative versions that were remarkably similar across organizations.

In arguments reminiscent of the emphasis on dualities in relational dialectics, Martin et al. (1983) suggest that narratives emerge from the need to reconcile the tensions and contradictions that surface from conflicts between organizational exigencies and the values of employees and society at large. Such tensions usually emerge over issues of equality, security, and control where the function of narrative goes beyond a simple description of contradiction, to an attempted reconciliation of what is frequently an irreconcilable world. As individuals offer self-enhancing attributions for organizational successes or failures in this sensemaking, they endow the organization with a uniqueness that is conveniently embraced or disparaged.

Martin et al. (1983) claim that highlighting uniqueness is not just an organizational phenomenon, but can also be seen on individual, cultural, and societal levels. As such, we should expect to find claims of uniqueness on a relational level for three reasons. First, the dualities reflected in stories about the organization's culture are also endemic to organizational relationships. Equality versus inequality reflects tensions over the differential amounts of social distance in high versus low quality LMX relationships (Fairhurst & Chandler, 1989). Security versus insecurity may reflect the ontological states of high versus low quality LMX members respectively, especially in an age of corporate downsizing. Finally, control versus lack of control has been a resource that traditionally distinguishes high from low LMX members (Graen & Scandura, 1987).

Second, Martin et al. (1983) found that although the organizational settings of the stories clearly vary, they share a set of common scripts that "specify a set of characters or roles and a causally connected sequence of events, sometimes with oppositional branches for alternative story components and events" (p. 441; see also Schank & Abelson, 1977). We suggest that scripts inform the nature of hierarchical relationships in the organization as much as they inform its culture because they are inseparable, with the former nested within the latter. Thus, common script elements should be found in LMX relationships, despite the fact that relationships are going to have their own idiosyncrasies. According to Edwards (1997), "People come to possess broadly the same cultural scripts . . . This kind of knowledge is clearly fundamental to any sort of cultural competence, and we surely use it in making sense of what people are doing, where, and why" (p. 143-144). Fairhurst (2001) called for better ways to study LMX so as to capture the interactive inputs of both culture (broadly defined) and dyad; the search for common scriptal elements in LMX stories may be one such solution.

Third, if, as Martin et al. (1983) discovered, individuals will cite and either embrace or disparage their organization's uniqueness to play into self-enhancing attributions for organizational successes or failures, why should a similar dynamic not operate with LMX? Idiosyncrasies surrounding the effectiveness or ineffectiveness of the relationship will likely be targeted positively or negatively as individuals engage in face saving and self-enhancing attributions as they explain their behavior. If the uniqueness paradox replicates itself in the context of LMX, the interactive inputs of both culture and dyad to LMX are reaffirmed once again.

In summary, this first narrative research agenda focuses on the elicitation of narratives through interviews. LMX actors would be given the opportunity to discursively reflect upon their relational experiences, thus reclaiming the ways that sensemaking and meanings for the relationship get worked out in communication and through discourse.

Stories Lived and Stories Told: Constructing the LMX

A second research agenda is predicated on the study of actual dialogue where LMX actors use narrative to construct high or low quality relationships. According to Ochs (1997):

> [T]he interactional production of narrative maintains and transforms persons and relationships. How we think about ourselves and others is influenced by both the message content of jointly told narratives and the experience of working together to construct a coherent narrative. (p. 185)

The reflexivity between thought and action implied by Ochs (1997) is reinforced by the notion of 'stories lived and stories told,' which reflects the idea that the telling of a story is part of a lived story (Cronen, 1995). To live within a story requires an understanding of the grammar of a relationship. Its rules and patterns of interaction are ongoing, unfinished, and subject to changes in meaning as actors respond to exigencies of situation or context (Pearce, 1995). Stories lived thus reflect the unfolding nature of relationships as story lines. By contrast, storytelling emphasizes the discursive means by which narrative may help construct relationships, that is, how they perform social actions in-the-telling (Boje, 1991; Edwards, 1997). It is unlike the usual study of narrative as full text garnered from autobiographies or ethnographic interviews, focusing instead on actual dialogue and the flexible, occasioned nature of discourse (Edwards, 1997).

Regarding LMX, discourse analysts should first look for the strategic ways in which narrative may be used to construct relationships of high or low quality *in situ*. Consider the following excerpt from Fairhurst's (1993) discursive analyses of LMX with women leaders.[3] Story telling is used quite strategically by a low LMX member (M) who happens to be male, white, older, less educated, and more tenured than his supervisor (L), who is female, black, young, more educated, and less tenured.[4]

D126, p. 22-23

1	M:	[uh I almost ended up on disability twice.]
2	L:	What happened?
3	M:	Going down the stairs, my leg gave out, and I went
4		flying down the stairs.
5	L:	Oh no! Let me see. Oh God.

6	M:	Grabbed onto the wall. Cut that.
7	L:	Oh God, I see. Let me see Let me see this hand ...
8		You're gonna have to be careful. You're gonna
9		hurt yourself real bad.
10	M:	Then I almost drowned ... Stayed in the pool until
11		I gave out ... I was swimmin' 80-80 foot length of
12		the pool and gave out when it was 9 feet deep.
13	L:	What happened?
14	M:	Just kept swimming.
15	L:	I'm glad you're okay, Herb. God you you scare me
16		sometimes.
17	M:	I almost drowned a lotta times. It doesn't stop
18		me.
19	L:	You better take care of yourself. You should do that
20		cause you scare me with some of those stories you tell
21		me. Oh no.
22	M:	I got a pill from the V.A. now. I could kill myself if I
23		wanted to.
24	L:	You got a pill that could kill yourself?
25	M:	Yeah, if I wanted to kill myself, I got a pill to do
26		it now ... Great big yellow pillow. No markings on it.
27	L:	SIGH. Mr. Cunningham, I don't know about you
28		sometimes. I wonder. Anyhow PAUSE let's get back
29		to this. As far as the associates with mechanical skills
30		working the line, who else can fill in?

This low LMX member relays stories of falling down stairs (line 3), bodily injury (line 6), near drowning (lines 10, 17), and potential suicide (line 22). However, these stories are a joint performance (Boje, 1991). The leader is a co-producer of these stories with each expression of strong interest and/or concern (lines 2, 5, 7, 13, 15, 19)—until the subject of suicide is introduced (line 22) at which point she changes the subject back to work related matters (lines 27-28)! To show more concern for a cut on the hand over talk of suicide makes sense only if the member has strained the bounds of credulity too far (Fairhurst, 1993).

The older, white male member is playing power games with the younger, black female leader, and with her help constructs an interactional pattern of deceit, distrust, and resistance to authority. This is brought off by the member's string of increasingly implausible narratives both prompted and unchallenged by the leader. As this pattern repeats itself in future conversations, as it apparently has in the past (lines 20-21), it comes to *constitute*, not merely reflect, this low LMX relationship. Thus, the stories told become part of an unfolding lived story line of low LMX quality.

Consider a second example from Fairhurst (1993), this time with a high LMX relationship. The use of narrative by the male member provides an opportunity for the female leader to stand behind previous commitments she has made.

```
1   L:   Even if we're not here, there oughta be a way to
2        cover it. So, if someone from the day shift who was
3        at the morning meeting could cover what happened
4        at the next meeting or for third shift, we'd be
5   M:   You gonna do that?
6   L:   [INDISTINGUISHABLE good shape. Do you want me to
7        ask somebody? Is that what you're sayin?]
8   M:   Yeah.
9   L:   Yeah, I can ask.
10  M:   My list . . . my list is getting long . . . you know, I'm
11       supposed to get my list shorter and remember
12  L:   I know.
13  M:   I'm not making any progress.
14  L:   [And so you can have a romantic interlude or
15       something INDISTINGUISHABLE]
16  M:   [I'm not. I don't have any time.]
17  L:   LAUGHTER . . . All right. I'll ask Shelly or Tom or
18       both of them.
```

The abbreviated use of narrative in this example is what Boje (1991) calls 'terse storytelling.' "A terse telling is an abbreviated and succinct simplification of the story in which parts of the plot, some of the characters, and segments of the sequence of events are left to the hearer's imagination" (Boje, 1991; p. 115). The member initiates a terse telling at lines 10-11 (" . . . my list is getting long . . . I'm supposed to get my list shorter . . . remember") immediately after he challenges the leader over shift coverage (line 5: "You gonna do that?"). The member uses this story to legitimate his unwillingness to cover the shift.

Interestingly, the leader not only acknowledges the abbreviated narrative over shortening his to do list (line 12: "I know"), but she more actively co-produces the narrative by humorously referencing the member's reasons for working less (lines 14-15: " . . . so you can have a romantic interlude or something"). When communicators choose parts of stories in a terse telling, it always raises questions about one's strategic goals in doing so (Boje, 1991). It is interesting in this case that the leader chose "the romantic interlude" reference in an attempt at humor, perhaps to diffuse the face threat introduced by the member at line 5 ("You gonna do that?"). When the humor that the leader initiates is then responded to in kind by the member at line 16 ("I'm not. I don't have any time."), it effectively achieves this goal. This is also an interesting example of leader support of the member because conditions are ripe for reneging on a prior commitment (Fairhurst, 1993). The leader could claim new circumstances, forcing the member to complete the task because of their contractual relationship. Instead, she stands behind her previous commitment (lines 17-18), and in so doing demonstrates support of the member as they co-construct this high quality LMX.

Boje (1991) hypothesizes that the more terse the story telling, the more shared the understanding of the social context because insiders know just what to leave to the imagination. This makes sense for a high quality LMX where leader and member communicate more frequently (Baker & Ganster, 1985; Schiemann & Graen, 1984), and thus could assume more about what the other knows. Thus, for this high LMX, the 'romantic interlude' story was tersely told, actively co-produced by leader and member, marked by in kind responses, and a signal that the leader would not renege on what she had agreed to in the past. This is but one instance of leader support of the member, however, many such incidents must have contributed to their unfolding story line of a trusting, high quality LMX.

Fairhurst (1993) also reports two other interesting examples of narrative use in a high quality LMX dyad that involve insider joking. Again, the leader is female and the member is male.

D 142, p. 1

```
1    M:   I wanted to talk about feasibility, PAUSE uhm PAUSE
2         update on uh making operation, my perspective on
3         that.
4    L:   Oh good. Mm-hmm
5    M:   Is this how you're gonna do this while we're taping?
6         Keep sayin' "Oh good" to everything I mention?
7    L:   LAUGHTER. That's what I told Carol. I said, "Hey,
8         I know you've already had this session already, so
9         if you do anything out of character, I'm going to call
10        you on it." Ok, now what else . . .
```

The leader's redundant backchanneling at line 4 ("Oh Good. Mm-hmm") prompts the member to humorously challenge her by narratively reflecting on her behavior (lines 5-6: "Is this how you're gonna do this while we're taping? Keep sayin' 'Oh good' to everything I mention?"). This is a prototype example of 'stories lived/stories told' or the telling of a story, in this case about the taping of their conversation, while living the story of actually doing so. It is also playful, but potentially face-threatening humor. Interestingly, the leader not only reacts positively to the attempted humor by the member with laughter, but produces her own narrative that she aligns with the sentiments of the member's (line 7: "That's what I told Carol . . . ."). In so doing, she joins in the co-production of the member's narrative and the threat to face dissolves.

However, consider a second example of humor intertwined with narrative by this same dyad. In this instance, the leader introduces the narrative (lines 11-15), while the member continues with playful, but potentially face-threatening challenges:

D 142, p. 8

11	L:	And I had requested him to write up a draft . . .
12		basically stating . . . we can meet production
13		requirements for test market, but we'll have
14		higher than normal scrap ratios scrap rates. And
15		he's gonna go do a draft for that and run it by you.
16	M:	Good weasel words.
17	L:	Aren't they?
18	M:	Higher than normal scrap rates?
19	L:	[Higher than normal, I know. Somebody would love to say, "Well
20		what does that exactly mean?"]

Frequently a privilege of the powerful, teasing is usually directed downward in a hierarchical relationship (Coser, 1960). Not only is the teasing directed upward, but the choice of words is a bald-on-record expression (line 16: "Good weasel words."). Note that the member in this instance could have chosen less face threatening, more strategically ambiguous language (e.g., "Interesting word choice") or could have selected something else from the leader's narrative to comment upon. However, once again the member's attempts at humor were met in kind by the leader, who joins in the co-production of the narrative (lines 17, 19-20).

Two points are noteworthy here. First, Fairhurst's (1993) argument is that insider joking is not just reflective, but constitutive of high quality LMXs. That the joking is initiated by a high quality LMX member is particularly noteworthy for the lack of social distance and power differentials it implies. Second, the member uses narrative quite strategically; in the first instance, knowing how to use narrative to accentuate, and in the second instance, knowing what to abbreviate in the leader's narrative for comment. Both instances resulted in playful, but face-threatening challenges to the leader, the nature of which suggests complex, subtle, and rhetorically powerful ways to use narrative.

In reflecting on the above LMX storytelling performances, Boje's (1991) observation that there are implicit rules in storytelling rings true. On the surface, LMX quality would appear to be a determining factor in who can tell a story, to whom, and where, with bias towards high LMX relationships and the interactional freedom both leaders and members enjoy. However, LMX alone appears insufficient to understand story performances because of the relational demography of the dyads. When leaders and members differ in gender and other social class variables such that individuals are high on one major dimension of social or occupational stratification and low on another, status inconsistency occurs (Fairhurst & Snavely, 1983; Fleishman & Marwell, 1977). Conflict can occur because interactants cannot agree as to whose status will serve as the basis for structuring their communication. As Fairhurst (1993) found in her analysis of low LMX dyads, status inconsistency was often the result of the organizational status/power of the leader being countered by the social status/power of the member. As demonstrated with the conversational excerpt from Dyad 126, the leader had higher organizational power, but her social status was relatively low; she was more educated, but she was female, black, young, and new (thus less knowledgeable of the culture). The member was less educated, but he was male, white, older, and more experienced. One cannot analyze the storytelling by this low LMX member without marveling at the narratively-organized power games he undertook in this and other instances (Fairhurst, 1993) and the interactional freedom he was permitted by this leader. Clearly, in this battle of the white male member's higher social status versus the organizational power of this black female leader, the member won out.[5] This brief example and the others in Fairhurst (1993) clearly indicate that the strategic use of narrative to construct LMX cannot be studied apart from the relational demography of the dyad.

Finally, these examples also demonstrate that story performances are always a co-production, their meanings are continuously negotiated, and competent communicators can use narrative to build or tear down a relationship. As such, the study of narrative in LMX construction will be difficult without in-depth, situated knowledge of context, relationship, and paraphrasing Harre (1984), leaders and members-in-conversation.

Stories as Discursive Formations

Cronen (1995) suggests a third narrative research agenda that describes the "special character" of certain types of stories lived and told based on Foucault's (1972) view of discourse. However, before going further it is important to clarify two broad definitions of the term *discourse* (Alvesson & Kärreman, 2000). The first definition of *discourse*, which we employ in the previous two narrative research agendas, focuses on talk and text in social practices where language in use and interaction process are central concerns. The second definition, which Alvesson and Kärreman (2000) refer to as *Discourses* to avoid confusion, focuses on Foucault's (1972; 1976; 1980) belief that they are general enduring systems for the formation and articulation of ideas in a historically situated time. More than just talk patterns, they are discursive formations—constellations of talk patterns, ideas, logics, and assumptions that constitute objects and subjects. Cronen (1995) is making reference to this second definition and suggests that some stories told may be discursive formations. He explains:

> Foucault used the term *discourse* to describe stories of a particular character. In my use of this term, a story can be regarded as a discourse if it includes a formalized set of grammatical relationships among utterances that is well instantiated in a group of users. The formalizations include the kind of relationships persons have with each other. The relationships that make up the discourse are widely known and available, carrying great authority and strong feelings for certain people. (p. 47)

What Cronen (1995) is suggesting is that some of the stories that people tell are "in-formed" by certain Discourses in society, giving the stories told a kind of authority vis-à-vis other stories lived and told. In the organizational arena, this becomes most apparent when we consider the Discourses of the corporate community, for example, the Discourse that characterizes the age of corporate downsizing and what it means for certain industries. To clarify this idea, consider three examples of senior management narratives from Fairhurst, Cooren, and Cahill's (2002) study of downsizing at an environmental remediation site. Formerly a governmental manufacturing facility of uranium metal products for the nation's defense programs, it became a construction site that met with considerable resistance from the workforce as it attempted to downsize.

```
1    L#1   What they have asked us to do is to clean the site up.
2          And they're asking us to do that very quickly, to bring some
3          private industry focus to this change. Our role is to clean . . . put a
4          fence around it . . . and get out of here. That's what they [the
5          Department of Energy] really want. So we were very candid
6          in that message. Probably it was not the best communication
7          strategy at the time because it caused a lot of dissension in the
8          workforce. They weren't really ready to deal with that.

9    L#2   This is a legacy workforce that feels like they will be here
10         forever. Even when they hear of layoffs, they are not
11         concerned because they know they'll still be here. We call
12         them "WeBe's." "We be here when you [the contractor]
13         came. We be here when you leave."

14   L#3   We were taking the traditional approach. The traditional
15         approach is, "Ok, looks like we need to reduce . . . Let's draw up
16         the list . . . rank 'em and start whacking from the bottom and start
17         handing them their notices and head 'em out the gate" . . . But in the
18         construction industry, employees don't take offense to that. It's
19         part of their lives. And so we come from that industry. It's so
20         hard for us to understand. Don't these employees know they're in
21         the construction industry? This is not a manufacturing plant.
22         "Just get your pink slip and get out of here. Get on with your life.
23         What do you think I am? Your mom and dad?"
```

In reading the narratives, it should immediately be apparent that language like "private industry focus" (line 3), "layoffs" (line 10), "the need to reduce" (line 15), and "handing them their notices" (line 17) are part of the Discourse on corporate downsizing. This Discourse not only has its own language (other well known examples include "rightsizing," "reengineering,' "reductions in force," etc.), but reflects and re-instantiates a belief system about organizational efficiency, competitiveness, and productivity that favors the elimination of jobs as business concerns dictate. This has been especially true of private industry. Likewise, Leader 3's counter posing of the construction industry with a manufacturing plant (lines 17-18: "But in the construction industry, employees don't take offense to that . . . ") comes from a related Discourse that normalizes downsizing as routine in the construction industry.

Thus, as these leaders are speaking, it is not solely their voices that we are hearing. It is also the voice of the corporate community, a voice that carries great authority for these leaders as they invoke its narratives (i.e., discursive formations) (Cronen, 1995). More importantly, it produces what is normal and what is reasonable for them. Consider

Leader 3's normalizing of construction industry downsizing when he calls it "the traditional approach" (lines 14-15). He also suggests the unreasonableness of the employees' position when he says, "Don't these employees know they're in the construction industry... what do you think I am? Your mom and dad?" (lines 20-23). In invoking the parent metaphor, the vice president pointedly marks the employee position as unreasonable to delegitimate the conflict (Fairhurst et al. 2002). Leader 2's pejorative reference to legacy employees as "WeBe's" (lines 12-13) is similarly critical.

While the leaders at this environmental remediation site were not asked specifically about their leader-member relationships, there is every reason to expect that the Discourses on downsizing in and outside of the construction industry would serve as interpretive resources in the context of their LMXs. However, there are other Discourses on other subjects within the corporate community (e.g., globalization, technology, etc.) and Discourses that are societal (e.g., health and modern medicine). These and other Discourses would be drawn upon by both leaders and members alike to define 'problems' based on what a discursive formation deems normal versus abnormal, reasonable versus unreasonable, etc. As these Discourses are drawn upon to set and solve problems in the context of an LMX, they reproduce themselves and reaffirm that the discursive business conducted in the context of an LMX relationship is not solely relational. At the same time, within the context of the LMX relationship we might expect that some actors would have more power than others to invoke and define certain Discourses. For example, leaders and high LMX members might have more such power than low and medium quality LMX members. However, as in the previous discussion of relational demography for stories lived and stories told, members with high social status/power may also have the ability to invoke and define certain Discourses. If either circumstance is true, the discursive business conducted in the context of an LMX relationship is not solely relational, but neither can the cultural be studied apart from it.

IMPLICATIONS AND CONCLUSIONS

In this chapter, we argued that extant measurement of LMX force-fits judgments of relational quality into numerical scales in ways that obscures the experience of LMX. As such, a discursive approach is required to reclaim this experience and the narrative basis for sensemaking in communication. Echoing organizational culture research, the uniqueness paradox may well apply to actors' sensemaking narratives suggesting some common scriptal elements over interpretation of high versus low quality LMX experiences.

We also took issue with the view that equates the study of individuals and their summary judgments with the study of the social. If leadership is an inherently social phenomenon, then communication is the primary social process. As such, actual dialogue and the interaction process of leaders and members require study as do the ways that narratives come to constitute, not merely reflect, LMX relationship quality.

Finally, we argued that leaders or members may be the storytellers, but it is not solely their voices that we are hearing. This is because the character of certain stories told will be influenced by the Discourses of the corporate community and society. These Discourses carry great authority as interpretive resources from which leaders and members draw to construct what is normal and reasonable as they set and solve problems in an LMX context.

The implications of this narrative agenda for future LMX research are threefold. First, although we have critiqued the psychological, empiricist orientation of mainstream leadership research, we believe it has made a significant contribution to the study of leadership. The arguments put forth in this paper could not have been made were it not for a long and rich tradition of this type of LMX research. Our concerns derive from the dominance and near-exclusivity of a psychological, empiricist orientation relative to the social constructionist, interpretive orientations of many discursive approaches.[6] Traditional LMX measurement is a viable means of studying LMX, just not the *only* means especially as its limitations become known. Our goal is not only to encourage more discursive LMX research, but also to consider a combination of perspectives such as found in Fairhurst (1993). Fairhurst (1993) elicited both LMX scale ratings and leader-member discourse in taped conversations, using the former to validate the latter. We believe that such a multi-perspective, multi-method approach would serve future discursive and psychological LMX research well. Interpretive and traditionally empiricist perspectives can compensate for the questions that each leaves unanswered.

Second, our narrative research examples are heavily leader-member, although we are mindful of relationship exchanges among team members and coworkers (Baugh & Graen, 1997; Dose, 1999; Graen & Uhl-Bien, 1995; Seers, 1989; Sherony & Green, 2002). There is every reason to expect that all three narrative research agendas outlined in this chapter would apply to team member and coworker exchanges. Clearly relationship dynamics will alter story content, but sensemaking about the relationship in communication and through narrative discourse should occur in team member and coworker interviews. Likewise, the strategic use of stories to construct these relationships should also occur in studying their actual dialogue, as would one or both members defining and invoking various Discourses to explain and justify their actions.

Finally, we have only touched the surface of the potential for narrative to inform LMX theory especially regarding diversity issues, the theme of this volume. For example, the narratives in the section on stories lived/stories told focused on LMX dyads with varying degrees of differences in relational demography. As Hiller and Day in this volume suggest, there are key diversity issues beyond the surface demographic characteristics of gender, race, education, or age. They argue that deep-level diversity in personality, values and attitudes has implications for team integration and cohesion and LMX relationships in the longer term. We heartily agree, but believe that the challenges associated with both surface- and deep-level diversity are not solely psychological. They are *heavily* communicative. An exploration of deep level diversity issues so critical to any leader, coworker, and team-member exchange would be well served by reclaiming the narrative and discursive basis of these exchanges, especially as organizations and teams deal with their tendency to drive out diversity over time (Schneider, Goldstein, & Smith, 1995). Narrative discourse will elicit the sensemaking surrounding these very thorny issues, and the study of narrative in leader-member interaction should show how similarities or differences in personality, values, and attitudes actually matter in the construction of the LMX.

Over twenty years ago, Mintzberg (1982) argued that leadership needed to be studied simply, directly, and imaginatively as he questioned the traditional methodologies of leadership researchers. We believe that reclaiming the narrative basis for LMX meets Mintzberg's standard in ways that perhaps he did not envision, but which continues to spotlight what leaders and members actually do and the inherently collaborative nature of managerial work itself.

{ack}The authors would like to thank Heather Zoller for her helpful comments on an earlier version of this chapter.

NOTES

1. To be clear, we are not against the gathering of perceptions about the LMX relationship. Our issue is with the implicit assumptions in this literature that actors' meanings take precedence over the study of social interaction and that these meanings are best captured in scaled judgments.

2. For example, member latitude in decision making is a form of autonomy that has been reframed as connection in high LMX relationships (Graen & Scandura, 1987). Arguing that the maintenance phase of the leader-member relationship could be in flux, high LMX members increase openness in escalating relationships, low LMX members come more closed in routine relationships, but use a combination of open/closed strategies including deception in deteriorating relationships (Lee & Jablin, 1995).

3. Fairhurst's (1993) original analysis of the data does very little with the role of narrative.

4. The transcript notation in this analysis closely resembles the notation by Rogers and Farace (1975). The number of symbols in the manuscript has been deliberately held to a minimum as a detailed focus on prosodics would not add substantially to the analysis. The symbols used are as follows:

[ ]	Successful talk-over (Similar to an interruption, a successful talkover is simultaneous speech where the interruptor gains the floor.)
( )	Unsuccessful talk-over (Similar to an interruption, an unsuccessful talkover is simultaneous speech where the interruptor does not gain the floor.)
...	Deletion
Italics	An emphasized word or phrase
PAUSE	A pause of one second or less within an utterance
?	A question or statement with an interrogative form
INDISTINGUISHABLE	An utterance that could not be heard clearly
Dxxx	Dyad number
L	Leader
M	Member

5. Fairhurst (1993) also examined the way that gender contributed to the construction of LMX relationships with male members through the ways they demonstrated support, shared decision making, and used humor to realign the relationship.

6. It is important to recognize that there are many forms of discursive analyses with wide ranging interpretive theoretical orientations and a few that are tradition-

ally empiricist. All represent more than just a methodology (for a review, see Putnam & Fairhurst, 2001).

REFERENCES

Altman, I., Vinsel, A., & Brown, B. B. (1981). Dialectic conceptions in social psychology: An application to social penetration and privacy regulation. In L. Berkowitz (Ed.), *Advances in experimental and social psychology* (pp. 107-160). New York: Academic Press.

Alvesson, M., & Kärreman, D. (2000). Varieties of discourse: On the study of organizations through discourse analysis. *Human Relations, 53,* 1125-1149.

Baker, D. D., & Ganster, D. C. (1985). Leader communication style: A test of average versus vertical dyad linkage models. *Group and Organization Studies, 10,* 242-259.

Barge, J. K., & Schleuter, D. W. (1991). Leadership as organizing: A critique of leadership instruments. *Management Communication Quarterly, 4,* 541-570.

Bauer, T. N., & Green, S. G. (1996). The development of leader-member exchange: A longitudinal test. *Academy of Management Journal, 39,* 1538-1567.

Baugh, S. G., & Graen, G. B. (1997). Effects of team gender and racial composition on perceptions of team performance in cross-functional teams. *Group and Organization Management, 22,* 366-383.

Baxter, L. (1988). A dialectical perspective on communication strategies in relationship development. In S. Duck, D. Hay, S. Jobfoll, W. Ickes, & B. Montgomery (Eds.), *Handbook of personal relationships: Theory, research, and interventions* (pp. 257-274). Chichester, UK: Wiley.

Baxter, L. (1990). Dialectical contradictions in relationship development. *Journal of Personal and Social Relationships, 7,* 69-88.

Baxter, L. (1992). Interpersonal communication as a dialogue: A response to the "social approaches" forum. *Communication Theory, 2,* 330-336.

Baxter, L. A., & Montgomery, B. M. (1996). *Relating: Dialogue and dialectics.* New York: Guilford.

Boden, D. (1994). *The business of talk: Organizations in action.* Cambridge, UK: Polity.

Boje, D. M. (1991). The storytelling organization: A study of story performance in an office supply firm. *Administrative Science Quarterly, 36,* 106-126.

Boje, D. M. (2001). *Narrative methods for organizational and communication research.* London: Sage.

Boland, R. J., & Tenkasi, R. T. (1995). Perspective making and perspective taking in communities of knowing. *Organization Science, 6,* 350-372.

Bruner, J. S. (1986). *Actual minds, possible worlds.* Cambridge, MA: Harvard University Press.
Bruner, J. S. (1990). *Acts of meaning.* Cambridge, MA: Harvard University Press.
Cooren, F. 2001. *The organizing property of communication.* Amsterdam: John Benjamins.
Coser, R. L. (1960). Laughter among colleagues: A study of the social functions of humor among the staff of a mental hospital. *Psychiatry, 23,* 81-95.
Cronen, V. E. (1995). Coordinated management of meaning: The consequentiality of communication and the recapturing of experience. In S. J. Sigman (Ed.), *The consequentiality of communication* (pp. 17-65). Hillsdale, NJ: Lawrence Erlbaum.
Czarniawska-Joerges, B. (1997). *Narrating the Organization: Dramas of institutional identity.* Chicago: University of Chicago Press.
Dansereau, F., Yammarino, F. J., & Markham, S. E. (1995). Leadership: The multiple-level approaches. *Leadership Quarterly, 6,* 97-109.
Dienesch, R. M., & Liden, R. C. (1986). Leader-member exchange model of leadership: A critique and further development. *Academy of Management Review, 11,* 618-634.
Dose, J. (1999). The relationship between work values similarity and team-member and leader-member exchange relationships. *Group Dynamics: Theory, Research and Practice, 3,* 20-32.
Edwards, D. (1997). *Discourse and cognition.* London: Sage.
Fairhurst, G. T. (1993). The leader-member exchange patterns of women in leaders in industry: A discourse analysis. *Communication Monographs, 60,* 321-351.
Fairhurst, G. T. (2001). Dualisms in leadership research. In F. M. Jablin & L. L. Putnam (Eds.), *The new handbook of organizational communication: Advances in theory, research, and methods* (pp. 379-439). Thousand Oaks: Sage.
Fairhurst, G. T. (2004, in press). Text, context, and agency in interaction analysis. *Organization, 11.*
Fairhurst, G. T., & Chandler, T. A. (1989). Social structure in leader-member interaction. *Communication Monographs, 56,* 215-239.
Fairhurst, G. T., & Cooren, F. (In press). Organizational language-in-use: A comparison of interaction analysis, conversation analysis and speech act schematics. In D. Grant, H. Hardy, C. Oswick, N. Phillips & L. L. Putnam (Eds.), *The Sage handbook of organizational discourse.*
Fairhurst, G. T., Cooren, F., & Cahill, D. (2002). Discursivness, contradiction, and unintended consequences in successive downsizings. *Management Communication Quarterly, 15,* 501-540.
Fairhurst, G. T., & Snavely, B. K. (1983). Majority and token minority group relationships: Power acquisition and communication. *Academy of Management Review, 8,* 292-300.

Fleishman, J., & Marwell, G. (1977). Status congruence and associativeness: A test of Galtung's theory. *Sociomerty, 40,* 1-11.

Foucault, M. (1972). *The archeology of knowledge* (A. M. S. Smith, Trans.). New York: Pantheon.

Foucault, M. (1976). *The archaeology of knowledge* (A. M. S. Smith, Trans.). New York: Harper & Row.

Foucault, M. (1980). *Power/knowledge: Selected interviews and other writings* (C. Gordon, Trans.). New York: Pantheon Books.

Gerstner, C. R., & Day, D. V. (1997). Meta-analytic review of leader-member exchange theory: Correlates and construct issues. *Journal of Applied Psychology, 82,* 827-844.

Graen, G. B., & Scandura, T. (1987). Toward a psychology of dyadic organizing. In B. Staw & L. L. Cummings (Eds.), *Research in organizational behavior* (Vol. 9, pp. 175-208). Greenwich, CT: JAI.

Graen, G. B., & Uhl-Bien, M. (1995). Relationship-based approach to leadership: Development of a leader-member exchange (LMX) theory of leadership over 25 years–Applying a multi-level multi-domain perspective. *Leadership Quarterly, 6,* 219-247.

Greimas, A. J. (1983). *Structural Semantics: An attempt at a method* (R. S. D. McDowell, & Alan Velie, Trans.). Lincoln: University of Nebraska Press.

Greimas, A. J. (1987). *On meaning: Selected writings in semiotic theory* (P. J. Perron & F. H. Collins, Trans.). London: Frances Pinter.

Gronn, P. (2002). Distributed leadership as a unit of analysis. *Leadership Quarterly, 13,* 423-452.

Harré, R. (1984). *Personal being.* Cambridge, MA: Harvard University Press.

Helmer, J. (1993). Story telling in the creation and maintenance of organizational tension and stratification. *The Southern Communication Journal, 59,* 34-44.

House, R. J., & Aditya, R. (1997). The social scientific study of leadership: Quo vadis? *Journal of Management, 23,* 409-473.

Jefferson, G. (1978). Sequential aspects of storytelling in conversation. In J. Schenkein (Ed.), *Studies in the organization of conversational interaction* (pp. 219-248). New York: Academic Press.

Keller, T., & Dansereau, F. (1995). Leadership and empowerment: A social exchange perspective. *Human Relations, 48,* 127-145.

Lee, J., & Jablin, F. M. (1995). Maintenance communication in superior-subordinate work relationships. *Human Communication Research, 22,* 220-257.

Liden, R. C., Sparrowe, R. T., & Wayne, S. J. (1997). Leader-member exchange theory: The past and potential for the future. In G. R. Ferris (Ed.), *Research in personnel and human resources management* (Vol. 15, pp. 47-119). Greenwich, CT: JAI.

Liden, R. C., Wayne, S. J., & Stilwell, D. (1993). A longitudinal study on the early development of leader-member exchange. *Journal of Applied Psychology, 78,* 662-674.

Martin, J., Feldman, M. S., Hatch, M. J., & Sitkin, S. B. (1983). The uniqueness paradox in organizational stories. *Administrative Science Quarterly, 28,* 438-453.

Martin, J., & Siehl, C. (1983). Organizational culture and counter culture: An uneasy symbiosis. *Organizational Dynamics, 12,* 52-64.

Mintzberg, H. (1982). If you're not serving Bill and Barbara, then you're not serving leadership. In J.G. Hunt, U. Sekaran, & C.A. Schriesheim (Eds.), *Leadership: Beyond establishment views* (pp. 239-259). Carbondale, IL: Southern Illinois University Press, 1982.

Montgomery, B. (1992). Communication as the interface between couples and culture. In S. A. Deetz (Ed.), *Communication yearbook 15* (pp. 475-507). Newbury Park, CA: Sage.

Mumby, D. K. (1987). The political function of narrative in organizations. *Communication Monographs, 54,* 113-127.

Mumby, D. K. (1988). Power, politics and organizational communication: Theoretical perspectives. In F. M. Jablin & L. L. Putnam (Eds.), *The new handbook of organizational communication* (pp. 585-623). London: Sage.

Ochs, E. (1997). Narrative. In T. A. v. Dijk (Ed.), *Discourse as structure and process* (Vol. 1, pp. 185-207). London: Sage.

O'Connor, E. S. (1997). Telling Decisions: The role of narrative in organizational decision making. In Z. Shapira (Ed.), *Organizational decision making* (pp. 304-323). New York: Cambridge University Press.

Orr, J. (1990). Sharing knowledge, celebrating identity: Community memory in a service culture. In D. S. Middleton & D. Edwards (Eds.), *Collective remembering: Memory in society* (pp. 169-189). Beverly Hills, CA: Sage.

Ouchi, W., & Wilkins, A. (1985). Organizational culture. *Annual Review of Sociology, 11,* 457-183.

Patriotta, G. (2003). Sensemaking on the shop floor: Narratives of knowledge in organizations. *Journal of Management Studies, 40,* 349-375.

Pearce, W. B. (1995). A sailing guide for social constructionists. In W. Leeds-Hurwitz (Ed.), *Social approaches to communication* (pp. 88-113). New York: Guilford Press.

Putnam, L. L., & Fairhurst, G. T. (2001). Discourse analysis in organizations: Issues and concerns. In F. M. Jablin & L. L. Putnam (Eds.), *The new handbook of organizational communication* (pp. 78-135). Thousand Oaks: Sage.

Rawlins, W. K. (1992). *Friendship matters: Communication, dialectics, and the life course.* New York: Aldine.

Rogers, L.E., & Farace, R.V. (1975). Relational communication analysis: New measurement procedures. *Human Communication Research, 1,* 222-239.

Roloff, M. E. (1981). *Interpersonal Communication: The social exchange approach.* Beverly Hills, CA: Sage.

Schank, R., & Ableson, R. (1977). *Scripts, plans and knowledge.* Hillsdale, NJ: Erlbaum.

Schein, E. (1985). *Organizational culture and leadership.* San Francisco: Jossey-Bass.

Schiemann, W. A., & Graen, G. B. (1984). *Structural and interpersonal effects in patterns of managerial communication.* Unpublished manuscript, Department of Management, University of Cincinnati.

Schneider, B., Goldstein, H.W., & Smith, B.D. (1995). The ASA framework: An update. *Personnel Psychology, 48,* 747-773.

Schriesheim, C. A., Castro, S. L., & Coglister, C. C. (1999). Leader-member exchange (LMX) research: A comprehensive review of theory, measurement, and data-analytic practices. *Leadership Quarterly, 10,* 63-114.

Schriesheim, C. A., Coglister, C. C., & Neider, L. L. (1995). "Is it trustworthy?" A multiple levels-of-analysis reexamination of an Ohio State leadership study with implications for future research. *Leadership Quarterly, 6,* 111-145.

Schriesheim, C. A., Neider, L. L., Scandura, T., & Tepper, B. J. (1992). Development and preliminary validation of a new scale (LMX-6) to measure leader-member exchange in organizations. *Educational and Psychological Measurement, 52,* 135-147.

Seers, A. (1989). Team-member exchange quality: A new construct for role making research. *Organizational Behavior and Human Decision Processes, 43,* 118-135.

Sherony, K.M., & Green, S.G. (2002). Coworker exchange: Relationships between coworkers, leader-member exchanges, and work attitudes. *Journal of Applied Psychology, 87,* 542-548.

Sias, P. M. (1996). Constructing perceptions of differential treatment: An analysis of coworker discourse. *Communication Monographs, 63,* 171-187.

Sparrowe, R. T., & Liden, R. C. (1997). Process and structure in leader-member exchange. *Academy of Management Review, 22,* 522-552.

Taylor, J. R., & Van Every, E. (2000). *The emergent organization: Communication as its site and surface.* Mahwah, NJ: Lawrence Erlbaum.

Tsoukas, H., & Hatch, M. J. (2001). Complex thinking, complex practice: The case for a narrative approach to organizational complexity. *Human Relations, 53,* 979-1013.

Uhl-Bien, M., & Graen, G. B. (1992). Self-management and team-making in cross-functional work teams: Discovering the keys to becoming an integrated team. *Journal of High Technology Management, 3,* 225-241.

Vecchio, R., & Gobdel, B. (1984). The vertical dyad linkage model of leadership: Problems and prospects. *Organizational Behavior and Human Performance, 34,* 5-20.

Weick, K. E. (1979). *The social psychology of organizing.* Reading, MA: Addison-Wesley.

Weick, K. E. (1995). *Sensemaking in organizations.* Thousand Oaks, CA: Sage.
White, H. (1987). *The content of the form.* Baltimore, MD: Johns Hopkins University Press.
Yukl, G. (1994). *Leadership in organizations* (3rd Ed.). Englewood Cliffs, NJ: Prentice Hall.
Zorn, T. E. (1995). Bosses and buddies: Constructing and performing simultaneously hierarchical and close friendship relationships. In J. T. Wood & S. Duck (Eds.), *Understudied relationships: Off the beaten path* (pp. 122-145). Thousand Oaks, CA: Sage.

Gail Fairhurst (gfairhurst@cinci.rr.com), PhD, University of Oregon, is a Professor of Communication at the University of Cincinnati. Her research interests include organizational leadership and discourse studies. Her articles have regularly appeared in both communication and management journals. She is also the coauthor of *The Art of Framing: Managing the Language of Leadership* (Jossey-Bass, 1996), which received the 1997 National Communication Association Organizational Communication Division Book of the Year Award.

Stephanie Hamlett (srhwc6@mizzou.edu), MA, University of Cincinnati, is a doctoral student in Communication at the University of Missouri. Her research interests include organizational, discourse studies, and narrative.

CHAPTER 6

INTERPERSONAL WORKPLACE THEORY AT THE CROSSROADS
LMX and Transformational Theory as Special Cases of Role Making in Work Organizations

George B. Graen

Thirty-five years of programmatic research on LMX has produced one of the most thoroughly studied theories of leadership and followership in the field. Ironically, LMX research began as a follower of traditional leadership style theory. Only after LMX research failed miserably to find empirical support for leadership style theory did it turn to leader and member exchange and found fertile soil for growth of understanding. This chapter focuses on the two dominant leadership theories: LMX and Transformational. Questions raised

---

Dealing with Diversity
A Volume in: LMX Leadership: The Series, pages 145–182.
Copyright © 2003 by Information Age Publishing, Inc.
All rights of reproduction in any form reserved.
ISBN: 1-930608-49-7 (hardcover), 1-930608-48-9 (paperback)

about both leadership formulations are recognized and discussed. Both theories are seen as having strengths and weaknesses, but they also are seen as complementary.

Role making as a general process for building interpersonal social relationships (Graen, 1976) has been de-emphasized somewhat in the research focus on documenting the LMX branches of relational theory. It seems to be the right time to attempt to broaden our foci to include dyadic relationships specified by other theories regarding leadership building in work organizations. To accomplish this, the "black box" (Rousseau, 1997) of interpersonal workplace theory including LMX and Transformational theory must be opened.

Before we open the "black box," the outline of the meta-theory that has been employed to cast light into the black box needs to be reviewed. This approach, called "strong inference" (Dunnette, 1966), prescribes the systematic scientific examination of unknown phenomena. It may be outlined roughly in five (5) steps:

1. carefully state the most plausible hypotheses,
2. perform well-informed critiques on both theory and methods,
3. carry out a series of empirical studies that successively appropriate critical tests,
4. carefully restate the most plausible hypotheses based on the tests, and finally
5. repeat steps 2 through 5 as often as necessary.

The definitions of "critical tests" are those that rule out some competing alternative explanation. Strong inference applies to programmatic research that builds carefully on the results of previous studies (Platt, 1963).

OPENING THE "BLACK BOX"

Illuminating the internal process of the dyadic "black box" was originally accomplished by teams of dedicated researchers using the strong inference approach. At that time the classical Average Leadership Style (ALS) approach was accepted as the most plausible theory for developing workplace interpersonal relationships.

According to this ALS approach, every leader has a profile of leadership behaviors that is applied equally to all direct reports. In addition, some leaders need to change their style by making it more individually considerate and stimulating and more or less structuring. When the best style depended on the particular situation facing the work unit, the ALS model was called situational.

According to this ALS model, leaders influence augmented performance of their followers through their behavior style, and all followers received the same treatment from the leader. The measurement assumptions were that the leader had a single style, that it was uniformly applied, and that all followers reacted the same to the leader's style. These assumptions produced the following prescribed measurement procedure: Sample at least three people from each follower group and use their average leadership descriptions to measure their leader's style in terms of consideration and structure or concern for people and concern for production or some other dichotomy of style (Stogdill, 1948).

Dissonant Results

Graen, Orris, and Johnson (1973) performed a longitudinal study of supervisors and new clerical hires focusing on the supervisor's effort profile expectations and the new hire's understanding of the same. Results over the six week probationary period showed that the same supervisors kept some new hires well informed regarding their expectations, but let other new hires flounder in progressively increasing ambiguity. Those who were kept well informed stayed on after the probationary period, whereas, those who floundered left the organization early. These results raised questions about treating all direct reports the same. Clearly, this assumption was shown to be invalid in this turnover study.

In an earlier field experiment (Graen, 1969), the same leader's behavior was reacted to differently by different direct reports, and these differences were predictive of improvements in hard performance from pretest to posttest. These findings raised questions about how direct reports reacted to the same leader's behavior. In this investigation, the leader's behavior was carefully controlled to be the same for all direct reports. Based on these results, a research design was proposed for a longitudinal investigation of leaders tailoring their behavior to the needs of their individual direct reports (Graen, 1968).

Questions Raised

These studies raised the following questions:

Q1: How variable are vertical dyadic (direct report), interpersonal relationships over time?

Q2: How variable are these relationships with the same leader?

Q3: Do these relationships predict organizational outcomes?

Q4: Do these relationships add any valid variance beyond what ALS in predicting about organizational outcomes?

Q5: Can these relationships predict organization outcomes better than individual's job satisfaction?

Q6: Are dyadic interpersonal relations changed over a developmental period?

These questions were investigated in the series of studies shown in Table 1. The results show support for diverse yet stable dyadic relationships within organizational units that are related to organizational outcomes. In addition, these dyadic relationships can add valid variance beyond ALS in predicting organizational outcomes. Moreover, these dyadic relationships were shown to predict turnover better than job satisfaction. Finally, the longitudinal studies suggested that dyad relations were strengthened selectively over time through a role-making process in which offers were not made to all direct reports by their leaders, and all offers made were not accepted.

This raised a new set of questions:

Q7: Can dyadic relationships be renegotiated over time?

Q8: Are certain followers more susceptible to dyadic role making?

TABLE 1
Systematic Documentation of the New Dyadic LMX Paradigm Using WABA

Year Published	Author(s)	Sample(s)	Number Size/Unit	Ind/Dep Variables	Study Design	Findings Between/Within
1973	Graen, Orris, & Johnson	Secretarial New Hires	64 24	Dyadic LMX Leadership/ Turnover	Longitudinal 6 months (5)	No Yes
1974	Haga, Graen, & Dansereau	Hotel Managers & Professionals	60 10	Dyadic Professionalism/Leader's rating of Follower's Actions	Longitudinal 9 months (4)	Yes Yes
1975	Graen & Cashman	Library Professionals	109 27	Dyadic LMX Leadership/ Leader's rating of Follower's Actions	Longitudinal 9 months (4)	No Yes
1975	Dansereau, Graen, & Haga	Hotel Managers & Professionals	60 10	Dyadic LMX Leadership/ Leader's rating of Follower's Action	Longitudinal 9 months (4)	No Yes
1977	Graen, Cashman, Ginsburgh, & Schiemann	Library Professional	103 27	Dyadic LMX Upper Dyad Dyadic LMX Lower Dyad/ Follower's Situation	Longitudinal 9 months (4)	Yes Yes
1978	Graen & Schiemann	Service Professionals	109/ 27 41/ 15	Dyadic LMX Leadership/ Agreement Between on Situations	Longitudinal 4 months (2)	No Yes

TABLE 1
Continued

Year Published	Author(s)	Sample(s)	Number Size/Unit	Ind/Dep Variables	Study Design	Findings Between/Within
1980	Liden & Graen	Maintenance Managers	41 15	Dyadic LMX Leadership/ Leader's rating of Follower's Action	Cross-Sectional (1)	No Yes
1981	Katerberg[a] Hom	National Guard	672 31	Dyadic LBDQ-XII/ Follower's Satisfaction	Cross-Sectional (1)	Yes Yes
1982	Vecchio[a]	US Air Force	192 48	Dyadic Individual LBDS (Rice & Chemers, 1975) / Follower's Behavior	Cross Sectional (1)	No No
1982	Graen,[b] Novak, & Sommerkamp	Account Technicians	132 7	Dyadic LMX Leadership Offer / Hard Productivity	Randomized Field Experiment 6 months (3)	No Yes
1982	Graen, Liden, & Hoel	Information Systems Professionals	48 17	Dyadic LMX Leadership/ Turnover	Longitudinal 3 years (3)	No Yes

Year	Study	N	Measure	Design	Replication
1984	Dansereau, Alutto, & Yammarino	276 / 83	Dyadic Leader Attention & Latitude (from Graen, 1976) / Leader's ratings of Follower's Behavior	Cross-Sectional (1)	Yes / Yes
1985	Ferris	68 / 18	Replication of Graen et al. (1982)	Longitudinal One Year (2)	No / Yes
1985	Vecchio	45 / 12	Replication of Graen et al. (1982)	Longitudinal One Year (2)	No / No
1986	Graen[b] Scandura & Graen	62 / 7	Dyadic LMX Leadership Offer/Hard Productivity	Randomized Field Experiment 6 months (3)	No / Yes

Notes: Supersedes Table 1 by Podsakoff and MacKinzie (1995).

Number in parenthesis under Study Design indicates waves of data collected. Graen, Scandura, & Graen (1986) was a "yoked-replication" of Graen, Novak, and Sommerkamp (1982) training the former control group to make LMX offers which replicated the 50% hard productivity gains. Moreover, Ferris (1985) replicated Graen, Liden, and Hoel (1982) independently and in all respects including the JDI (Smith, 1967) versus LMX wash out contest. After the Ferris' replication the empirical base for dyadic LMX leadership within groups as a valid construct and measure was firmly established and additional replications could add little to our knowledge.

[a] All same-source correlations which cannot be interpreted using WABA II.

[b] True field experiment with randomization of groups and producing 50% hard productivity gains from LMX training high of growth need strength.

These questions were tested and replicated in two field experiments, each over six-months in length. It was found that dyadic relationships can be renegotiated over time, and dyads can change relationships dramatically (Graen, Scandura, & Graen, 1986). In these experiments, the programmed offering of relational role making by the manager elicited hard productivity as well as relational gains. This was especially the case for the high growth need (Hackman & Oldham, 1976) technicians. This change in the quality of the relational role was further elaborated by Scandura and Graen (1984) and Graen and Scandura (1987). This susceptibility of high growth need (GNS) followers was replicated by Graen and Scandura (1986).

Stock Taking

What was learned at this point was that dyadic, interpersonal relational role making is different from the formal organizationally prescribed process of job relational role taking (Graen, 1976). This was suggested by the findings that different people in similar jobs demonstrated different interpersonal dyadic relations with their direct reports and performed different extra-role tasks. This was conceptualized as two different processes: (1) Everyone was offered and accepted the job relational role taking, but (2) not everyone was offered or accepted the interpersonal relational role making. Thus, this role making was an optional process and an extra organizational one which changed the way different people performed on the same job. The results of the two field experiments in Table 1 suggested that only high growth need (GNS) followers were susceptible and would likely accept role making offers.

Findings from these studies also suggest that this optional process of role making was not restricted to direct reporting relationships. Peers and coworkers also appeared to practice role making selectively. When this process occurred between direct reports it was called leader-member exchange (LMX), when it occurred between peers in the same unit it was called member-member exchange (MMX), and when it was between coworkers, it was called coworker exchange (CWX). All three were seen as dyadic interpersonal relational role making which could influence role relationships and consequentially how people behave on their jobs. Because the products of role making were demonstrated so clearly in the vertical case, this was the situation of choice for most research.

An unforeseen problem with this emphasis on the LMX case at the expense of the MMX and CWX cases has been the common assumption that the process underlying these three cases is vastly different. On the contrary, we assume that they are three cases of dyadic, interpersonal role making differing mainly in comparative power and interdependence. We assume that they are three cases of dyadic influence development.

Turning to LMX within organizational units, the findings clearly indicate the optional nature of role making. Within the same unit, LMX can vary widely among direct report dyads. None of the organizations studied had formal role making procedures except our experimentally imposed ones in the field experiments. Thus, mostly naturally occurring role making was studied. In some units, the differences between those who had benefited from role making and those who had not were so strong that we called them "In" and "Out" dyadic relations. This did not mean that new role making could not move people from weak (Out) to strong (In) relationships and vice versa. This was intended to differentiate those who had successfully undergone role making from those who had not.

Within units, the findings demonstrated that those with strong LMX (with role making) and from those with weak LMX (without role making) differed significantly on work outcomes such as performing extra-role and more responsible tasks, and collaborating with their leader on their leader's critical decisions and projects (Dansereau, Graen, & Haga, 1975; Graen & Cashman, 1975; Graen & Schiemann, 1978; Graen & Novak, 1982; Liden & Graen, 1980; Graen, Novak, & Sommerkamp, 1982; Graen, et al., 1986). In addition, almost all groups contained members who had undergone role-making and others who had not, judging from their job role and relationships.

Critical Test

A Strong Inference "critical" test based on Graen, Orris, and Johnson (1973) was finally completed which necessarily employed an experimentally unconfounded criterion variable, which was measured by a different method of assessment, namely, turnover. Results of this study showed that *within* group dyadic leadership (i.e., LMX) contributed to follower turnover, whereas the *between* group leadership (i.e., average unit LMX) did not contribute to turnover. This relationship between *within* group LMX and turnover was both statistically ($p < .01$) and practically significant. Moreover, *within* LMX contributed more strongly to turnover than any of the competing Job Descriptive Index (JDI) satisfaction scales (Smith, 1967). LMX was stronger than JDI in predicting turnover. This was shown by LMX statistically washing out the JDI relations when entered first on turnover, but not the reverse. Also, "critical" support of the Graen, Liden, and Hoel (1982) study was provided by a rigorous replication by an independent investigator (Ferris, 1985). Ferris' results were virtually identical to the Graen, et al. (1982) study. Even the findings of washing out of the JDI predictions of turnover by *within* LMX, but not the reverse, were replicated. This was a strictly independent replication.

Results of these rigorous tests of theory-derived hypotheses strongly supported the proposition that leadership at the dyad level (LMX) can contain valid variance. In short, leadership also lives at the dyadic (i.e., two-person) level as well as the group (i.e., all members of the unit including the leader) level. This *within* group effect held even under the restriction of partialling out a large amount of potentially valid dyadic variance from the LMX score by taking out all between group variance. Let us be clear, this does not mean that leadership (LMX) at the group level cannot also be valid. Clearly, this has been demonstrated before on experimentally unconfounded dependent variables (Stogdill, 1948). Thus, LMX theory assumes that leadership can exist at either or both levels depending on the situation: (a) leaders can develop different LMXs with different followers, and (b) different leaders can develop different compositions of LMX within their group. Thus (a) and (b) can happen at the same time for the same people.

The role-making frame of reference is a general social reference group, and is not restricted to any particular work group. Therefore, LMX can be analyzed as within a group (i.e., by partialling out *between* group), but also it can be analyzed as within an organization (i.e., by partialling out between organizations) or within a culture (i.e., by partial out between cultures). Analogously, asking for a single child's description of his/her relationship with his/her mother does not require a family reference because a societal reference is more appropriate. Without a doubt, the question of how good was one's communications with one's mother could be answered relative to those of one's grade school chums or relative to any cohort member known, or heard about, or read about.

LMX as a measure of the quality of the dyadic interpersonal relationship can be interpreted relative to one's work group chums or relative to anyone one has heard or read about. It is not restricted by temporary group or organization. However, we believe that it may need cross-cultural adjustments to make it comparable across cultures (Graen, Hui, Wakabayashi, & Wang, 1997). In this, we agree with House and Aditya, (1997). Clearly, role-making theory works in Japan (Wakabayashi, Minami, Hashimoto, Sano, Graen, & Novak, 1980; Wakabayashi & Graen, 1984; 1988; Wakabayashi, Graen, Graen, & Graen, 1988; Wakabayashi, Graen, & Uhl-Bien, 1990), but different behaviors are involved.

Misunderstanding the In and Out

In the role-making literature, there is no line of research about managers purposefully forming an in-clique and treating members of such an in-group more favorably from members of the rest of the work group. In fact, we know of no such study. Graen (1976) suggested no reified in-group and out-group within the leader's group of direct reports. This in-group/out-group dichotomy was semantic only, and was employed by Graen in the past to emphasize that leader-member relationships vary in quality from high to low depending on the developed levels of mutual trust, respect, and commitment. Clearly, no research evidence supporting this dichotomy of favored clique and disfavored clique exits in the empirical literature.

In contrast, many studies support the alternative explanation of a continuous construct of LMX relationship quality (For a meta-analysis on LMX theory and research, see Gerstner & Day, 1997). In fact, Gerstner and Day concluded, in their meta-analytic review, that LMX7, a continuous and unidimensional measurement scale, was superior to all other measurement devices in terms of reliability and validity, and was recommended as the best. Therefore, LMX7 is now the accepted standard. Overall, attempts to ask about favored cliques and disfavored cliques have been few and quite uniformly ineffective. Generally, leaders refuse to admit that they systematically and intentionally disadvantage any of their direct reports.

Indeed, it would be difficult to construe them as effective leaders if they did so.

Prescriptively, using LMX theory and research, it would be dysfunctional for teamwork for a leader to purposefully create two such cliques. In contradiction to Northhouse (2001), the existence of such opposite cliques threatens that: the productive contributions of the leader and the favored clique would be undermined by the disfavored clique. In contrast, LMX theory and research predict and find that leaders attempt to prevent the emergence of such cliques because they lead to conflict and wasted resources, both human and material. In those few cases where cliques are present before the leader assumes the role, the leader is directed by LMX theory to dismantle them and bring all direct reports into the fold of high LMX

To seriously propose that we study leadership groups that contain favored and disfavored cliques assumes that we can identify them empirically. We know of no research which has established the base rate of such groups or has developed acceptable measures of this construct. According to Schriesheim, Castro, and Cogliser (1999), two opposite cliques are present when the leader:=

1. recognizes them as different cliques,
2. behaves differently to members based on clique membership alone, and
3. behaves consistently to favor one clique's members and to disfavor the other clique's members.

In all our years of leadership research and consulting, we have never found a leader who would ascribe to such dysfunctional behavior. In sum, this appears to be an extremely rare event in leadership groups and clearly not popular leadership practice. This being the case, it would be difficult to find enough cases to research properly. Clearly, the third type, proposed by Schriesheim and his associates, is rare and may be a null set. Clearly, it has never been successfully studied to our knowledge.

In Sum

Understanding of the contents of the processes inside the black box of LMX, MMX, and CWX can be summed up by describing the appropriate dyadic, interpersonal role making. For the LMX case, it was described by Graen and Uhl-Bien (1995) and the MMX and CWX cases were described by Uhl-Bien, Graen, and Scandura (2000). In all three cases, role making involves social exchange based on respect, trust, and commitment. This social exchange is different from transformational leadership (Bass, 1985), which is not based on social exchange of any kind, but is based on member-accepted leader behavior.

TWO COMPETING MODELS

Strong inference advances theory construction by testing competing hypotheses. In the case of LMX leadership, the closest competing model is transformational leadership (Bass, 1985). Both models employ follower descriptions of dyadic leader-follower relationships, and predict leadership and organizational outcomes. We can best discover and document how they agree and differ when investigated within the same study.

What are the similarities and differences between these two approaches? Both use the concept of leadership as emergent influence of a person over a follower's thinking, feeling, and doing in some area of human endeavor. As outlined above, leadership is not part of the role-taking process of a follower accepting a prescribed job. It is a different process of emotional attachment and identification with the leader which involves a social exchange process of role making, and produces the above emergent influence. However, they do differ in their leadership outcomes.

LMX theory specifies that in addition to emergent influence, leader and member engage in collaboration on mission activities, build strong relational outcomes of affect, trust, respect, and commitment. Transformational theory specifies that in addition to emergent influence, leader and member engage in a conversion process in which the follower comes to identify with and emulate the leader and accept his prescriptions for thinking, feeling, and acting, and to have strong affection and emotional attachment toward the leader. At the extreme, the self-esteem of the follower is dependent on his or her leader's consideration.

For both theories, organizational outcomes predicted are the same, namely, satisfaction, commitment, performance, motivation, and turnover. Thus, the theories differ in their predicted leadership outcomes, which is where studies testing the two competing models should be focused. What behavioral categories are specified in each theory (House & Aditya, 1997)? LMX prescribes negotiating an offer of emergent leadership which involves seeking value agreement, sharing of nonroutine problem solving and decision making, engaging in reciprocal support for thinking, feeling, and doing, developing dyadic language, performing mutual role negotiation, discussing choice framing, considering suggestions, and doing career mentoring (Fairhurst, Rogers, & Sarr, 1987; Graen, 1989).

In contrast, transformational prescribes symbolic leader behavior, visionary and inspirational appeals to ideologies, intellectual stimulation, Pygmalion expectations, confidence, and image building (House & Shamir, 1993). Clearly, these behavioral categories need to be refined to permit competing hypothesis testing. For example, seeking value agreement may be included in visionary and inspirational appeals to ideologies, and engaging in reciprocal support for thinking, feeling, and doing may be included in Pygmalion expectations and confidence.

Both theories require a role-making process to allow leader and follower to interact on relevant issues. One difference appears to be that LMX prescribes a social exchange between two active participants, whereas transformational prescribes a conversion process between an active leader and a passive follower. This difference in followers suggests a strong inference test. Next, we turn to new formulations of transformational leadership that may further clarify the nature of the difference in followers.

Transformational leadership was refined by Kark and Shamir (2002) based on a general self-concept theory proposed by Lord, Brown, and Freiberg (1999). According to this theory, transformational leaders must have high self-esteem and high self-concept clarity which was defined by Campbell (1990) as the degree to which the contents of the individual's self-concept are clearly and confidently defined, internally consistent, and temporally stable. In other words, it is a classic human trait. It is highly related to, but not the same as, self-esteem which is the evaluative component of self-concept (Gecas, 1982). Both are assumed to be stable characteristics of individuals.

Transformational leaders tend to be characterized as high self-esteem and high self-concept clarity. Transformational followers tend to be best characterized as low self-esteem and low self-concept clarity (Freemesser & Kaplan, 1976; Galanter, 1982). These weak followers are particularly susceptible to the influence of charismatic ideologies (Erickson, 1980). Transformational leaders are most effective in influencing such followers, and seek them out to execute their personal agenda. They accomplish this by providing self-relevant social cues that fulfill needed self-direction and identification with an attractive and powerful leader (Brockner, 1988).

When transformational leaders must deal with followers with low self-esteem and low self-concept clarity, the behaviors that give the leader charismatic power are communicating a new ideological vision, intellectually challenging followers to think outside the box, sending Pygmalion expectations, praising the follower's worth and role modeling (Bass, 1985; Conger & Kanungo, 1998; House & Shamir, 1993; Shamir, House, & Arthur, (1993).

Compared to transformational leaders, LMX leaders cannot be characterized as single-minded, but they tend to have at least moderate self-esteem and rather clear self-concepts. LMX partners cannot be characterized as low self-esteem and low self-concept clarity. Each appears to have at least moderate self-esteem, and low self-concept clarity followers tend not to invite nor accept LMX offers. LMX leaders make offers of partnership to strong followers which involve a negotiated mission based on shared values and the relational attributes of respect, trust, and commitment in the relationship. Thus, when the leader is a strong personality and the true followers are weak personalities, the transformational method works to generate the required increments in influence. When the leader is moderate in strength of personality and so are the partner followers, the LMX method works to generate the required increments in influence.

What is needed to test this two-factor model is research that measures the appropriate variables in the same design: MFQ, LMX7, Self-concept clarity, and Self-esteem of leaders and followers, and follower behavior and performance. An interesting study of this kind, by Howell and Hall-Merenda (1999), showed that LMX leadership was a better predictor than transformation of follower performance 12 months later. With 317 Canadian bankers, the standardized path coefficients for partial least square (PLS) on performance were

a. LMX = .34 (p < .0005), Transformational = .12 NS, Contingent Reward = -.03 NS, Active Management by Exception = .15 NS, and Passive Management by Exception = -.12 NS. LMX components for PLS were

a. Transformational = .54 (p < .0005),
b. Contingent Reward = .45 (p < .0005),
c. Active Management by Exception = -.38 (p < .0005), and Passive Management by Exception = -.35 (p<.0005).

In addition, LMX worked for both established (i.e., distant office) and developing (i.e., home office) managers, but transformational only worked for home office managers. This may reflect stronger and weaker self-concepts. These results are in agreement with Gerstner and Day's (1997) meta-analysis of LMX theory and Graen and Uhl-Bien's (1995) review of LMX theory and research. That is, they suggest that LMX taps into a critical relationship at work between leader and follower and this relationship has a strong impact on follower performance.

Moreover, transformational measures are about a follower's view of the leader's behavior, and this has less impact on the follower's performance. Unless the leader's behavior, according to LMX theory, is appropriately contingent with leader and follower's dyadic relationship, it tends to have less impact on strong followers performance. As in Pygmalion theory (Eden, 1993), a leader's sending strong performance expectations to a strong follower may fall on deaf ears unless the LMX is appropriately developed. Leadership behavior to the wrong audience is a poor predictor of follower performance.

Clearly, we need more competing hypothesis investigations testing transformational with LMX leadership theory. By performing tests comparing the two, the relative strengths and weakness of each theory will be systematically revealed. Next, we turn to the common dimensionality question using factor analysis.

DIMENSIONALITY OF THE LMX CONSTRUCT

As Borchgrevink and Boster (1998) mapped the terrain of LMX leadership characteristics, they found the pattern of evaluations by followers of the LMX leaders shown in Table 2. As can be seen in this Table, LMX was most highly correlated with *Respect* and *Trust* (.92), *LMX Relationship Satisfaction* (.87), *Self-Efficacy* (.79), *Commitment* (.74), *Paladin* (.65), *Fairness*, (.64), *Confidant* (.67), and *Dyadic Communications* (.63). At the other extreme, those characteristics of

TABLE 2
Characteristics of LMX Free-Dyads as Seen by Followers (N=236)

Scale	NS	Alpha	LMX Correlation
Trust and Respect...	8	.90	.92***
LMX Satisfaction...	4	.89	.87***
Self-Efficacy...	2	.84	.79***
Mutual Commitment...	2	.87	.74***
Confidant...	5	.77	.67***
Paladin...	3	.75	.65***
Fairness...	3	.82	.64***
Dyadic Communications...	3	.78	.63***
Championing...	3	.83	.59**
Enjoyment...	2	.82	.54**
Care...	2	.64	.52**
Reciprocity...	3	.85	.51**
Idiosyncratic...	2	.74	.45*
Ambivalence...	3	.79	.42*
Portfolio...	3	.63	.26
Maintenance...	3	.62	.23
Mutual Coercion...	2	.70	.22
Jealous...	3	.63	.22
Charisma...	3	.76	.16
Sexual Intimacy...	2	.82	.09

Notes: Scales with less than three items are not completely defined, but are shown for hypothesis generation purposes.
*Significant LE .05, two-tailed.
**Significant LE .01, two-tailed.
***Significant LE .001, two-tailed.

the free dyadic relationship which were seen as less highly correlated with LMX were *Sexual Intimacy* (.09), *Charisma* (.16), *Jealousy* (.22), *Mutual Coercion* (.22), *Maintenance* (.23), and *Portfolio of Leader* (.26). In the middle were characteristics such as leader *Championing* (.59), *Mutual Enjoyment* (.54), taking *Care* (.52), *Reciprocity* of assistance (.51), *Idiosyncratic* (.45), and *Ambivalence* of feeling (.42).

This supports the underlying dimensions of LMX theory in that *Trust* and *Respect* were proposed as two separate scales, but could not be separated empirically using CFA. In addition, *Trust* and *Respect* as a combined scale (alpha = 90) correlated the highest with the *LMX*

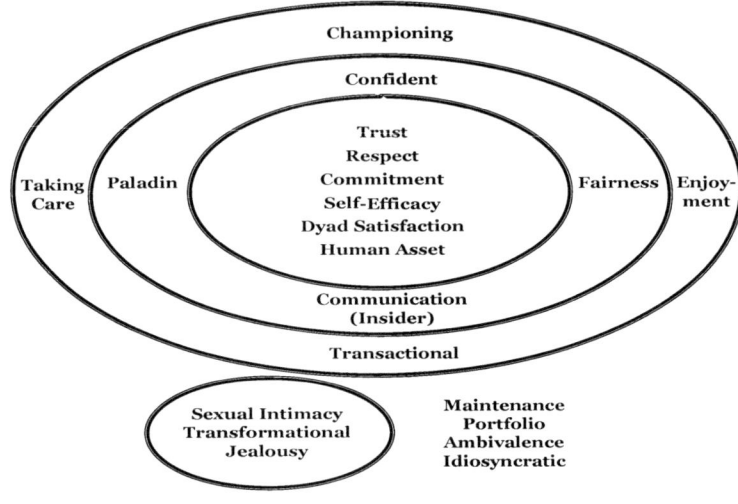

FIGURE 1
LMX Construct

(alpha = .92) measure. Moreover, *Commitment* (alpha = .87) correlated fourth highest with *LMX* and correlated highly with *Trust and Respect* (.68). Therefore, the three theoretical dimensions underlie the LMX free-dyad relationships which are mutual trust, respect and commitment were supported in this study. Finally, the strong correlation of *Self-Efficacy* (alpha = .84) with *LMX* (.79) suggest that a fourth dimension should be considered in addition. Although, it contained only two items, it correlated highest with *Trust and Respect* (.71) and with *Commitment* (.77). Also in this set was satisfaction with the dyadic relationship. Therefore, five factors may underlie the LMX leadership and followership relationship. Future studies should test this strong inference.

As shown in Figure 1, the inner core of LMX is *Mutual Trust, Respect, Commitment* and possibly *Self-Efficacy* and *Dyad Satisfaction*. The first ring around the inner core contains *Confidant, Paladin, Fairness,* and *Insider Communication*. The second ring around the inner core includes *Championing, Reciprocity, Enjoyment,* and *Taking Care* of each other. Finally, those outside of the second ring are most distant from the inner core. Some support was found for the Liden and Maslyn (1998) dimension of Loyalty. No support was found for House and Aditya's (1997) criticism of Trust, Respect, and Commitment underlying LMX7.

Bass' (1990) and House's (1991) model of transformational was not significantly correlated with *LMX* (.16), although the items clearly contain the content of their construct. The specific items were

1. "My supervisor dominates my thoughts,"
2. "I think about my supervisor even when I am not with my supervisor."
3. "It gives me pleasure to watch my supervisor."

This appears to be the behavioral results that the Bass' and House's models specify. In addition, *Charisma* is strongly correlated with *Jealousy* (.86), and *Sexual Intimacy* (.50). In addition, Eden's (1993) work on self-efficacy appears to be compatible with LMX theory, as is his work on the Pygmalion effect.

Construct validity of LMX7 has been repeatedly confirmed (Graen et al., 1982; Graen, et al., 1982; Novak, 1985; Scandura & Graen, 1984; Ferris, 1985; Scandura, Graen, & Novak, 1986; Seers & Graen, 1984; Tierney, 1999; Uhl-Bien, 1991). Finally, the Gerstner and Day (1997) meta-analysis found LMX7 to be psychometrically sound and superior to all other measures of LMX. Clearly, with Cronbach Alphas in the nineties, LMX7 is homogeneous with the four (4) LMX4 items and the additional three (3) LMX7 items. This unidimensionality has been shown repeatedly over a large number of different studies (Gerstner & Day, 1997). Although Liden and Maslyn (1998) suggest their MDX measure of LMX is multidimensional, its Cronbach Alpha suggests that it is unidimensional. LMX taps into domains called *trust, respect,* and *commitment,* its Alpha in the nineties suggests that these domains are highly correlated. In response to the Schriescheim et al. (1999) questions about LMX7 validity, the above should be sufficient to answer them.

OVERLAPPING VARIANCE BETWEEN LMX AND TRANSFORMATIONAL

Transformational Form and Contingent Reward (scales) of the MLQ (Bass & Avolio, 1990) were factor analyzed because several different studies found different factor structures (Howell & Avolio, 1993; Lowe, Kroek, & Sivasubramaniam, 1996; Yammarino, Spangler, & Bass, 1993; Yammarino & Dubinsky, 1994). The factoring

(Yammarino, Spangler, & Dubinsky, 1998) began with 47 items of the MLQ and ended with 9 items (MLQ9) which accounted for most of the reliable and valid variance. (Transformational has 5 items and Contingent Reward has 4 items.) It should be noted that in this study, these scales are factor scored and hence uncorrelated for follower's and leader's reports. The factoring worked well, producing two independent and homogeneous factors (.92 and .92 for follower's alphas and .77 and .84 for leader's alphas on Transformational and Contingent Reward, respectively).

As shown in Table 3 this new short-form MLQ9 clarifies the meaning of the two measures. Consider the items. Transformational asks for endorsements on a five-point agreement scale to the following five statements: (#15) I have complete faith in him/her, (#22) He/she has a special gift of seeing what it is that is really important for me to consider, (#9) His/her vision spurs me on, (#29) He/she is a symbol to me of success and accomplishment, (#64) I trust him/her to overcome obstacles. Note that none of these specifies particular behaviors. Dimensionally, this is quite similar to LMX7 (Graen & Uhl-Bien, 1995). The corresponding LMX7 items are shown in Table 3. By using the items shown in Table 3 to define the operational measures of Transformational, we can see why it is so highly correlated with LMX7.

It appears that the short form of MLQ reduces Transformational to two of the three components of LMX7. As shown, LMX7 taps the three components of mutual trust, respect, and commitment between follower and leader, and the focus is on the follower, the leader, and the working relationship between them. Similarly, Transformational taps *trust* and *respect,* but not the *commitment* component which may explain part of the difference between the two theories.

LMX theory specifies leader and follower interaction patterns in the development of dyadic (commitment) relationships between followers and leaders; whereas, Transformation Leadership theory specifies leader-only behavior patterns in the development of an appropriate follower. The two theories agree at the operational definition (measurement) level that two of the critical components of LMX and Transformational Leadership are followers Trust and Respect of leader, but they disagree in that LMX theory goes beyond this and specifies that leader's reciprocate follower's evaluations about Trust and Respect and Commitment.

TABLE 3
Dimensionality of Content of Yammarino's MLQ (short form) and Graen's LMX7 (short form)

Yammarino's MLQ (short form)	*Graen's LMX7 (short form)*
\multicolumn{2}{c}{*Trust In Leader*}	
a. Follower trusts leader to overcome obstacles #64	a. Follower trusts leader to do the right thing #6
	b. Follower trusts leader to help with job problem #4
	c. Follower trust leaders to "bail them out" at leaders expense #5
\multicolumn{2}{c}{*Respect For Leader*}	
b, Follower has great faith in leader #15	d. Follower has respect in that leader understands job problems and needs #2
c. Leader is seen by follower as successful #29	e. Follower has respect for leader's ability to recognize follower's potential #3
d. Leader has a special gift for seeing follower's best interests #22	
e. Leader's vision spurs on follower #9	
\multicolumn{2}{c}{*Commitment To Relationship*}	
	f. Leader is delighted with follower's performance (LMX7). #1
	g. Follower and leader have a great working relationship (Centroid). #7

Note: Both operational measures tap two of the same sources of variation and all three relational components are highly correlated with Cronbach alphas in the eighties and above. Relational components are appropriately measured by LMX theory but not by the leader-based theory of Bass (1985). In contrast, Bass' theory purports to measure leader behavior and not dyadic working relationships. Numbers after LMX7 items are LMX order (#1 to #7). Centroid indicates defining dimension of LMX7.

Clearly, Transformational has been reduced to its basic dimension in this seminal investigation. The other LMX7 items, identified by their components are shown at the bottom of Table 3. It should be noted that the main operational differences between LMX7 and MFLQ-short form of Transformational Leadership is that MFLQ-short form purports to tap leader behavior directly and LMX7 purports to tap the relational components of *mutual trust, respect,* and *commitment.* MLQ-short form does not ask about behavior directly judging from the items, but asks about the relational components of *mutual trust* and *respect,* but not *commitment.*

In both theories, what is needed to achieve these relational components is specified, and it is here that the two theories differ. Transformational theory prescribes that leaders develop a specified leader behavior style to transform the group into a loyal subordinates ready to do the leader's bidding. In contrast, LMX theory prescribes that leaders interact with followers to build mature dyadic partnerships and assemble these mature dyads into a team which is committed to group plans and goals.

At this operational level, Transformational theory taps into the same sources of variance that LMX measures have mined for over 35 years. The mother lode of leadership resides in the leader and follower dyadic relationship. Defining items of the short form transformational scale were not behavior descriptions as theorized, but role-making outcomes, (e.g., having faith, seeing special gift, accepting vision, and becoming a success symbol). As Yammarino and his colleagues (1998) found, the defining items of the short form transformational scale were not behavior descriptions.

Transformational theory suggests that a leader's behavior should be measured directly through observation or videotape or both, and doing a Bales-type coding. They might also have leaders, followers, and others in the workplace keep diaries of actions by leaders and their consequences in a critical incident fashion (Bales, 1949).

It is interesting that MLQ (short form) purports to contain four dimensions of transformational leadership called:

1. charisma,
2. inspirational,
3. individualized consideration and
4. intellectual stimulation.

the long form measures these four (4) using 37 items, but they were able to cull this down from 37 to 5 items. What did this factoring process omit and what are the implications for construct validity?

As shown in Table 4, we classified the 5 best items into the four underlying dimensions and found that only two dimensions were needed: Inspirational (priest role) and charisma (shaman role). The omitted dimensions were individualized consideration (social worker role) and intellectual stimulation (teacher role). Apparently,

TABLE 4
Classifying MLQ-Short Form on Constructs

#15	I have complete faith in him/her...	(Inspirational)
#9	His/her vision spurs me on...	(Inspirational)
#22	He/she has a special gift of seeing What it is that is really important For me to consider...	(Charisma)
#29	He/she is a symbol of success... and accomplishment...	(Charisma)
#64	I trust him/her to overcome Obstacles...	(Charisma)

Notes: We had the most difficulty classifying #22, because it had both "special gift" and "me", but the former was dominant for us. Also, #9 had both "vision" and "me", but again the former was dominant for us.

the dimensions of intellectual stimulation and individualized consideration were superfluous to the overall short form. Thus, they may need to train leaders to gain the faith of group members in two roles: (1) they as leaders in their vision and (2) the magic of charisma for the group members as holding special gifts to see what was best for people, to overcome obstacles and to be a symbol of success.

Q AND A ABOUT ROLE MAKING AND LMX

Q1: "Four stage model suggested by Graen and Uhl-Bien (1995): we maintain that the development of the theory within each of its stages of development is equally if not more important. While Graen and Uhl-Bien categorized various LMX studies, it is difficult to follow the development of the construct from their presentation, the discussion of Stages #1, #2 and #3 all contain references to papers within the same time frame (1984-1987). This chronological mixing of studies thus appears to contradict the assertion that the theoretical development of the LMX construct has been chronologically progressive and based on previous LMX theory; there does not appear to have been a clear development and refinement of ideas over time." (Schriesheim et al., 1999, p. 69).

A1: Figure 2 illustrates the branching progression of LMX theory and research over 35 years. It shows that it began with average leadership style (ALS), the trunk of the tree, and spun off branch #1 in 1967 (published first on this in 1969), spun off branch #2 in 1972 (published first on this in 1975), spun off branch #3 in 1973 (published first on this in 1976), and spun off branch #4 in 1975 (published first on this in 1977). Research continues on ALS, branches #1, through #4, and spun off branch #5 in 1999 (published first in 2000). Hence, the progression was not ALS - stop - branch #1 - stop, branch #2 - stop, branch #3, and stop branch #4. Rather the branching progression is (1) ALS plus #1, (2) plus #2, (3) plus #3, (4) plus #4, and (5) plus #5. The branches are ALS, #1 Dyadic leader and member interactions, #2 Relationship Outcomes, #3 LMX Partner Building Process, #4 LMX Groups and Networks, #5 Strategic Assets. Research continues in all branches and in ALS. In fact, research on each stage easily can be found. This concept of branching is a standard technique in programming, and creative thinking (Kaplan, 1963; Popper, 1950).

Q2: LMX theory has studied the relationship between the leader and two groups of his or her direct reports in which the leader treats one subgroup as favored and the other as disfavored (Northhouse, 2001)

A2: LMX research discovered that different kinds of direct reports respond differently to their leader's offer of role

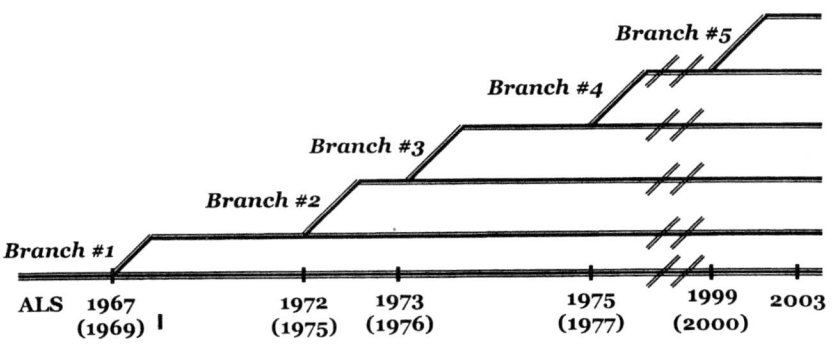

FIGURE 2
Branching Progression of LMX Theory and Research

making. Those with high growth need strength (GNS) respond positively by taking on extra-job responsibilities and duties and developing strong social exchanges of trust, respect, and commitment with their leader. In contrast, those with low GNS respond less positively by taking on less extra-job responsibilities and duties and developing weak social exchanges (SX). Thus, the leader and his or her direct reports develop into a starting team and a reserve team to use a sports metaphor. When a member of the starting team needs to be replaced, someone from the reserve team must be ready to play the role. If this requires new role making, this will be done.

Although the starting team gets the most attention from the leader, the reserve team is not disfavored in any way. In fact, this is the way leaders develop additional human assets for their organization. Most people have more to contribute than required by their jobs and this something more is the stuff of human assets (Uhl-Bien et al., 2000).

In support of this interpretation of role-making attention by those most interested in growth needs (high GNS), Maslyn and Uhl-Bien (2001) found that LMX was predicted by both leader's and follower's amount of effort. The more both contributed the higher their LMX. Thus, both were highly active as predicted by LMX. Those who made the starting team clearly earned their position through both their effort and that of their leader. They also developed greater team-interest and less self-interest (Sparrowe & Liden, 1997).

Q3: What are organizational and environmental conditions affecting LMX?

A3: In terms of organizational and environmental contexts, Table 5 shows the predictions of Transactional leadership, and Leader-Member Exchange (LMX) Leadership. According to this Table, the likelihood of LMX will be more under conditions of high stress for the people in the organization. In contrast, Transactional leadership will be more likely under conditions of low stress. The true test of leadership is: When you really need your followers are they there for you?" (Graen, 1989). Following this test, only LMX calls on follow-

TABLE 5
The Likelihood of LMX and Transformational Leadership Emergence Under Different Environmental and Organizational Conditions

Situational Conditions	Likelihood of LMX and Transformational Leadership	
Environmental		
Stable	Low	
Unstable	High	
Political/Legal	Low	
Not Political/Legal	High	
Collectivistic	High	
Individualistic	Low	
Organizational		
Consistent With Cultural Values	High	
Inconsistent With Cultural Values	Low	
Mechanistic	Low	
Organic	High	
Reactive Processing	Low	
Proactive Monitoring	High	
Hierarchical Authority	Low	
Dispersed Authority	High	
Centralized Decision-Making	Low	
Decentralized Decision-Making	High	
Vertical Communication	Low	
Lateral Communication	High	
Task Characteristics		
Standardized, Routine	Low	
Complex, Changing	High	
Well-Defined Performance	Low	
Poorly-Defined Performance	High	
Goals		
Ambiguous Performance	High	
Mostly Extrinsic Rewards	Low	
Mostly Intrinsic Rewards	High	
	Transformational	LMX
Leader-Subordinate Relations		
Leader Power Greater	High	Low
Follower Power Greater	Low	High
Leader Information Greater	High	Low
Follower Information Greater	Low	High

Notes: (Adapted from Howell, 1997)

ers for extra effort in time of leader weakness; whereas, Transactional headship calls on followers in times of leader strength. Clearly, LMX Leadership can be considered relational leadership, but Transactional must be called something else, such as savior (Graen & Hui, 2001).

Q4: Why isn't loyalty included as a defining dimension of LMX (Dienesch & Liden, 1986)

A4: The study of LMX dimensionality presented above shows that loyalty of keeping confidences and defending were related but not defining. What were defining were trust, respect, commitment, self-efficacy, and satisfaction.

Q5: What's the proper mix of starting and reserve teammates using LMX? (Liden, Berrin, Wayne, & Sparrowe, 2000).

A5: The question of how much differentiation is good for team performance was researched by Liden and his associates (Liden et al., 2000). Results shown in Figure 3 reveal that the dominant relationship was between percent of high LMX in a team and team performance with the largest difference in performance between about 10% teams and the

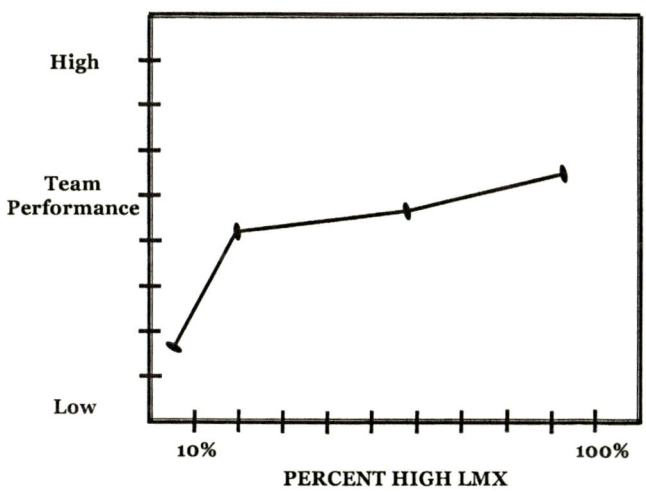

FIGURE 3
LMX Composition and Team Performance

others. Hence, the minimum percentage of high LMX without a decrement to team performance was about 20% in this study. Moreover, the study found that the correlations between the mean team LMX (ALS) and performance was .16 (<.05) and between the team LMX standard deviation (a measure of differentiation) and performance was .09 (NS). Finally, the correlation between ALS and differentiation above was -.49 ($p<.05$). The smaller the standard deviation the larger the ALS. We speculate that the standard deviation is truncated by the ceiling effect of team LMX (ALS).

Q6: How might transformational and LMX theory be combined?

A6: Avolio and Bass (1991) proposed eight leadership styles under three categories in their multi-factor theory (M-F). The three categories are Laissez-Faire (Benign Neglect), Transactional (Management-by-Exception, and Contingent Reward), and Transformational (Individualized, Intellectual, Inspirational, Vision, and Charisma). These are shown in Table 6 as Laissez-faire (allow everything), Management-by-Exception (wait for mistakes and correct), Contingent Reward (pay the winner only), Individualized (know their names), Intellectual (talk ideas to them), Inspirational (convert them), Vision (big picture) and Charisma (charm, amaze, and intimidate them). Finally, Graen and Hui (2001) in theory Leader Option Exchange (LOX) proposed five leadership options of Full Partner (LMX) (negotiate all with followers including basic vision for unit or team), Team Player (LMX) (negotiate goal setting and all but vision development with follower, Supporter (LMX) (negotiate rule and procedure setting and all but vision and goal setting), Associate (LMX), (negotiate process development and change and all but vision, goals, and rules and procedures with follower) and Hired Hand (negotiate only details of delegated assignments with follower. Thus, both types of theories offer multiple choices.

Clearly, the main distinction here on leadership is between leader behavior focused models which seek "the one best way" for leaders to behave toward all followers, and reciprocal agreement focused models which seek "the one best way" for leaders and followers to

TABLE 6
Multiple Model of Leadership Under Leader-Based and
Relationship-Based Approaches (28 Options)

Leader-Based (Leader Behavior)	Relationship-Based (Reciprocal Agreements)
Average Leadership Style (ALS) (Stogdill, 1948)	
.	Leader-Member Exchange (LMX) (Graen, 1968; 1969; 1976)
.	Leader Bureaucratic Exchange (LBX) (Graen, 1968; 1969; 1976)
.	
Path-Goal (P-G) (House, 1971)	
Charismatic Leadership (CL) (House, 1977)	
Transactional Leadership (T-Act) (Burns, 1978)	
Transformational Leadership (T-Form) (Burns, 1978)	
Full Range of Leadership (M-F)	*Leadership Options Exchange (LOX)*
• Laissez-Faire	• Partner LMX (Vision)
• Management-by-Exception	• Team Player LMX (Goals)
• Contingent Reward	• Supporter LMX (Rules and Procedures)
• Individualized	
• Intellectual	• Associate LMX (Processes)
• Inspirational	• Hired Hand LMX (Delegation)
• Vision	(Graen, & Hui 2001)
• Charisma	
(Avolio & Bass, 1991)	

Note: Leaders have eight options under Leader-Based and five options under Relationship-Based. Leaders can use all eight (8) options of M-F with Hired Hand, but only specified combinations of M-F with the other four (4) LOX in that Laissez-Faire Management-by-Exception, and Contingent Reward are compatible with only Hired Hand. The bottom listed five (5) (M-F) styles of leader behavior toward a follower can be combined with any of the top listed four (4) (LOX) Leader-Follower relationship. This results in twenty-eight (28) options with the most developed being Partner LMX with Charisma.

behave toward each other to find "the Third Way" (Graen & Wakabayashi, 1994). Moreover, the environmental and organizational conditions highlight the major difference between hired hand managership roles (a.k.a. Management by Exception and Contingent Reward) and the leadership roles such as LMX (a.k.a. top four levels of LOX) and T-Form (a.k.a. top five types of M-F). Finally, LMX and Transformational can be complimentary in the ways shown below in Table 7.

As shown in Table 7, the twenty-eight combinations of leader behavior and leader-follower negotiations produce specified levels of Leader-Member Exchange (LMX) quality with dyads and result in various levels of developmental opportunities for the follower and the leader. As shown, hired hand involves lower levels of LMX and low developmental opportunities, whereas, the top four LOXs produce higher levels of LMX and progressively higher developmental opportunities.

In practice, leaders and followers during negotiations of top four LOXs develop corresponding high levels of trust, respect of the other, and commitment to the relationship. These three underlying

TABLE 7
Compatible Combinations of Multi-Factors (M-F) and Leader Option Exchange (LOX)

Multi-Factor (M-F)	Leader Option Exchange (LOX)	Leader-Member Exchange (LMX)	Developmental Opportunities	Number of Options
Benign Neglect				
Laissez-Faire	Hired Hand	Lower	Low	1
Transactional				
Management-by-Exception	Hired Hand	Lower	Low	1
Contingent Reward	Hired Hand	Lower	Low	1
Transformational				
Top 5 Transformational	Hired Hand	Lower	Low	5
Top 5 Transformational	Associate	Higher	Moderate	5
Top 5 Transformational	Supporter	Higher +	Moderate +	5
Top 5 Transformational	Team Player	Higher ++	High	5
Top 5 Transformational	Partner	Higher +++	High +	5
Total				28

Notes: Multi-Factor (M-F) refers to the behavioral style of the leader toward a follower and Leader Option Exchange (LOX) refers to the content of the negotiated agreement relationship between leader and follower.

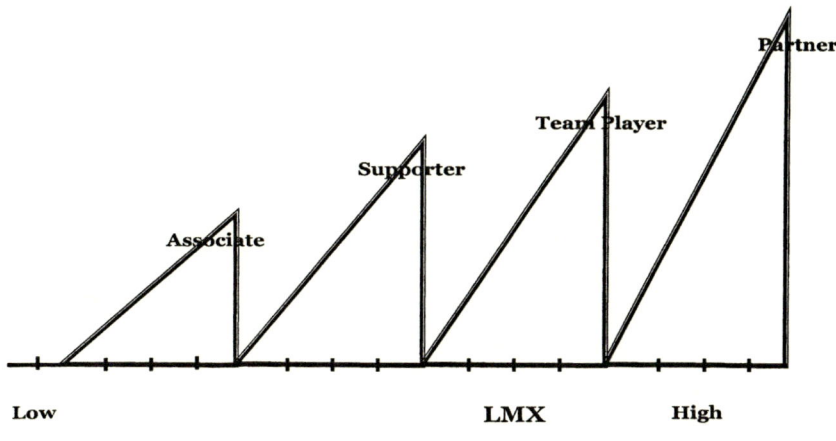

FIGURE 4
Relationship between Scope of Role Making and LMX7

components of LMX have been found consistently to be highly correlated. Also, in practice, leaders tend to employ corresponding levels of all five of the top M-F styles. Hence, the top five M-F style are found consistently to be highly correlated. In sum, we appear to have two packages: (a) the LMX package of corresponding levels of reciprocal trust, respect, and commitment for leaders and followers, and (b) the M-F style package of the top five in corresponding amounts. Thus, LMX7 appears as one homogeneous factor including trust, respect, and commitment and T-Form shows as one homogeneous factor including individualized, intellectual, inspirational, visioning, and charismatic behavior of leader.

Finally, the average hired hand LMX will demonstrate the lowest LMX7, partner LMX will reveal the highest LMX7, and the in-between order from lower to higher LMX7 should be associate, supporter, and team player. As illustrated in Figure 4, the relationship between scope of role making and LMX7 is positive and progressively stronger from Associate (low scope) to partner (high scope). Although the Figure shows no overlap between different scope functions, some overlap is expected.

CONCLUSION

Thirty-five years of programmatic research on LMX theory (Gerstner & Day, 1997; Graen, 1968, 1969, 1976, 1989; Graen, Orris, &

Johnson, 1973; Graen & Uhl-Bien, 1995; Graen & Wakabayashi, 1994; Liden & Maslyn, 1998; Liden, Sparrowe, & Wayne, 1997; Uhl-Bien et al., 2000) has contributed a new and tested LMX leadership followership/relationship paradigm to our scientific leadership domain. Before this programmatic research and theory, scientific research in leadership was dominated by the Average Leadership Style (ALS) paradigm (Graen, 1976,). Since the last review of LMX theory and research (Graen & Uhl-Bien, 1995) twelve (12) papers (including Engle & Lord, 1997, House & Aditya, 1997; Liden & Maslyn, 1998; and Schriesheim et al., 1999) have contained questions about the development of this theory.

We herein answered these questions and presented a brief description of the programmatic research process over the past 35 years in hopes of demonstrating the roles of serendipity, multiple hypothesis testing, and branching theory development through strong influence research. This chapter suggested that LMX and transformational theory have developed into useful leadership models but remains promising special cases of interpersonal role making in work organizations. Moreover, suggestions were offered to improve both formulations by using competing hypotheses testing as prescribed by strong inference (Graen, 2002).

REFERENCES

Avolio, B. J., & Bass, B. M. (1991). The full range of leadership development. *Basic and advanced manuals*. Binghamton, NY: Bass, Avolio, & Associates.

Bales, R. F. (1949). *Interaction Process Analysis: A Method for the Study of Small Groups*. Reading.

Bass, B. M. (1985). *Leadership and performance beyond expectations*. New York: Free Press.

Bass, B. M. (1990). *Bass and Stogdill's handbook of leadership: Theory, research, and managerial applications*. New York: Free Press.

Bass, B. M., & Avolio, B. J. (1990). *Transformational leadership development: Manual for the Multifactor Leadership Questionnaire*. Palo Alto, CA: Consulting Psychologist Press.

Borchgrevink, C. P., & Boster, F. J. (1998). Leader-member exchange and interpersonal relationships: Construct validity and path model. *International Journal of Hospitality and Leisure Marketing*, 5(1), 53-79.

Brockner, J. (1988). *Self esteem at work: Research theory and practice*. Lexington, MA: Lexington.

Burns, J. M. (1978). *Leadership*. New York: Harper & Row.
Campbell, J. D. (1990). Self-esteem and clarity of the self-concept. *Journal of Personality and Social Psychology, 59* 538-549.
Conger, J. A., & Kanungo, R. N., (1998). *Charismatic leadership in organizations*. Thousand Oaks, CA: Sage.
Dansereau, F., Alutto, J. A., & Yammarino, F. J. (1984). *Theory testing in organizational behavior. The varient approach*. Englewood Cliffs, NJ: Prentice-Hall.
Dansereau, F., Graen, G., & Haga, W. (1975). A vertical dyad linkage approach to leadership within formal organizations—A longitudinal investigation of the role making process. *Organizational Behavior and Human Performance, 13*, 46-78.
Dienesch, R. M., & Liden, R. C. (1986). Leader-member exchange model of leadership: A critique and further development. *Academy of Management Review, 11*, 618-634.
Dunnette, M. D. (1966). Fad, fashions and folderol in psychology. *American Psychologist, 21*, 343-352.
Eden, D. (1993). Leadership and expectations: Pygmalion effects and self-fulfilling prophecies in organizations. *Leadership Quarterly, 56*, 215-239.
Engle, E. M., & Lord, R. G. (1997). Implicit theories, self-schemas, and leader-member exchange. *Academy of Management, 40*(4), 988-1010.
Erickson, E. (1980). *Identity and the life cycle*. New York: Oxford University Press.
Fairhurst, G. T., Rogers, L. E., & Sarr, R. A. (1987). Manager–subordinate control patterns and judgments about the relationship. *Communication Yearbook, 10*, 395-415.
Ferris, G. R. (1985). Role of leadership in employee withdrawal process: A constructive replication of Graen's study. *Journal of Applied Psychology, 70*, 777-781.
Freemesser, G. F., & Kaplan, H. B. (1976). Self-attitudes and defiant behavior: The case of the charismatic religious movement. *Journal of Youth and Adolescence, 5*(1), 1-9.
Galanter, M. (1982). Charismatic religious sects and psychiatry: An overview. *Journal of Psychiatry, 139*, 1539-1548.
Gecas, V. (1982). The self-concept. In R. H. Turner & J. F. Short, Jr. (Eds.), *Annual Review of Sociology, 8*, 1-33.
Gerstner, C. R., & Day, D. V. (1997). Meta-analytic review of leader-member exchange theory: Correlates and construct issues. *Journal of Applied Psychology, 82*, 827-844.
Graen, G. B. (1968). Approach for testing multiple hypotheses concerning the motivational effects of work role treatments on managerial behaviors. James McKeen Cattell Award Winner, American Psychological Association, Division of Industrial and Organizational Psychology.

Graen, G. B. (1969). Instrumentality theory of work motivation: Some experimental results and suggested modifications. *Journal of Applied Psychology, 53,* (whole no. 2, part 2).

Graen, G. B. (1976). Role making processes within complex organizations. In M. D. Dunnette (Ed.), *Handbook of Industrial and Organizational Psychology,* (pp. 1201-1245). Chicago: Rand-McNally.

Graen, G. B. (1989). *Unwritten rules for your career: 15 secrets for fast-track success.* New York: John Wiley & Sons.

Graen, G. B. (2002). It's about LMXs stupid: Collect high quality data, follow it, trust LMXs and seek serendipity always. In A. Bedeian (Ed.) *Management laureates: A collection of autobiographical essays* (Vol. 6, pp. 52-81). Greenwich, CT: JAI Press.

Graen, G. B., & Cashman, J. F. (1975). A role-making model of leadership in formal organizations: A developmental approach. In J. G. Hunt & L. L. Larson (Eds.), *Leadership Frontiers* (pp. 143-165). Kent, OH: Kent State University.

Graen, G. B., Cashman, J., Ginsburgh, S., & Schiemann, W. (1977). Effects of linking-pin quality upon the quality of working life of lower participants: A longitudinal investigation of the managerial understructure. *Administrative Science Quarterly, 22,* 491-504.

Graen, G. B., & Hui, C. (2001). Approaches to leadership: Toward a complete contingency model of face-to-face leadership. In M. Erez & P. C. Earley (Eds.), *Work Motivation and Clinical Language.* New York: Erlbaum.

Graen, G. B., Hui, C., Wakabayashi, M., & Wang, Z. M. (1997). Cross-cultural research alliances in organizational research: Cross-cultural partnership-making in action. In C. Earley & M. Erez (Eds.), *Cross-Cultural Research in Industrial Organizational Psychology* (pp. 160-189). San Francisco: Jossey Bass.

Graen, G., Liden, R., & Hoel, W. (1982). Role of leadership in the employee withdrawal process. *Journal of Applied Psychology, 67,* 868-872.

Graen, G. B., & Novak, M. (1982). The effects of leader-member exchange and job design on productivity and satisfaction: Testing a dual attachment model. *Organizational Behavior and Human Decision Processes, 30*(1), 109-132.

Graen, G., Novak, M. A., & Sommerkamp, P. (1982). The effects of leader-member exchange and job design on productivity and satisfaction: Testing a dual attachment model. *Organizational Behavior and Human Performance, 30,* 109-131.

Graen, G., Orris, J., & Johnson, T. (1973). Role assimilation in a complex organization. *Journal of Vocational Behavior, 3,* 395-420.

Graen, G. B., & Scandura, T. A. (1987). Toward a psychology of dyadic organizing. In L. L. Cummings & B. M. Staw (Eds.), *Research in Organizational Behavior,* (Vol. 9, pp. 175-208). Greenwich, CT: JAI Press.

Graen, G. B., Scandura, T., & Graen, M. R. (1986). A field experimental test of the moderating effects of growth need strength on productivity. *Journal of Applied Psychology, 71*, 484-491.

Graen, G. B., & Schiemann, W. (1978). Leader-member agreement: A vertical dyad linkage approach. *Journal of Applied Psychology, 63*, 206-212.

Graen, G. B. & Uhl-Bien, M. (1995). Development of leader-member exchange (LMX) theory of leadership over 25 years: Applying a multi-level multi-domain perspective. *Leadership Quarterly, 6*, 219-247.

Graen, G. B., & Wakabayashi, M. (1994). Cross-cultural leadership making: Bridging American and Japanese diversity for team advantage. In H. C. Triandis, M. D. Dunnette, & L. M. Hough (Eds.), *Handbook of Industrial and Organizational Psychology* (Vol. 3, pp. 415-446). Chicago: Rand-McNally.

Hackman, J. R., & Oldham, G. R. (1976). Motivation through the design of work: Test of a theory. *Organizational Behavior and Human Performance, 16*, 250-279.

Haga, W. J., Graen, G. B., & Dansereau, Jr., F. (1974). Professionalism and role making within service organizations: A longitudinal investigation. *American Sociological Review, 39*, 122-133.

House, R. J. (1971). A path-goal theory of leadership effectiveness. *Administrative Science Quarterly, 16*, 321-328.

House, R. J. (1977). A 1976 theory of charismatic leadership. In J. G. Hunt & L. L. Larson (Eds.), *Leadership: The cutting edge.* (pp. 189-207). Carbondale, IL: Southern Illinois University Press.

House, R. J. (1991). The distribution and exercise of power in complex organizations: A meso theory. *Leadership Quarterly, 2*, 23-58.

House, R. J., & Aditya, R. N. (1997). The social scientific study of leadership: Quo vadis? *Journal of Management, 23*, 409-473.

House, R. J. & Shamir, B. (1993). Towards the integration of transformational, charismatic, and visionary theories. In M. M. Chemers & R. Ayman (Eds.), *Leadership theory and research* (pp. 81-107). San Diego: Academic Press.

Howell, J. M. (1997). Organizational contexts, charismatic and exchange leadership. *Academy of Leadership Press* (pp. 1-36). KLSP: Transformational Leadership Working Papers

Howell, J. M., & Avolio, B. J. (1993). Transformational leadership, transactional leadership, locus of control and support for innovation. *Journal of Applied Psychology, 78*, 891-902.

Howell, J. M., & Hall-Merenda, K. E. (1999). The ties that bind: The impact of LMX, Transformational and Transactional leadership, and distance on predicting follower performance. *Journal of Applied Psychology, 84*(5), 680-694.

Kaplan, A. (1963). *The conduct of inquiry: Methodology for behavioral science,* New York: Harper & Row.

Kark, R., & Shamir, B. (2002). The dual effect of transformational leadership: Priming relational and collective selves and further effects on followers. In B. J. Avolio & F. J. Yammarino (Eds.), *Transformational and charismatic leadership: The road ahead* (pp. 67-91). Oxford: Elsevier.

Katerberg, R., & Hom, P. W. (1981). Effects of within-group and between groups variation in leadership. *Journal of Applied Psychology, 66*, 218-223.

Liden, R. C., Berrin, E., Wayne, S. J., & Sparrowe, R. T. (2000). LMX differentiation: Implications for group effectiveness. Paper presented at the annual meeting of the Academy of Management, Toronto, Canada.

Liden, R., & Graen, G. B. (1980). Generalizability of the vertical dyad linkage model of leadership. *Academy of Management Journal, 23*, 451-465.

Liden, R. C., & Maslyn, J. M. (1998). Multidimensionality of leader-member exchange: An empirical assessment through scale development. *Journal of Management, 24*, 43-72.

Liden, R. C., Sparrowe, R. T. & Wayne, S. J. (1997). Leader-member exchange theory: The past and potential for the future. *Research in Personnel and Human Resources Management, 15*, 47-119.

Lord, R. G., Brown, D. J., & Freiberg, S. J. (1999). Understanding the dynamics of leadership: The role of follower self-concepts in the leader/follower relationship. *Organizational Behavior and Human Decision Process, 78* 167-203.

Lowe, K. B., Kroek, K., & Sivasubramaniam, N. (1996). Effectiveness correlates of transformational and transactional leadership: A meta-analytic review of the MLQ literature. *Leadership Quarterly, 7*, 385-425.

Maslyn, J., & Uhl-Bien, M. (2001). Leader-member exchange and its dimensions: Effects of self and other effort on relationship quality. *Journal of Applied Psychology, 86*(4), 697-708.

Northhouse, R. G. (2001). *Leadership: Theory and practice*, (2nd Ed.). Thousand Oaks: Sage Publications.

Novak, M. A. (1985). A study of leader resources as determinates of leader-member exchange. Doctoral Dissertation, University of Cincinnati.

Platt, J. R. (1963). Strong inference. *Science, 146*, 347-352.

Podsakoff, P. M., & MacKenzie, S. B. (1995). An examination of substitutes for leadership within a levels-of-analysis framework. *Leadership Quarterly, 6*(3), 289-325.

Popper, K. R. (1950). *Logic of Science*. Amsterdam: Turbingen.

Rousseau, D. (1997). LMX meets the psychological contract: Looking inside the black box of leader-member exchange. Working paper, Carnegie Mellon University.

Scandura, T. A., & Graen, G. B. (1984). Moderating effects of initial Leader-Member Exchange status on the effects of a leadership intervention. *Journal of Applied Psychology, 69*, 428-436.

Scandura, T. A., Graen, G. B., & Novak, M. A. (1986). When managers decide not do decide autocratically: An investigation of leader-member exchange and decision influence. *Journal of Applied Psychology, 71*, 579-584.

Schriescheim, C. A., Castro, S. L., & Cogliser, C. C. (1999). Leader-member exchange (LMX) research: A comprehensive review of theory, measurement and data analytic practices. *Leadership Quarterly, 10*(1), 63-113.

Seers, A., & Graen, G. B. (1984). The dual attachment concept: A longitudinal investigation of the combination of task characteristics and leader-member exchange. *Organization Behavior and Human Performance, 33*, 283-306.

Shamir, B., House, R. J,, & Arthur, M. B. (1993). The motivational effects of charismatic leadership: A self-concept based theory. *Organization Science, 4*, 577-594.

Smith, P. C., (1967). The development of a method of measuring job satisfaction: The Cornell studies, (pp. 343-350). In (E. Fleishman, Ed.) *Studies in Personnel and Industrial Psychology.* Homewood, IL: Dorsey Pres.

Sparrowe, R. T., & Liden, R. C. (1997). Process and structure in leader-member exchange. *Academy of Management Review, 22*, 522-552.

Stogdill, R. M. (1948). Personal factors associated with leadership: A survey of the literature. *Journal of Psychology, 25*, 35-71.

Tierney, P. (1999). Work relations as a precursor to a psychological climate for change. *Journal of Organizational Change Management, 12*(2), 120-133.

Uhl-Bien, M. (1991). Teamwork of the future: An investigation into teamwork processes of professional work team in knowledge-based organizations. Doctoral Dissertation, Department of Management, University of Cincinnati.

Uhl-Bien, M., Graen, G., & Scandura, T. 2000. Implications of leader-member exchange (LMX) for strategic human resource management systems: Relationships as social capital for competitive advantage. In G. R. Ferris (Ed.), *Research in personnel and human resources management* (Vol. 18, pp. 137-185). Greenwich, CT: JAI Press.

Vecchio, R. P. (1982). A further test of leadership effects due to between-group and within-group variation. *Journal of Applied Psychology, 67*, 200-208.

Vecchio, R. P. (1985). Predicting employee turnover from leader-member exchange: A failure to replicate. *Academy of Management Journal, 28*, 478-485.

Wakabayashi, M., & Graen, G. B. (1984). The Japanese career progress study: A seven-year follow up. *Journal of Applied Psychology, 69*, 603-614.

Wakabayashi, M. & Graen, G. B. (1988). Human resource development of Japanese managers: Leadership and career investment. In K. M. Rowland & G. R. Ferris (Eds.), *International Human Resources Management.* Greenwich, CT: JAI Press.

Wakabayashi, M., Graen, G. B., Graen, M. R., & Graen, M. G. (1988). Japanese management progress: Mobility into middle management. *Journal of Applied Psychology, 73,* 217-227.

Wakabayashi. M., Graen, G. B., & Uhl-Bien, M. (1990). Generalizability of the hidden investment hypothesis among line managers in five leading Japanese corporations. *Human Relations, 43,* 1099-1116.

Wakabayashi, M., Minami, T., Hashimoto, M., Sano, K., Graen, G. B., & Novak, M. (1980). Managerial career development: Japanese style, *International Journal of Intercultural Relations, 4,* 391-420.

Yammarino, F. J., & Dubinsky, A. J. (1994). Transformational leadership theory: Using levels of analysis to determine boundary conditions. *Personnel Psychology, 47,* 787-811.

Yammarino, F. J., Spangler, W. D., & Bass, B. M. (1993). Transformational leadership and performance: A longitudinal investigation. *Leadership Quarterly, 4,* 81-102.

Yammarino, F. J., Spangler, W. D., & Dubinsky, A. J. (1998). Transformational and contingent reward leadership: Individual, dyad, and group levels of analysis. *Leadership Quarterly, 9*(1), 27-54.

George B. Graen began his career at the University of Minnesota (Minneapolis), where he received his PhD in Organizational Psychology. In 1967 Graen joined the Psychology and Industrial Relations Faculty of the University of Illinois (Champaign). During his tenure at Illinois, he received a Distinguished International Exchange Professorship and spent 1972 at Keio University in Tokyo. He left the University of Illinois in 1977 to found the University of Cincinnati Center, continuing his research in Japan after receiving the first Johnson's Wax Fulbright Research Fellowship in 1984. For the last eight years he and his cross-cultural research and consulting team have been engaged in projects to understand joint venture businesses in China, Hong Kong and Taiwan and to help them build effective local "Third Cultures" to enhance their competitiveness. In 1997 he was named the Gene Brauns Endowed Chair Professor of International Management at the University of Louisiana.

He is a Fellow of the American Psychological Society and enjoys membership in other professional societies including the Academy of Management, the International Association of Applied Psychology, the American Association for the Advancement of Science, the Society of Organizational Behavior, and the Association of Japanese Business Studies (President, 1992-1995).

CHAPTER 7

THE NEW CONDUCT OF BUSINESS
How LMX Can Help Capitalize on Cultural Diversity

Diane M. Sullivan, Marie S. Mitchell, and Mary Uhl-Bien

The growing number of culturally diverse organizations has spawned an interest in cross cultural research. In this chapter, we examine this new conduct of business by incorporating leadership and cultural diversity. Specifically, we view how leader-member exchange (LMX), as explained through social exchange theory, is coupled with Hofstede's (1980a) four main cultural dimensions (uncertainty avoidance, power distance, individualism, and masculinity). We propose that these cultural dimensions hold many similarities to the processes of exchange in terms of reciprocity (e.g., equivalence, immediacy, and interest) and the currencies of exchange in LMX (e.g., contribution, professional respect, loyalty, and affect). Within this framework, we discuss how these ideas can be used to develop an agenda for future research that explores issues of leadership diversity and cross-cultural relationship development.

> The word 'globalization' was not talked about 10 years ago... Now it's become extremely important, almost to the point of being cliché... Managers today are in daily communication with counterparts all around the world... Leaders in a new, more global company will need some level of geographic flexibility.
> —John Pepper, former CEO and current Chairman of the Board, Proctor & Gamble (From Bingham, Felin, & Black, 2000).

INTRODUCTION

The US exports roughly $850 billion to other nations every year, and is the home of the largest amount of foreign investment in the world (Javidan & House, 2001; House, Javidan, Hanges, & Dorfman, 2002). Experts predict that trade between nations will exceed that of the total business transactions within nations, and by 2005 world exports are expected to exceed $11 trillion (House et al., 2002). As globalization continues to spread throughout the world, issues of diversity and cross-cultural leadership take on new importance. Global enterprise demands that leaders and managers be responsive to the practices, norms, and values of their foreign business partners. However, responsiveness is not enough—global leadership requires true understanding and appreciation of others' culture. Because of this, there is a growing need for leadership theories that address the challenges of multinational management, particularly issues of managing cultural differences (Dorfman, 1996; House et al., 2002; Triandis, 1993).

Recent leadership and cultural diversity research suggests that leader-member exchange (LMX) theory can be a useful theoretical framework from which to view diversity leadership (Chen & VanVelsor, 1996; Hui & Graen, 1997; Pillai, Scandura, & Williams, 1999; Scandura & Lankau, 1996). According to Chen and Van Velsor (1996), LMX can make distinctive contributions to diversity leadership for three primary reasons. First, LMX uses a dyadic approach, which may help cross-cultural leadership research move beyond comparative work. Second, LMX focuses on relationship building, which provides substantive meaning to diversity leadership beyond the people approach of many traditional leadership theories. Third, LMX theory draws from the dynamics of in-group/out-group relations, which can yield important insights into the complexities of managing and leading diversity in cross-cultural contexts.

Contrasting this point of view, House and Aditya (1997) argued that although the dyadic nature of LMX makes it appear applicable to diversity, LMX theory currently reflects Western values and assumptions (e.g., individualism and emphasis on rationality) rather than those applicable to cultural diversity (e.g., tradition, spirituality, or superstition). As such, they contend that LMX is not conducive in cross-cultural contexts. They argue that in order for LMX to apply to cross-cultural research, we must first understand what constitutes desired, acceptable, and effective relationships between managers and subordinates in different cultures. For instance, in collectivistic cultures individuals may define their self-concept relative to a group rather than individual identification. House and Aditya believe that this failure to identify the nature of expected relationships among members of diverse cultures limits LMX theory's application, leading to a potential breakdown in the predicted course of LMX relationship-building for multicultural environments.

We argue that LMX research has advanced since House and Aditya's (1997) review, such that it is now appropriate to develop a theoretical framework applicable to cross-cultural contexts using LMX theory. In particular, LMX researchers have recently begun to dig deep into the social exchange roots of LMX (e.g., Liden, Sparrowe, & Wayne, 1997; Maslyn & Uhl-Bien, 2001; Uhl-Bien, Graen, & Scandura, 2000; Uhl-Bien & Maslyn, 2003; Wayne, Shore, & Liden, 1997). This research allows for broader interpretations and implications of LMX relationship building, not limited to those only reflective of Western values and assumptions. As a result, we believe that LMX is now well positioned to address diversity leadership, especially issues of cross-cultural social exchange.

In the present chapter we describe how LMX theory can provide a framework for examining cross-cultural relationship building. We do this by integrating social exchange elements of LMX theory and Hofstede's (1980a, 1981, 2001) model of cultural dimensions. Hofstede's (1980a, 1981, 2001) model was chosen because it (1) appears to be the most widely accepted and representative model of cultural dimensions available to date (see Hofstede 1980a, 1981, 2001 for reviews), and (2) provides a concise typology that can be manageably integrated with an LMX social exchange framework. While we do not believe this integration will provide a full or complete explanation of the complexities of cross-cultural dyadic relationship building, we do believe it offers a good start in identifying potentially fruitful directions for advancing understanding in this area (Erdogan & Liden, 2002).

The chapter begins by describing the elements of social exchange highlighted in LMX theory. This is followed by a brief review of Hofstede's (1981, 2001) cultural dimensions. The two perspectives are then integrated, with a specific discussion of how we could expect the cultural dimensions identified in Hofstede's model to be related to cross-cultural social exchanges and LMX. The framework we present describes LMX relationship building and cultural diversity from the standpoint of the influence of Hofstede's cultural dimensions on both social exchange (Liden et al., 1997; Uhl-Bien et al., 2000) and the valued currencies of a relationship, as described in LMX theory (Liden & Maslyn, 1998). Finally, we offer suggestions for how to build a research agenda to investigate cross-cultural relationship development.

THEORETICAL OVERVIEW

As businesses push forward into global enterprise, demand for culturally diverse leaders rises (House et al., 2002). Companies need managers who understand and appropriately respond to their business partners' cultural values, practices, and norms. Practitioners emphasize that managers in a multinational environment must have the flexibility to react in effective ways in order to advance company goals (Carpenter, Sanders, & Gregersen, 2000; Connor, 2000; Bingham et al., 2000). Cross-cultural leadership, however, presents unique challenges for managers, as those with whom they interact (employees, peers, suppliers, customers) bring to the table embedded cultural aspects that guide their attitudes and behaviors (Trice & Beyer, 1993). Thus, a difficulty in managing cross-culturally is learning and appreciating the fact that effective leadership qualities will vary depending on the norms and values of the individuals involved (House & Aditya, 1997; Schein, 1992).

In particular, what makes cross-cultural leadership difficult is that expected, accepted, and effective leadership behaviors can and likely will vary based on the cultural backgrounds of the individuals (House & Aditya, 1997). This can affect leadership on two levels: (1) there will be varying preferences in individuals' culturally endorsed implicit theories of leadership (CILTs), and thus their reaction to demonstrated management and leadership practices, and (2) it presents challenges relative to how managers and subordinates interact and build relationships, influencing how well they can work with one another (House & Aditya, 1997). While the first issue, culturally endorsed ILTs, is the subject of extensive investigation by House and colleagues and the GLOBE project (Den Hartog, et al., 1999), there is a general void in understanding of the second issue, cross-cultural managerial relationship building.

We believe LMX theory can be useful in filling this void. On a general level, the basic applications of LMX to diversity leadership have already been made (Chen & Van Velsor, 1996; Scandura & Lankau, 1996). For example, Chen and Van Velsor (1996) argue that diverse leaders need to build high LMX with followers in order to competently address cultural diversity. They believe that LMX can be used as a tool to uncover dynamics that create diversity competence, ultimately developing effective leadership. According to these authors, LMX may hold a key to understanding the true skills and abilities necessary in developing culturally diverse leaders. Scandura and Lankau (1996) highlighted the exchange and role making foundation of LMX as it relates to diversity. They argued that LMX developmental processes are highly relevant to understanding diversity leadership, and that diverse leaders need to focus on the creation and maintenance of one-on-one leader-member relations.

For work to advance in this area, we need to delve deeper into the processes by which cross-cultural dyadic relationship building occurs. To do this, we need to better define the process of relationship building in terms of cultural differences. Therefore, we turn next to a brief overview of LMX and its underlying social exchange processes. We then examine certain types of cultural differences within this LMX-social exchange framework, focusing specifically on the *processes* of social exchange (through reciprocity) and the LMX dimensions that are valued as *currencies* of social exchange.

EXCHANGE PROCESSES AND CURRENCIES IN LMX

Leader-member exchange (LMX) defines the quality of the relationship that develops between the direct supervisor and a subordinate (Graen & Scandura, 1987; Graen & Uhl-Bien, 1991, 1995). As supervisors and subordinates interact with one another, these interactions develop each member's role, forming the basis of the work relationship. Social exchange is the foundation of these interactions and frames the overall relationship between the parties (Wayne et al., 1997). At its core, social exchange theory dictates that when individuals are treated well by another, they build an obligation to return the goodwill (Blau, 1964). The norm of reciprocity (Gouldner, 1960) generates this sensation of goodwill, and quid pro quo imitation grows the interactions into a committed and trusting relationship. Generally, research demonstrates that high quality LMX relations encompass higher levels of trust, respect, and loyalty, which thereby positively affect outcomes (e.g., Gerstner & Day, 1997, Liden et al., 1997; Masterson, Lewis, Goldman, & Taylor, 2000).

LMX relationship building has been the topic of extensive discussion in the literature (Graen & Scandura, 1987; Graen & Uhl-Bien, 1991, 1995; Liden, Wayne, & Stilwell, 1993; Liden et al., 1997; Uhl-Bien et al., 2000). To summarize, LMX development begins through the interactions between the manager and subordinate. These interactions constitute exchange sequences. Exchange sequences form and refine perceptions, attributions, and attitudes about exchange partners and the overall relationship (Uhl-Bien et al., 2000). Over time, repeated interactions provide for reevaluations, which ultimately determine the LMX quality. The amount and quality of interaction are a part of developmental testing (Uhl-Bien et al., 2000) and form the basis of how quickly the relationship develops (Liden et al., 1993). Generally, once formed, LMX relations remain stable (Liden et al., 1993), and the formative testing processes settle into maintenance evaluations. However, if violations of relational expectations are perceived, active testing resumes (Uhl-Bien et al., 2000).

Recent research on leader-member exchange has revisited and emphasized the social exchange underpinnings of LMX theory (Liden et al., 1997; Maslyn & Uhl-Bien, 2001; Uhl-Bien et al., 2000; Uhl-Bien & Maslyn, 2003). Based on this work, in the present paper we consider LMX relationship building relative to two main categories of social exchange. First, we discuss the *processes* governing the exchange between managers and subordinates, grounded in the norm of reciprocity (Gouldner, 1960; Homans, 1958). Second, we expand on the *currencies* of social exchange, which involves what is valued and exchanged within dyads (Liden & Maslyn, 1998).

LMX Exchange Processes

The nature of LMX exchange sequences is described by social exchange theory. Social exchange theory indicates that individuals generate an obligation to return good faith behavior when treated well by another (Blau, 1964). In essence, relationship development is governed by the "norm of reciprocity," in which imbedded obligations are created by exchanges of benefits and favors among individuals (Homans, 1958; Gouldner, 1960; Liden et al., 1997; Simmel, 1950; Thurnwald, 1932). The obligations evoked are based on past behaviors, such that "...when one party benefits another, an obligation is generated. The recipient is now *indebted* to the donor, and he remains so until he repays" (Gouldner, 1960, p. 174). According to Gouldner (1960), the act of being indebted is a *status duty*. Social structure develops through these status duties. Thus, the norm of reciprocity serves to initiate and stabilize social interaction among exchange parties.

In some cases, the norm of reciprocity can develop LMX positively, but it can also develop relationships negatively (Gouldner, 1960; Sahlins, 1972; Uhl-Bien & Maslyn, 2003). The quality of the relationship differs based on several factors that comprise reciprocity: the equivalence, immediacy, and interests involved in the exchange (Graen & Uhl-Bien, 1991; Liden et al., 1997; Sahlins, 1972; Sparrowe, 1998, Uhl-Bien & Maslyn, 2003). These factors constitute the formative and maintenance elements of LMX processes, thus helping to establish the quality of the relationship.

Equivalence

LMX researchers discuss the importance of equivalence in terms of relational testing. In order for LMX to develop into a higher quality, the exchange must be considered to be valuable and balanced (Graen & Scandura, 1987). This means that dyad members must perceive the value of what they get from the exchange to not be consistently less than the value of their contribution to the exchange. In other words, they have to feel they are receiving as well as giving. Throughout the course of the developing relationship, individuals engage in "active testing," in which the value and equivalence of exchanges are calculated. As LMX matures to a higher quality, scorekeeping and worries about whether exchanges will be paid back diminish (Uhl-Bien et al., 2000). Instead, individuals in high-quality relationships trust and respect one another. Their commitment supercedes concerns about whether exchanges are of equal value, and mutual interests eventually replace concern for equivalence.

Immediacy

The amount of time between the receipt of an exchange and when reciprocation occurs greatly influences leader member relations. Liden and colleagues (1997) indicate that the time of reciprocation ranges from instantaneous (high immediacy) to an indefinite amount of time (low immediacy). Like equivalence, as LMX quality improves, the importance of immediacy also lessens (Liden et al., 1997; Sparrowe & Liden, 1997). Graen and Uhl-Bien (1991, 1995) argue that in the early stages of LMX, exchange partners expect reciprocity within a short period of time because the relationship is still in an active testing phase (Uhl-Bien et al., 2000). As individuals begin to build trust in one another, the time span of reciprocation lengthens, and if the relationship reaches high quality, concern about when reciprocation occurs becomes less important.

Interest

The third component of reciprocity, interest, speaks directly to the motivations driving the exchange partners (Liden et al., 1997). According to Liden et al. (1997), as relationship quality increases, the motive moves from *self-interest* to *mutual-interest*. Self-interested parties seek to maximize individual interests at the sake of others'. In mutual interest, parties emphasize the benefit of both exchange partners. They predict that in the highest quality relationships, the interest focus is on the other member of the relationship, reflected by an unselfish devotion and deep concern for the other, i.e., *other-interest*. Graen and Uhl-Bien (1991, 1995) agree with this conceptualization, but limit the range the interest motive can take as extending from self-interest to mutual interest. According to these authors, the highest level of relationship quality would be characterized as *partnerships*, reflected by a high level of mutual interest in which each party acts in the best interests of the relationship.

Taken together, the three components of reciprocity build the quality of LMX. Consistent with this, a recent study by Uhl-Bien and Maslyn (2003) used a configural approach to examine reciprocity in manager-subordinate relationships, and found support for predicted patterns of immediacy, equivalence and interest in LMX relationships. For interest, findings supported self-interest as a key driver in low quality LMX relationships and mutual-interest in high LMX relationships, but did not find support for other-interest. Findings also showed differences in relationships with work outcomes (e.g., performance, citizenship) depending on the reciprocity configuration, with higher quality exchange relationships having higher levels of perceived organizational support and altruism (but not organizational commitment) than the lower and negative exchange groups, and the negative reciprocity group showing lower levels of performance and conscientiousness as rated by the manager.

LMX Currencies

In addition to the processes governing exchange (e.g., reciprocity), cross-cultural relational research can also benefit from the examination of the *currencies* of LMX. In their development of a multidimensional perspective of LMX, Liden and Maslyn (1998) suggested that identification and empirical support for multiple dimensions of LMX could help increase understanding of LMX development and maintenance. Building on Dienesch and Liden (1986), they developed a framework to describe "currencies of exchange," which highlight different relational elements that are valued by LMX members. In particular, these currencies address four specific task- and socially-related dimensions of leader-member exchanges: contribution, professional respect, loyalty, and affect.

Contribution

The contribution dimension of LMX describes the perceived "amount, direction, and quantity of work-oriented activity each member puts forth toward mutual goals (explicit or implicit)" (Dienesch & Liden, 1986, p. 624) within the dyad. This is an important dimension as it represents a member's willingness and ability to contribute task-oriented behavior necessary to progress work commitments. Within the context of social exchange theory, contribution is highly relevant to building relational quality. A manager's assessment of subordinate contributions directly impacts future invitations of valuable work assignments and the delegation of valuable resources (Dunegan, Duchon, & Uhl-Bien, 1992; Graen & Cashman, 1975; Liden & Graen, 1980; Scandura, Graen, & Novak, 1986). Here again, we see reciprocity in action, as subordinates who receive such invitations and resources are likely to reciprocate with more contributions.

Respect

Professional respect is a critical factor in building work relationships. Liden and Maslyn (1998) argue that it represents the perceived degree to which each member of the dyad has built a reputation of excelling at his or her line of work, whether the reputation is built within or outside the organization. Perceptions of professional respect can be based on historical data, personal experience, comments from others, or awards or professional recognition. Therefore, it is possible for this LMX dimension to develop apart from any interaction. Liden and Maslyn describe this as the expert power component (French & Raven, 1959) of the relationship. Since individuals with power possess valuable resources, these authors argue that exchange partners are drawn to these individuals in order to gain the benefits of the association and potential exchange. However, for the relationship to develop and maintain, perceptions of respect must also be reinforced through interactions.

Loyalty

A third dimension of LMX is the extent to which each member of the exchange is loyal to the other. Loyalty is thereby defined as an obligation or expression of public support for the goals and the personal character of the other member of the dyad (Liden & Masyln, 1998). It involves faithfulness and public support of the other's action and character. The more loyal a subordinate is to the manager, the more likely the manager will reciprocate with more autonomous tasks and responsibility (Liden & Graen, 1980; Scandura et al., 1986). Likewise, the more loyal the manager is to the subordinate, the more the subordinate will want to give to the relationship.

Affect

Like professional respect, affect is a socially-related LMX dimension. It represents the mutual affection and liking members hold for one another based primarily on interpersonal attraction (unlike professional respect, which is based on work or professional values) (Liden & Maslyn, 1998). The amount of affect one holds in the other also indicates a desire for friendship with the dyad partner. Although affect may play a dominant or small role in LMX, as compared to the other dimensions, research indicates it is important in

LMX development and maintenance (e.g., Dockery & Steiner, 1990; Liden et al., 1993). Regardless of its importance, LMX researchers suggest that some dyad members may have a greater need for affect in LMX development than others (Graen & Uhl-Bien, 1995; Uhl-Bien, 2003).

Research using the multidimensional measure (LMX-MDM) has demonstrated that all of the dimensions influence subordinate ratings of LMX quality (Liden & Maslyn, 1998; Colella & Varma, 2001). Further, research combining these dimensions found a significant relationship between sources of support and performance, as mediated by LMX (Kraimer, Wayne, & Jaworski, 2001), as well as a significant relationship between interactional justice perceptions and social loafing as mediated by LMX (Murphy, Wayne, Liden, & Erdogan, 2003). In a study using the LMX-MDM examining mentee relationships with other parties in the workplace, Raabe and Beehr (2003) found significant relationships between the dimensions in the LMX-MDM and mentee outcomes of job satisfaction, organizational commitment, and turnover intent as they relate to the mentee's relationship with their immediate supervisor and their best-liked coworker.

Taken together, this discussion of reciprocity and dimensions illustrates that consideration of the processes and currencies of LMX can provide a fruitful means to understand how leader-member relationships develop. These concepts provide a framework to consider whether, and how, members of different cultural backgrounds differentially value these exchanges and their currencies, which then can provide a basis for understanding how leaders can manage relationships in multicultural environments. However, before discussing how we can consider these processes (e.g., reciprocity) and currencies (e.g., LMX dimensions) relative to cross-cultural contexts, we need to first understand the dimensions of culture.

VALUES AND CULTURE

Culture is a holistic concept that taps into the historically determined, socially constructed, and enduring belief systems, values, and norms that guide individual perceptions, attitudes, and behavior (Hofstede, 1980a; Schein, 1992; Trice & Beyer, 1993). In short, culture provides for what is valued in an environment, making values the building blocks of a society, nation, or organization (Hofstede, 1980a). Many culture scholars have advanced research by evaluating and isolating clusters of values within national environments. Hofstede (1983, 2001), in particular, has conducted a great deal of research refining universal categories of culture.

In extensive studies of work-related value patterns of employees across a wide range of countries, Hofstede (1983, 2001; cf. Holt, 1997; Lam, Shaubroeck, & Aryee, 2002; Singhapakdi, Marta, Rao, & Cicic, 2001) identified four basic dimensions for considering cultural values. These dimensions are: uncertainty avoidance, power distance, individualism (versus collectivism), and masculinity (versus femininity). The four dimensions help explain different motivations within organizations, ways of structuring organizations, and issues faced by different societies. They are grouped within cultural clusters that represent beliefs held by members in different countries who share similar cultural perspectives of what is valued.

Uncertainty Avoidance

This dimension of culture indicates the extent to which a society feels threatened or uncomfortable by uncertain and ambiguous situations. Hofstede (1985, 2001) identified various value orientations that characterize uncertainty avoidance. They are time, work ethic, acceptable behavior, emotional displays, rules and regulations, and derivation of knowledge. Cultures depicting high uncertainty avoidance attempt to establish greater career stability, require more formal rules, do not tolerate deviant ideas and behaviors, believe in absolute truths and the attainment of expertise, and are generally characterized by higher levels of anxiety and aggressiveness. In an effort to reduce uncertainty, these cultures generate a strong inner urge to work; thus, time is money. In contrast, cultures characterized by low uncertainty avoidance are not bound by rules, are free with time, and do not hold a strong work ethic. Aggressive and emotional displays are frowned upon, and knowledge is driven by generalist, common sense principles. While investigating marketing ethics, Armstrong (1996) examined the relationship between uncertainty avoidance and ethical perceptions. His findings support Hofstede's characterization of this value orientation in that individuals with higher levels of uncertainty avoidance perceive higher levels of importance with regard to ethical problems.

Power Distance

Power distance indicates the extent to which power in institutions and organizations is distributed unequally. Hofstede (1983) characterizes power distance through a number of values: relational orientation, power acceptance and use, and trustworthiness. Cultures characterized by high power distances are less interested in participative management techniques. Instead, superiors take on the sole responsibility of determining and delegating work across subordinates (Hofstede, 1980b). High power distance cultures embrace power as a basic fact of society, and powerful people yield their power in order to illustrate their influence over others. Not surprisingly then, coercive and referent power (French & Raven, 1959) are emphasized, decreasing the amount of trust members hold in one another. As a result, there is an innate conflict between the powerful and the powerless. In contrast, low power distance cultures see relatively few differences from subordinates to supervisors, and use power only to progress legitimate means. Therefore, legitimate and expert power (French & Raven, 1959) are emphasized, which enhances the amount of trust people hold in others. In an investigation of power distance on work-related outcomes, Lam and colleagues (2002) demonstrated power distance as a moderator between justice perceptions and outcomes of satisfaction, performance, and absenteeism, where the impact of justice on outcomes was, not surprisingly, stronger for individuals lower in power distance.

Individualism

Hofstede (1983) describes the values in this third dimension based on the "interest" orientation of the society or organization. The ultimate social goal is to progress the individual person's interests (and those in the individual's family). Highly individualistic cultures are those where the identities, consciousness, and emphasis are driven by self-interests and initiatives. Individual involvement in organizations is primarily calculative, which means autonomy, variety, pleasure, financial security, and friendships all envelop this goal. In contrast, *collectivism* describes low levels of individualism, in that interests are based on group identities, consciousness, and benefits. As such, membership, order, duty, and security in the clan (or organization) provide stability, and are the primary goal. Demonstrating these differences between two samples of US (individualistic) and Chinese (collectivistic) entrepreneurs, Holt (1997) found that the value orientations between these two samples differed on many values relevant to the entrepreneurial process.

Masculinity

This dimension represents the extent to which the dominant values in the society are reflected by a preference for achievement, heroism, assertiveness, and material success (as opposed to caring for others). Thus, values characterized by this dimension of culture are materialism, dependency, sympathy, and quality of life. Masculine cultures value money and material objects, growth, independence, and a constant drive for excelling, which means they feel sympathy only to those who achieve. *Femininity* depicts "low masculinity" in that individuals prefer relationships, modesty, caring for the weak, and a quality of life (Hofstede, 1985). Here, service to others is ideal, which means sympathy for the unfortunate is emphasized. Head and Sorenson (1993) examined the cultural values of masculinity-femininity in relation to organizational development. Results revealed that preferences for developmental interventions (task versus process-oriented interventions) varied based on value orientation relative to Hofstede's masculine-feminine dimension, indicating the importance of considering cultural diversity to ensure intervention effectiveness.

Overall, Hofstede's work identifies clusters of universal cultural values. We believe these categorizations can be integrated with the social exchange elements of LMX in order to address cross-cultural leadership. Within the context of Hofstede's dimensions, we can now begin to consider how individuals from different cultural backgrounds value and emphasize different levels of the processes and currencies within LMX. We emphasize, however, that this attempt at integration is just a start, and that empirical work will be needed to identify the exact nature of these relationships. We offer the discussion below to spark thinking about how research on cross-cultural relationship building can advance beyond the current status of comparative research. Moreover, this framework allows us to better address House and Aditya's (1997) questions regarding what constitutes desired, acceptable, and effective behavior in relationships between managers and subordinates of different cultural backgrounds.

LMX AND CROSS-CULTURAL SOCIAL EXCHANGE

Using the review provided previously, we now outline some ideas about how the cultural dimensions may relate to reciprocity processes of exchange and the LMX currency dimensions, focusing on the initiating stage of the relationship (rather than established relationships, where rules developed during social exchange would take over). In Table 1, we have integrated these concepts in order to better illustrate potential relationships. It is important to note that not all of the cells in Table 1 are filled. Only those associations that emerged more obviously are addressed here. As we mentioned earlier, we believe that these relationships can be better elaborated through a program of empirical investigation, and would expect the elements of Table 1 to be refined and modified based on empirical findings.

Figure 1 illustrates the expected association of relationship quality building in terms of cross-cultural leader-member relations. Culture has an enduring impact on what is valued in a relationship. As Figure 1 illustrates, these cultural characteristics that are valued within an individual's culture provide a foundation for which processes of reciprocity and currencies of LMX build relationship quality. As such, we expect that each dimension will contribute to factors that impact the overall leader-member relationship quality that emerge across cultures. The model presented in Figure 1 illustrates

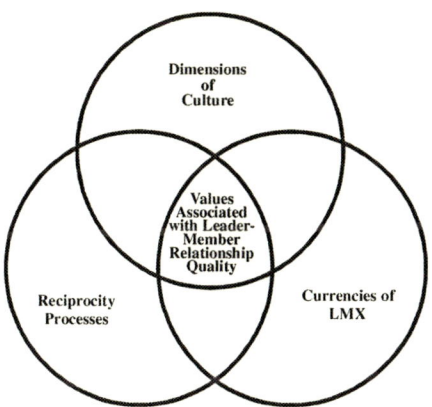

FIGURE 1
Compensatory Model of Valued Dimensions of Culture, Processes of Reciprocity, and Exchange Currencies Relevant to Leader-Member Relationship Quality

TABLE 1
Integration of the Dimensions of Culture and the Processes and Currencies of Leader-Member Exchange.

Leader-Member Exchange (LMX)	Dimensions of Culture				
	Values of LMX in Uncertainty Avoidance	Values of LMX in Power Distance	Values of LMX in Individualism	Values of LMX in Masculinity
Processes of Reciprocity:				
Equivalence	• Calculated behavior and scorekeeping to reduce uncertainty	• Powerless (subordinates) are not equivalent to the powerful (superiors).	• "Me" calculative attempts to provide for maximum pay off in exchange for the individual interest.	• Exchanges are based on the amount and quality of performance.
Immediacy	• Immediate return of exchange in order to reduce uncertainty and establish stability; time is money.	• The nature of time is dependent on those with power (superiors).		
Interest		• Work goals derive from and suit those in power.	• High self-interest orientation.	• Independence and individual excellence drive behavior.
Currencies of Exchange:				
Contribution	• Strong inner urge to work to reduce uncertainty.	• Work is determined and delegated by those in power.	• Initiatives and behavior seek to maximize individual interests.	• Achievement, performance, and growth are embraced.

Professional respect	• Beliefs derive from certainty, rules, and expertise; expert knowledge reduces uncertainty.	• Power is a resource; individuals who yield power are respected.		
Loyalty	• Deviant behaviors and ideas are frowned upon because it heightens uncertainty.	• Conflict between powerful (superiors) and powerless (subordinates) results, as members do not trust one another.	• Loyalty is to the self.	• Loyalty is given to those who perform; high femininity cultures attempt to ensure quality of life, so caring for the weak is a priority.
Affect	• Emotion displayed through anxiety and aggression.	• Although power is respected, the powerful (superiors) are not trusted.	• No real interest in others; relationship-building is a moral virtue in highly collectivistic cultures.	• Caring for others and the weak is a moral virtue only valued in femininity cultures.

the compensatory relationship between valued cultural dimensions, reciprocity processes, and currencies of exchange, indicating that each factor should be taken into account when considering those values composing leader-member relationship quality across cultures. For example, when referring to the integration of these factors in Figure 1, we would expect the Venn diagram for an individualistic individual to emphasize individualistic cultural values, reciprocity processes of equivalence and self-interest, and exchange currencies of contribution, loyalty, and affect. Together, these dimensions should able to indicate what is valued, and which factors should be especially considered when building quality leader-member relations.

Uncertainty Avoidance and LMX Relations

As described above, cultures characterized by uncertainty avoidance are not comfortable with uncertainty and ambiguity (Hofstede, 1980b). Therefore, individuals from high uncertainty avoidance cultures concentrate their efforts on avoiding tentative situations. Of particular relevance to LMX and social exchange are Hofstede's (1983) findings that persons who scored high on uncertainty avoidance tend to be sensitive to time, possess an inner urge to work hard, display and embrace aggressive behavior, view deviant persons and ideas as dangerous, and hold a strong belief in expert knowledge.

Uncertainty Avoidance and Equivalence

Equivalence involves the extent to which the amount of the return is roughly equal to what has been received. Given these definable value characteristics of high uncertainty avoidance cultures, we believe that the equivalence component of reciprocity would be particularly important in social exchanges. Individuals who are concerned with equivalence are also calculative of the value and appropriateness of the exchanges within LMX relations. Because of this, we expect that individuals who are from high uncertainty avoidance cultures would highly value equivalent exchanges in order to reduce any ambiguity associated with exchanges in the relationship. In other words, it is possible that individuals higher in uncertainty avoidance will require more equivalent exchanges in a leader-member exchange relationship than individuals lower in uncertainty avoidance.

Uncertainty Avoidance and Immediacy

Immediacy involves the amount of time between the receipt of an exchange and when reciprocation occurs (Sahlins, 1972). Individuals in relationships characterized by high immediacy are concerned with scorekeeping and paybacks. Similar to the characteristics valued in uncertainty avoidance cultures, high immediacy relationships reciprocate in a more timely fashion to avoid uncertainties associated with future interactions. Due to these similarities, we believe individuals from high uncertainty avoidance cultures may be more concerned with the timing (immediacy) of reciprocation within LMX relations than individuals in low uncertainty avoidance.

Uncertainty Avoidance and Contribution

We also believe that the LMX dimension of contribution would be important for relationship development in high uncertainty avoidance cultures. Again, high uncertainty avoidance cultures have a strong work ethic and have an aggressive nature. By working hard they can reduce uncertainty about their futures. Similarly, the exchange currency of contribution refers to an individual's willingness and ability to contribute effectively to work activities and goals, as well as contributing beyond the job description (Liden & Maslyn, 1998). In essence, contribution is defined in terms of proactivity and an aggressive work ethic. Based on this, individuals who are from high uncertainty avoidance cultures may value contributions more in work relationships than those from lower uncertainty avoidance cultures.

Uncertainty Avoidance and Professional Respect

Individuals high in uncertainty avoidance focus on expert knowledge, along with prescribed rules (Hofstede, 1983). Expert knowledge creates a level of respect among workers and colleagues (Liden et al., 1997) and enhances the work relationship through the LMX dimension of professional respect. Since expert knowledge and adherence to prescribed rules are emphasized in high uncertainty avoidance cultures, and since professional respect involves perceptions of workplace excellence and expert power (Liden & Maslyn, 1998), we believe that individuals from high uncertainty avoidance cultures may place greater value on professional respect in a leader-member exchange relationship than individuals lower in uncertainty avoidance.

Power Distance and LMX Relations

Cultures characterized by high power distances accept the fact that power in institutions and organizations is not distributed equally (Hofstede, 1983). As a result, these cultures are interested in establishing the differential attributes that distinguish superiors from subordinates, to include attributing blame to the powerless, providing lower status individuals with little participation, distrusting subordinates, and rewarding the more powerful (superiors). Low power distance cultures seek to enhance trust and members see each other on equal ground. Thus, low power distance cultures are much more egalitarian and participative than high power distance cultures.

Power Distance and Equivalence
Power distance involves an inherent inequality with respect to societal roles. Those with power rule, and those without power are at the mercy of the powerful. As such, high power distance cultures purposefully delineate the powerful (supervisors) from the powerless (subordinates). This presents an interesting challenge in terms of work relationships. Both social exchange and LMX theories suggest that in order for relationships to progress, especially initially, exchanges should be equivalent. But what will this mean for those from high power distance cultures? The expectation of equivalent exchanges within high power distance cultures, particularly from the manager to the subordinate, is not likely. The process of equivalence in reciprocity emphasizes egalitarianism (Uhl-Bien et al., 2000), whereas inequality is the norm within high power distance cultures. Therefore, individuals from high power distance cultures may not expect or demonstrate equivalent exchanges from managers to subordinates. In other words, individuals higher in power distance may place less value on equivalent exchanges in a leader-member exchange relationship than individuals lower in power distance.

Power Distance and Immediacy
Within high power distance cultures, superiors are held in high regard such that subordinates provide unquestioned compliance. This blatant role of submission also is accompanied with the expectation that, once a superior has demonstrated some form of exchange, the subordinate is required to reciprocate in a timely

fashion. On the other hand, that same expectation does not hold for a supervisor in his/her exchanges with the subordinate. Put simply, the roles are not viewed as equal. Therefore, it is possible that subordinates from high power distance cultures will exhibit high immediacy when interacting with their supervisors, while high power distance supervisors will not reciprocate in a similar fashion since they are in the power position and do not need to respond immediately.

Power Distance and Professional Respect

Since in high power distance cultures differences between superiors and subordinates are highlighted, we expect the LMX currency of professional respect will also be an essential component in these work relationships. As stated earlier, professional respect is a dimension of LMX that builds work relationships. The more professional respect a subordinate holds for the supervisor, and vice versa, the higher the quality of LMX (Liden & Maslyn, 1998). Perceptions of individuals who hold power (real or not) inherently yield respect. Liden and Maslyn (1998) argue that professional respect generates from "expert power" and that individuals seek out those whom they respect professionally in order to gain benefits associated with a relationship with that individual. We believe that professional respect will be highly valued in cultures characterized by high power distance since higher levels of power within the organization will likely lead to higher perceptions of professional respect.

Power Distance and Affect

Lower power distance cultures embrace similarities between subordinates and superiors, decrease levels of power in an effort to increase trust, and maintain harmony between the powerful and the powerless. The LMX dimension of affect focuses on the mutual affection members have for one another based on interpersonal attraction (Liden & Maslyn, 1998). Interestingly, the similarity-attraction paradigm asserts that those perceived as similar will subsequently be more highly liked interpersonally (Ferris & Judge, 1994; Stone, Stone, & Dipboye, 1992; Tsui & O'Rielly, 1989; Turban & Jones, 1988; Wayne & Liden, 1995), and this sense of liking may contribute to relationship building (Wayne & Liden, 1995). Because of this, we believe that individuals in low power distance cultures may more highly value affect in their relationships than individuals in high power distance cultures.

Individualism and LMX Relations

Cultures characterized as highly individualistic prefer a loosely knit social framework in which individuals are supposed to take care of themselves and their immediate families primarily. Highly individualistic cultures exhibit a self-orientation where they are conscious of themselves, involve themselves with organizations and other individuals based on calculated motives, and desire strong levels of autonomy and variety. This is opposed to a collectivistic society, or one with low levels of individualism, where there is a preference for a tightly knit social framework in which the expectation is that their relatives, clan, or other in-group members will look after them in exchange for unquestioning loyalty. In highly collectivistic societies, emphasis is on the group, or a collective-orientation and a "we" consciousness. Members of society tend to be involved within their collectives due to moral obligations and a membership ideal characterized by a sense of security and duty (Hofstede, 1980b, 1983).

Individualism and Interest

The social exchange reciprocity component of interest examines the motive of individuals (Liden, et al., 1997; Shalins, 1972). When individuals are self-interested, they tend to focus on obtaining benefits for themselves (Liden et al., 1997; Graen and Uhl-Bien, 1991, 1995). Individuals within highly individualistic cultures are characterized by a self-orientation and an "I" consciousness. This could play out as a desire to develop high quality relationships because they benefit the individual's self-interest. More collectivistic cultures focus on others and the group. Since collectivistic cultures have a "we" consciousness coupled with an emotional dependence on the organization, and since the social exchange reciprocity interest component of other-interest reflects an unselfish devotion and deep concern for those within the collective (Liden, et al., 1997; Graen and Uhl-Bien, 1991, 1995), cultures characterized as more collectivistic might exhibit more other-interest than cultures characterized as more individualistic. This possibility is of particular interest since Uhl-Bien & Maslyn (2003) did not find support for other-interest, yet their study utilized a sample from the US, which is characterized as a more individualistic culture according to Hofstede's (1980, 1983, 1985) work. It may be that some null research findings are due to the cultural composition of the samples in which the studies are conducted. Perhaps a study examining reciprocity dimensions of interest within a collectivistic culture would find more support for other-interest.

Individualism and Loyalty

Collectivistic cultures embrace the expertise of individuals, support group decisions, and emphasize a sense of duty to the group (Hofstede, 1983). Additionally, it is believed that the group of which one is a part will provide a sense of security in exchange for unquestioning loyalty. For example, Hui and Graen (1997) propose that Chinese management values emphasize loyalty, and China was identified as a collectivistic culture according to Hofstede's research program. Alternatively, more individualistic cultures have been found to emphasize autonomy, calculated relationships, support for individual decisions, and emotional independence from institutions or the group. As such, we could expect that individuals who are collectivist in nature would place greater value on loyalty than individuals higher in individualism, since loyalty (or obligation) involves the expression of support for the members of the exchange relationship (Liden and Maslyn, 1998) and since support for group decisions and others' expertise is emphasized in more collectivistic cultures.

Masculinity and LMX Relations

Cultures characterized by high masculinity prefer achievement, heroism, assertiveness, and material success. Emphasis is placed on performance, independence, decisiveness, and excellence (trying to be the best) of the individuals in the group. Alternatively, cultures that are low on masculinity, or high on femininity, tend to emphasize service, interdependence, a people orientation, quality of life, and sympathy for the unfortunate (Hofstede, 1983). These values seem highly appropriate to both the processes and currencies of LMX relations.

Masculinity and Equivalence

Individuals high in masculinity seek to distinguish themselves and their efforts. Contribution and quality of work are aggressively pursued in order to reap rewards associated with these efforts. Individuals from masculine cultures, however, expect to be appropriately appreciated for their efforts. As such, equivalence may be an essential social exchange component in masculine cultures. Both equity theory (Adams, 1965) and principles of distributive justice (Cropanzano & Greenberg, 1997) support this contention, as they indicate that individuals assess their work contributions to others' and compare the rewards received for those contributions. Accordingly, when the distributed rewards are perceived as inequitable in comparison to others, individuals attempt to restore equity in other ways (e.g., leave the organization, push work off on others). Thus, equity or *equivalence* is important to ensure that contributions are valued. Based on this, we believe that individuals from masculine cultures may find equivalence of exchanges to be highly important in building LMX relations. In contrast, individuals low in masculinity (femininity) seek an egalitarian life and hold sympathy for the misfortunate. Restoring equity is not vital. Thus, quality and quantity of work may not be as important in building relationships, since caring and quality of life are emphasized in these types of individuals.

Masculinity and Interest

Following a similar logic, high masculinity cultures focus on assertiveness, independence, and individual excellence. As a result, one would not expect individuals to be very interested in the outcomes for the whole organization. High femininity cultures, on the other hand, emphasize a people orientation, quality of life for all, service, and interdependence (Hofstede, 1983). This suggests that the interest in high femininity cultures is in the group. Stated simply, the interests are much more mutual. As such, we might expect that cultures higher in masculinity would be more reflective of an individual or mutual-orientation (because mutual interest also benefits the individual), and those higher in femininity would be more reflective of a mutual- or other-interest orientation.

Masculinity and Contribution

High masculinity cultures appear to hold many similarities to the LMX currency of contribution. While masculine cultures place value on achievement, performance, and growth (Hofstede, 1983), the contribution dimension of LMX emphasizes the amount, direction, and quality of work activity toward the achievement of work goals (Liden & Maslyn, 1998). Given the similarities between cultural masculinity and the contribution currency of LMX, we believe that individuals from highly masculine cultures will be more likely to value work contribution within leader-member relationships as compared to low masculinity (i.e., high femininity) cultures where work outcomes are less emphasized.

Masculinity and Affect

Low masculinity cultures (i.e., femininity) focus on relationships, caring, and sympathy. More masculine cultures stress assertiveness, heroism, and material success. Therefore, concern for others is not a top priority among individuals of more masculine cultures, which means liking others is also not a top priority. The LMX-MDM dimension of affect, however, is the socially related dimension to a relationship and it represents a desire or manifestation of friendship and interpersonal attraction (Liden & Maslyn, 1998). This dimension may be important to building quality leader-member exchanges for individuals who desire friendship or interpersonal attraction in manager-subordinate relationships. We believe lower masculinity cultures (femininity) may hold such a value, as more feminine cultures emphasize relationship-building and caring, as opposed to assertiveness, independence, and material success. Because of this, affect may be more important in leader-member exchange development in low masculinity than high masculinity cultures.

In sum, cultural values likely influence how individuals engage in relationship development through social exchange—what they value and how they approach exchanges with the dyad partner. Individuals from different cultural backgrounds may find themselves in situations of conflicting values, and if they do not understand these differing values, may not be able to develop effective work relationships with one another. In the next section we discuss these issues more fully, and provide additional ideas for how the concepts presented here can be developed into an agenda for future research.

A RELATIONAL APPROACH TO CULTURAL DIVERSITY

According to Hiller and Day's chapter in this volume, advancement of leadership and LMX research relative to diversity would be facilitated by consideration of "deep-level diversity." Deep-level diversity refers to underlying differences among individuals, such as in personality, values, and attitudes, in contrast to "surface-level diversity," which denotes the existence of differences in readily observable characteristics such as race, gender, or age (Jackson, May, & Whitney, 1995). Hiller and Day argue that researchers need to dig deeper into the underlying variables influencing relationship development, rather than examining only surface differences such as age, gender, and race under the assumption that these will necessarily influence LMX relationships (Lawrence, 1997; Byrne, 1971; McPherson & Smith-Lovin, 1987). Moreover, they suggest that relational demography approaches (Tsui, Xin, & Egan, 1995), which consider the context of the interpersonal system, are preferable to approaches that focus on demography in isolation, since demography of the dyad needs to be considered relative to the context of the group.

We agree with Hiller and Day that more work needs to explore deep-level diversity, and believe the present paper provides an avenue for building such a research program. Our focus is not on demography, however, for we believe demography still overemphasizes surface-level diversity at the expense of deep-level diversity (e.g., values). Rather, we consider cultural values (Hofstede, 1983)—a deep-level diversity perspective—relative to concepts of social exchange (e.g., reciprocity and currencies of exchange). Using this approach, we hope to push research beyond surface-level demographic issues and toward exploration of underlying factors that influence cross-cultural relationship-building.

The leadership-making model of Graen and Uhl-Bien (1991, 1995; Uhl-Bien et al., 2000) can be used as an overarching framework for this research program. According to the leadership-making model (Graen & Uhl-Bien, 1995), in order for mature relationships to develop, the preliminary perceptions and testing that occurs in the initial stages of the relationship must be successful. An offer must be made by one of the parties to move the relationship to a higher level of maturity. Although there is no evidence that leader or member demographic characteristics show any consistent patterns with LMX when considered alone (Gerstner & Day, 1997), consideration of cultural diversity and its impact on value preferences in relationship-building might yield larger effects.

At the initial appraisal stage of LMX development, when the dyad members are strangers, the influence of cultural values and how they relate to social exchange preferences is likely to be of importance. Both the leader and the member are likely to make assessments of the other through their cultural lens, and this will influence how they make offers and how they evaluate receipts in social exchange processes. They will begin to assess the underlying information about values, attitude, and belief congruence with the other at this stage. Based on the similarity-attraction paradigm (Ferris & Judge, 1994; Tsui & O'Rielly, 1989), if there is perceived congruence, the leader and member will have an easier time in relationship-building. If there is not congruence, however, this does not have to mean the relationship is doomed. If individuals at least understand the others' cultural preferences, they may still be able to navigate through the testing processes of early relationship development by adjusting their behaviors to the dyad partner.

Uhl-Bien (2003) describes this relative to "relational favorability." She says that it is possible some relationships are easier, or more "natural" to form than others. In some relationships individuals may "hit it off" from the beginning for whatever reason. This could be because they have complimentary personalities, common values, congruent perspectives or interpersonal styles, similar backgrounds, etc., such that the relationship gets off to a good start and just keeps going, with neither member really thinking about or consciously managing the process. Other relationships, however, may be much harder to develop due to personality differences, style differences, incongruent values, etc., that make it more difficult for dyad members to build the relational components necessary for higher quality relationships, i.e., relational unfavorability.

Extending the logic to this paper, in situations of cross-cultural relationship building, relational favorability may vary depending on the individuals and their cultural backgrounds. Some combinations of cultural backgrounds may be naturally unfavorable for relationship development. The obvious examples are cultures that are opposite in value dimensions (e.g., high versus low power distance or uncertainty avoidance, masculine versus feminine, individualistic versus collectivistic). Other combinations may not be detrimental to relational favorability, such as collectivistic and feminine.

According to Uhl-Bien (2003), in situations that are unfavorable, if the individual or individuals are high in what she calls "relational skills," the dyad members may be able to navigate around potential obstacles in relationship development and still form high quality exchanges. She defines relational skills as the abilities necessary to build effective and lasting work relationships that are mutually beneficial and enduring with a variety of different types of people and across varying task situations. She distinguishes these from interpersonal, or social, skills (Riggio, 1986; Riggio & Zimmerman, 1991) in which the focus is on interacting to present a good image of oneself, to be able to persuade and influence the other person to meet one's interpersonal goals. Relational skills are said to include characteristics such as:

1. An understanding of the testing process in relationship-building (reciprocity) (Uhl-Bien et al., 2000).
2. Social skills (Riggio, 1986; Riggio & Zimmerman, 1991).
3. Relational self-management skills (e.g., self-correcting behavior, ability to accept negative feedback from a dyad partner and use it to adapt accordingly, taking blame/accepting responsibility for failed actions in the relationship).
4. Relational feedback-giving (effectiveness in addressing difficult/sensitive issues in a way that the other will listen; not avoiding difficult subjects with the other).

Relational skills may also involve awareness of one's "implicit relational schemas" and the ability to manage the potential inhibiting effects of these schemas. Uhl-Bien (2003) adapts the concept of implicit leadership theory (Eden & Leviatan, 1975; Lord & Maher, 1991; Lord & Emrich, 2001) to the idea of an implicit relational theory, or the beliefs and assumptions about the characteristics of effective relationships (distinguishing between work and personal relationships). An individual's implicit relational schema consists of prototypical traits and behaviors that he/she expects relational partners to demonstrate. When dyad partners exhibit these prototypes, interpersonal favorability is higher, and relationship development to more advanced stages of relationship-building is facilitated.

Examination of implicit relational theories and how they are associated with concepts of cross-cultural relationship-building may prove a fruitful avenue for future investigation. In situations of cultural diversity, for example, one's implicit relational schema may be heavily influenced by their cultural values, and understanding these values can help individuals negotiate relationships with dyad partners. Individuals high in relational skills would recognize the need to develop high quality relationships and manage/adjust their schema to disregard or downplay mismatches with their relational prototype. Those lower in relational skills may not understand the effect their relational schema is having on them and, therefore, they perceive the dyad partner as not a good match and engage in behaviors that would not lead to the development of a higher quality relationship (potentially without ever realizing what happened). By examining how cultural values and relational theories operate, researchers may also be able to develop training programs to better help individuals understand how to develop relationships in situations of cultural diversity. Relating these ideas to Figure 1, it is intuitive to imagine that to the extent that the Venn diagram of dyad members overlaps on the valued dimensions of culture, reciprocity processes, and exchange currencies, as examined in this chapter, or whatever is valued within dyad members' implicit relational schemas, the better the quality of leader-member relationship that might emerge. Alternatively, if values are not overlapping, but dyad partners are high in relational skills, they may be able to assemble the pieces of Venn of their exchange partner, and thus be better able to develop an understanding of how to relate to them.

Another important issue for future research is to consider how these issues vary for leaders and followers. In the present paper we did not differentiate between leaders and followers. However, we believe that in some cases the variables may operate differently depending on the dyad member. For example, power distance may operate differently for managers and subordinates, with subordinates high in power distance being highly responsive to managers but managers not reciprocating for subordinates. Therefore, research should not assume that the relationships described above will be the same for leaders and followers, but rather should allow for exploration of differences depending on position in the dyad.

Finally, consistent with the suggestion of Erdogan and Liden (2002), any research addressing cross-cultural social exchanges should not assume that because an individual is from a certain culture that they embrace the predominant cultural values. Rather, investigation of these issues needs to assess Hofstede's dimensions for each individual and then examine them relative to the individual's perspectives of and preferences in the social exchanges.

CONCLUSION

We began this chapter with a quote from John Pepper (Bingham, Felin, & Black, 2000), who noted that leaders in a global economy are more important than ever, and that they will require a level of geographic flexibility. The ideas in this chapter first introduced exchange processes, currencies of LMX, and values and culture, and then integrated them into a framework of LMX and cross cultural social exchange. We then introduced a relational approach to culture diversity by including deep-level diversity in the form of values in relationships among diverse cultures. We hope that these developments may assist leaders and researchers in developing this flexibility, not only geographically, but also *culturally* in the rapidly growing diverse marketplace.

The present chapter, additionally, provides an avenue for building a research program for examination of deep-level diversity in situations of cultural diversity. We have developed a framework for evaluating leader-member quality within a culturally diverse framework utilizing Hofstede's cultural dimensions. The proposed integration of Hofstede's dimensions, reciprocity processes, and exchange currencies represented in Table 1 provides a foundation for researchers interested in testing the bounds of leader-member exchange theory and cultural diversity. In fact, with further development, the integration illustrated in Table 1 might act as a starting point for the construction of propositions and hypotheses that may be empirically tested in future research.

In a recent communication with Geert Hofstede (personal communication, August 4, 2003), in a statement about the future of culture research, he noted, "Culture will always be here…" It is with this confidence that we complete this chapter with our belief that leadership, too, will always be here and it is our intention and hope that our integration of these two domains will provide an enlightening path for future elaboration in both, nudging them further into their inevitable immortalities.

Acknowledgment: We would like to thank John Maslyn for discussing ideas that led to development of this paper.

REFERENCES

Adams, J. S. (1965). Inequity in social exchange. In L. Berkowitz (Ed.), *Advances in experimental social psychology* (Vol. 2, pp. 267-299). New York: Academic Press.

Armstrong, R. W. (1996). The relationship between culture and perception of ethical problems in international marketing. *Journal of Business Ethics, 15*(11), 1199-1208.

Bingham, C. B., Felin, T., & Black, J. S. (2000). An interview with John Pepper: What it takes to be a global leader. *Human Resource Management, 39*(2-3), 287-292.

Blau, P. M. (1964). *Exchange and power in social life.* New York: Wiley.

Byrne, D. (1971). *The attraction paradigm.* New York: Academic Press.

Carpenter, M. A., Sanders, W. G., & Gregersen, H. B. (2000). International assignment experience at the top can make a bottom-line difference. *Human Resource Management, 39*(2-3), 277-285.

Chen, C. C., & Van Velsor, E. (1996). New directions for research and practice in diversity leadership. *Leadership Quarterly, 7*(2), 285-302.

Colella, A., & Varma, A. (2001). The impact of subordinate disability on leader-member exchange relationships. *Academy of Management Journal, 44*(2), 304-315.

Connor, J. (2000). Developing the global leaders of tomorrow. *Human Resource Management, 39*(2-3), 147-157.

Cropanzano, R., & Greenberg, J. (1997). Progress in organizational justice: Tunneling through the maze. In L. T. Robertson & C. L. Cooper (Eds.), *International review of industrial and organizational psychology* (pp. 317-372). New York: John Wiley & Sons.

Den Hartog, D., House, R. J., Hanges, P. J., Ruiz-Quintanilla, S. A., & Dorfman, P. W. (1999). Culture specific and cross-culturally generalizable implicit leadership theories: Are attributes of charismatic/transformational leadership universally endorsed? *Leadership Quarterly, 10*(2), 219-257.

Dienesch, R. M., & Liden, R. C. (1986). Leader-member exchange model of leadership: A critique and further development. *Academy of Management Review, 11*, 618-634.

Dockery, T. M., & Steiner, D. D. (1990). The role of the initial interaction in leader-member exchange. *Group and Organization Studies, 15*, 395-413.

Dorfman, P. W. (1996). International and cross-cultural leadership research. In B. J. Punnett & O. Shenkar (Eds.), *Handbook for international management research* (pp. 267-349). Oxford, UK: Blackwell.

Dunegan, K. J., Duchon, D., & Uhl-Bien, M. (1992). Examining the link between leader-member exchange and manager performance: The role of task analyzability and variety as moderators. *Journal of Management, 18*, 59-76.

Eden, D., & Leviatan, U. (1975). Implicit leadership theory as a determinant of the factor structure underlying supervisory behavior scales. *Journal of Applied Psychology, 60*, 736-741.

Erdogan, B., & Liden, R. C. (2002). Social exchanges in the workplace: A review of recent developments and future research directions in leader-member exchange theory. In L. L. Neider & C. A. Schriesheim (Eds.), *Leadership* (pp. 65-114). Greenwich, CT: Information Age Publishing.

Ferris, G. R., & Judge, T. A. (1994). Subordinate influence and the performance evaluation process: Test of a model. *Organizational Behavior and Human Decision Processes, 58*(1), 101-136.

French, J. R. P., & Raven, B. H. (1959). The bases of power. In D. Cartwright (Ed.), *Studies in social power* (pp. 150-167). Ann Arbor: University of Michigan Press.

Gernster, C. R., & Day, D. V. (1997). Meta-analytic review of leader-member exchange theory: Correlates and construct issues. *Journal of Applied Psychology, 82*, 827-844.

Gouldner, A. (1960). The norm of reciprocity: A preliminary statement. *American Sociological Review, 65*(2), 176-177.

Graen, G. B., & Cashman, J. F. (1975). A role making model in formal organizations: A developmental approach. In J. G. Hunt & L. L. Larson (Eds.), *Leadership frontiers* (pp. 143-165). Kent, OH: Kent State Press.

Graen, G. B., & Scandura, T. A. (1987). Toward a psychology of dyadic organizing. In L. L. Cummings & B. M. Staw (Eds.), *Research in Organizational Behavior* (Vol. 9, pp. 175-208). Greenwich, CT: JAI Press.

Graen, G., & Uhl-Bien, M. (1991). The transformation of professionals into self-managing and partially self-designing contributors: Toward a theory of leadership-making. *Journal of Management Systems, 3*(3), 33-48.

Graen, G., & Uhl-Bien, M. (1995). The transformation of professionals into self-managing and partially self-designing contributors: Toward a theory of leadership-making. *Journal of Management Systems, 3*(3), 33-48.

Head, T. C., Sorenson, P. F. (1993). Cultural values and organizational development: A seven-country study. *Leadership and Organization Development Journal, 14*(2), 3-7.

Hofstede, G. H. (1980a). *Culture's consequences: International differences in work-related values.* Beverly Hills, CA: Sage.

Hofstede, G. H. (1980b). Motivation, leadership, and organization: Do American theories apply abroad? *Organizational Dynamics, 9*(1), 42-63.

Hofstede, G. H. (1981). Culture and organizations. *International Studies of Management and Organizations, 10*(4), 15-41.

Hofstede, G. H. (1983). National cultures in four dimensions: A research-based theory of cultural differences among nations. *International Studies of Management and Organizations, 13*(1-2), 46-74.

Hofstede, G. (1985). The interaction between national and organizational value systems. *Journal of Management Studies, 22*(4), 347-357.

Hofstede, G. (2001). *Culture's consequences: Comparing values, behaviors, institutions, and organizations across nations.* Thousand Oaks, CA: Sage.

Holt, D. H. (1997). A comparative study of values among Chinese and US entrepreneurs: Pragmatic convergence between contrasting cultures. *Journal of Business Venturing, 12*(6), 483-505.

Homans, G. C. (1958). Social behavior as exchange. *The American Journal of Sociology, 63*(6), 597-606.

House, R. J., & Aditya, R. N. (1997). The social scientific study of leadership: Quo vadis? *Journal of Management, 23*(3), 409-474.

House, R. J., Javidan, M., Hanges, P., & Dorfman, P. (2002). Understanding cultures and implicit leadership theories across the globe: An introduction to project GLOBE. *Journal of World Business, 37*(1), 3-10.

Hui, C., & Graen, G. (1997). Guanxi and professional leadership in contemporary Sino-American joint ventures in Mainland China. *Leadership Quarterly, 8*(4), 451-465.

Jackson, S. E., May, D. E., & Whitney, K. (1995). Understanding the dynamics of diversity in decision-making teams. In R. A. Guzzo & E. Salas (Eds.), *Team decision-making effectiveness in organizations* (pp. 204-261). San Francisco: Jossey-Bass.

Javidan, M., & House, R. J. (2001). Cultural acumen for the global manager: Lessons from Project GLOBE. *Organizational Dynamics, 29*(4), 289-305.

Kraimer, M. L., Wayne, S. L., & Jaworski, R. A. (2001). Sources of support and expatriate performance: The mediating role of expatriate adjustment. *Personnel Psychology, 54*(1), 71-99.

Lam, S. S. K., Schaubroeck, J., & Aryee, S. (2002). Relationship between organizational justice and employee work outcomes: A cross-national study. *Journal of Organizational Behavior, 23*(1), 1-18.

Lawrence, B. S. (1997). The black box of organizational demography. *Organization Science, 8*, 1-22.

Liden, R. C., & Graen, G. B. (1980). Generalizability of the vertical dyad linkage model of leadership. *Academy of Management Journal, 23*, 451-465.

Liden, R. C., & Maslyn, J. M. (1998). Multidimensionality of leader-member exchange: An empirical assessment through scale development. *Journal of Management, 24*(1), 43-72.

Liden, R. C., Sparrowe, R. T., & Wayne, S. J. (1997). Leader-member exchange and human resource management: The past and potential for the future. *Research in Personnel & Human Resources Management, 15*, 47-119.

Liden, R., Wayne, S., & Stilwell, D. (1993). A longitudinal study on the early development of leader-member exchanges. *Journal of Applied Psychology, 78*(4), 662-674.

Lord, R., & Emrich, C. (2001). Thinking outside the box by looking inside the box: Extending the cognitive revolution in leadership research. *Leadership Quarterly, 11*(4), 551-579.

Lord, R. & Maher, K. (1991). *Leadership and information processing: Linking perceptions and performance.* Boston: Unwin-Hyman.

Masterson, S. S., Lewis, K., Goldman, B. M., & Taylor, M. S. (2000). Integrating justice and social exchange: The differing effects of fair procedures and treatment of work relationships. *Academy of Management Journal, 43*, 738-748.

Maslyn, J., & Uhl-Bien, M. (2001). Leader-member exchange and its dimensions: Effects of self and other effort on relationship quality. *Journal of Applied Psychology, 86*(4), 697-708.

McPherson, J. M., & Smith-Lovin, L. (1987). Homophily in voluntary organizations: Status distance and the composition of face-to-face groups. *American Sociological Review, 52,* 370-379.

Murphy, S. M., Wayne, S. J., Liden, R. C., & Erdogan, B. (2003). Understanding social loafing: The role of justice perceptions and exchange relationships. *Human Relations, 56*(1), 61-84.

Pillai, R., Scandura, T. A., & Williams, E. A. (1999). Leadership and organizational justice: Similarities and differences across cultures. *Journal of International Business Studies, 30*(4), 763-779.

Raabe, B. & Beehr, T. A. (2003). Formal mentoring versus supervisor and coworker relationships: Differences in perceptions and impact. *Journal of Organizational Behavior, 24*(3), 271-293.

Riggio, R. (1986). Assessment of basic social skills. *Journal of Personality and Social Psychology, 51*(3), 649-660.

Riggio, R., & Zimmerman, J. (1991). Social skills and interpersonal relationships: Influences on social support and support seeking. *Advances in Personal Relationships, 2,* 133-155.

Sahlins, M. D. (1972). *Stone Age Economics.* New York: Aldine Publishing Company.

Scandura, T. A., Graen, G. B., & Novak, M. A. (1986). When managers decide not to decide autocratically: An investigation of leader-member exchange and decision influence. *Journal of Applied Psychology, 71,* 579-584.

Scandura, T. A., & Lankau, M. J. (1996). Developing diverse leaders: A leader-member exchange approach. *Leadership Quarterly, 7*(2), 243-263.

Schein, E. H. (1992). Organizational culture and leadership. San Francisco: Jossey-Bass.

Simmel, G. (1950). *The Sociology of Georg Simmel.* New York: Free Press.

Singhapakdi, A., Marta, J. K. M., Rao, C. P., & Cicic, M. (2001). Is cross-cultural similarity an indicator of similar marketing ethics? *Journal of Business Ethics, 32*(1), 55-68.

Sparrowe, R. T. (1998). Leader-member exchange, social networks, and differentiation. Unpublished doctoral dissertation, University of Illinois at Chicago.

Sparrowe, R. T., & Liden, R. C. (1997). Process and structure in leader-member exchange. *Academy of Management Review, 22,* 522-552.

Stone, E. F., Stone, D. L., & Dipboye, R. (1992). Stigmas in organizations: Race, handicaps, and physical unattractiveness. In K. Kelley (Ed.), *Theory, research, and practice in industrial and organizational psychology* (pp. 449-511). Amsterdam: Elsevier.

Thurnwald, R. (1932). *Economics in Primitive Communities.* London: Oxford.

Triandis, H. C. (1993). The contingency model in cross-cultural perspective. In M. M. Chemers & R. Ayman (Eds.), *Leadership theory and research: Perspectives and directions* (pp. 167-188). San Diego: Academic Press.

Trice, H. M., & Beyer, J. M. (1993). *The cultures of work organizations.* Englewood Cliffs, NJ: Prentice Hall.

Tsui, A. S., & O'Reilly, C. A. (1989). Beyond simple demographic effects: The importance of relational demography in superior-subordinate dyads. *Academy of Management Journal, 32*(2), 402-423.

Tsui, A. S., Xin, K. R., & Egan, T. D. (1995). Relational demography: The missing link in vertical dyad linkage. In S. E. Jackson & M. N. Ruderman (Eds.), *Diversity in work teams: Research paradigms for a changing workplace* (pp. 97-129). Washington, DC: American Psychological Association.

Turban, D. B., & Jones, A. P. (1988). Supervisor-subordinate similarity: Types, effects, and mechanisms. *Journal of Applied Psychology, 73*, 228-234.

Wayne, S. J., & Liden, R. C. (1995). Effects of impression management on performance ratings: A longitudinal study. *Academy of Management Journal, 38*(1), 232-260.

Wayne, S. J., Shore, L. M., & Liden, R. C. (1997). Perceived organizational support and leader-member exchange: A social exchange perspective. *Academy of Management Journal, 40*(1), 82-111.

Uhl-Bien, M. (2003). Relationship development as a key ingredient for leadership development. In S. E. Murphy & R. E. Riggio (Eds.), *The future of leadership development* (pp. 129-147). Mahwah, NJ: Erlbaum.

Uhl-Bien, M., Graen, G. B., & Scandura, T. (2000). Implications of leader-member exchange (LMX) for strategic human resource management systems: Relationships as social capital for competitive advantage. In G. Ferris (Ed.), *Research in Personnel and Human Resource Management* (Vol. 18, pp. 137-185). Greenwich, CT: JAI Press.

Uhl-Bien, M., & Maslyn, J. (2003). Reciprocity in manager-subordinate relationships: Components, configurations, and outcomes. *Journal of Management, 29*(4), 511-532.

Diane Sullivan is a doctoral student in the Management Department at the University of Central Florida, specializing in strategy/entrepreneurship. She earned her MBA and BSBA from the University of Central Florida. Her work has appeared in the *Journal of Organizational Behavior.* Her research interests include entrepreneurship, creativity and innovation, teams, leadership, and diversity.

Marie Mitchell is a doctoral student in the Management Department at the University of Central Florida, specializing in organizational behavior. She earned her BA from George Mason University and MAHR from Rollins College. She initiated doctoral studies at the University of Texas at Austin, and then transferred to the University of Central Florida in 2001. Her primary research interests include social exchange, organizational justice, relational leadership, and deviance.

Mary Uhl-Bien is an Associate Professor of Management at the University of Central Florida. She received her MBA and PhD from the University of Cincinnati. Her work has appeared in *The Academy of Management Journal, Journal of Applied Psychology, Journal of Management, Leadership Quarterly, Research in Personnel and Human Resources Management,* and *Human Relations,* among others. She serves on the Editorial Board of the *Academy of Management Journal* and *Leadership Quarterly.* Her research interests include relational leadership theory, social exchange, and complex leadership. She has consulted to companies including State Farm Insurance, Walt Disney World, British Petroleum, Sears, and the US Fish and Wildlife Service.

CHAPTER 8

LMX AND ORGANIZATIONAL CITIZENSHIP BEHAVIOR
Examining the Links Within and Across Western and Chinese Samples

Rick D. Hackett, Jiing-Lih Farh,
Lynda J. Song, and Laurent M. Lapierre

Despite organizational citizenship behavior (OCB) figuring prominently in conceptualizations of leader-member exchange (LMX) theory, little is known about either the magnitude of the LMX-OCB relationship, or the paths by which the two constructs are related. Our meta-analysis of the literature shows a population correlation of +.32 between LMX and overall measures of OCB, and no evidence for moderators. Modeling of the LMX-OCB relationship should better integrate published findings, and give due prominence to the role of employee "affect." While the fundamental tenets of LMX theory appear to apply to the highly relationship-oriented culture of the Chinese, the leader-member relational roles may be more culturally prescribed among the Chinese and more "negotiated" in Western cultures. Cross-cultural differences in exchange processes and currencies should be explored.

Dealing with Diversity
A Volume in: LMX Leadership: The Series, pages 219–264.
Copyright © 2003 by Information Age Publishing, Inc.
All rights of reproduction in any form reserved.
ISBN: 1-930608-49-7 (hardcover), 1-930608-48-9 (paperback)

To *lead* is to "take charge of"—to direct operations, activities, or performance of people. A *leader*, traditionally speaking, is someone who has a commanding *authority* or *influence* over others. While we commonly think of leadership in terms of "downward" influence on followers, leadership can be exercised laterally and from the "bottom-up." An example of the former is the individual who, with no formally assigned authoritative role, leads her peers of a self-managing project-team to accomplishing common goals. Moreover, her leadership may be shared with one or more members of the team. An example of "bottom-up" leadership is someone low in the formal hierarchical structure successfully influencing the "higher ups" to adopt changes in organizational policies and practices to the benefit of peers and the overall organization.

As described above, leadership entails the exercise of *power*—which we may define as the capacity of one individual to influence another. Typically, power results from the dependency of one person on another. The base or source of the power varies across relationships. For example, one can coerce behavior in others by threatening harm, force, or restriction of movement, or cause others to behave in desired ways by exercising legitimately ascribed authority (through title, appointment, or social standing). In the later case, there may be a felt obligation to "fall in line" to maintain the "social order" (while reaping the benefits of compliance, and avoiding the negative consequences of non-compliance). Power may also derive from the control and allocation of scare resources that are highly valued and sought-after (e.g. expertise, money, social recognition); or from the admiration, trust, and respect that one commands from others—originating from perceived ability, integrity, benevolence, and overall "moral character." The capacity for social influence may draw from *one or more* of the above sources (French & Raven, 1959).

Leadership, however, is more than the exercise of power. Few would describe a dictator or tyrant as a "leader." Nor does political appointment or ascription by social status bestow leadership on the incumbent, though both provide for social influence. Initiating behavioral change through promising valued resources (contingent-reward), or threatening punishment (contingent-punishment) also falls short of commonly held notions of leadership. In the above cases, behavioral compliance is likely to be fleeting (diminishing when threat of punishment and contingent rewards are removed, and/or when the "social order" changes), and minimally satisfying of behavioral prescriptions.

Influence exercised through the trust, respect, and admiration that one has for another (supplemented with contingent-reward) is likely to be more enduring, and more likely to result in greater efforts to exceed minimal behavioral requirements. In this case, the dependence of followers on the leader derives from followers' self-identity being linked to the leader's implicit (and perhaps explicit) approval of them. It is this sort of influence that is frequently associated with notions of "leadership" (cf. Cogliser & Schriesheim, 2000). Hence, while leadership inherently requires the exercise of power, clearly power does not inherently entail the exercise of leadership.

Reduced to its simplest form, leadership is the ability to influence a group of individuals toward the achievement of shared goals (cf. Bryman, 1996)—whether the direction of influence is downward, upward, or lateral. For the Chief Executive Officer (CEO) of an organization, leadership involves creating a vision, setting broad objectives, aligning resources to the vision, and inspiring organizational members to "own" the vision. Leaders at other levels throughout the organization are required to translate the broader organizational vision into more specific objectives for their units, transforming the self-interest of individual members into the collective interests of their team, department, and overall organization.

What does it mean to "*transform*" self-interest into collective interests? One interpretation is to align the interests of the individual with those of their unit, such that behaving in a way that benefits the unit also benefits the individual. Accordingly, leadership in organizations entails energizing, harnessing and directing the efforts of individuals toward achieving a common cause that transcends (*and advances*) individual interests. It follows further that, in order to be effective, leaders must know: (1) how to transform individual interests into collective interests and; (2) what is behaviorally expected of employees for them to contribute to the collective.[1] Let us now turn our attention briefly to these two issues, and, in so doing, establish the foundation and framework of this chapter.

Behavioral strategies for moving followers beyond their self interests for the good of the group, organization or society, are found in the transactional-transformational leadership paradigm (Bass, 1985, 1997; Burns, 1978). Drawing on the "transactional" side of this paradigm, leaders establish goals, clarify role and task requirements, reward desired behavior, and provide constructive feedback to keep followers on task. While these goal-focused behaviors can be of a pro-social nature, the exchange is largely economic, with promotion of self-interest the primary motivating force. Accordingly, behavioral commitment may be shallow, and fleeting. Moreover, this predominantly economic exchange requires that behavioral expectations for employees be clearly defined within the "contract." There are myriad pro-social discretionary behaviors that contribute to unit objectives that are difficult to define, measure and monitor in any comprehensive and systematic way (George & Brief, 1992).

The *transformational* side of the transactional-transformational leadership paradigm focuses largely on the *socio-emotional* bond between the leader and follower. Transformational leaders attend to the concerns and the individual developmental needs of their followers (individual consideration). They change followers' awareness of issues by helping them to look at old problems in new ways (intellectual stimulation). Moreover, transformational leaders are able to arouse and inspire followers to expend effort well beyond their individual task responsibilities to the benefit of their unit(s) (charisma) (Bass, 1985, 1997).[2] Transformational leadership builds on transactional leadership, with the most effective leaders demonstrating both (Bass, 1985; Waldman, Bass & Yammarino, 1990). Most notable, however, is the affective-emotional engagement that transformational leaders elicit from their followers. That is, this relationship extends beyond a predominantly economic, self-interest-driven exchange arrangement.

While transformational leaders have been described as "other-oriented," in as much as they "continually adjust their behavior to the level to which the follower has been developed" (Avolio & Bass, 1995, p. 207), leader-member-exchange-theory (LMX), gives more specific attention to the relationship initiation and maturation process. LMX theory posits that leaders develop differentiated relationships, of varying quality, with their followers, with the quality of the relationship determined by the nature and level of reciprocal exchanges over time (Uhl-Bien, Graen, & Scandura, 2000).[3] LMX research has aimed to better understand this process (Dienesch & Liden, 1986; Graen & Uhl-Bien, 1995). Understanding, at the dyad level, the factors contributing to—and detracting from—high-quality relationships, is important to ascertaining how best to bring about effective leadership.

Both transformational leadership and LMX prescriptions underscore the importance of establishing an affective connection or personal "bonding" between leader and follower. This recognizes that the most effective employees are not merely "task proficient," but also behave in many ways that enhance the social and psychological environment of their workplace. These behaviors often are discretionary, falling outside of written job descriptions (e.g. extra-role), and not explicitly or formally rewarded (cf. Podsakoff, MacKenzie, Paine, & Bachrach, 2000). An example is the worker who voluntarily assists a new hire in becoming acquainted with work procedures. Behaviors of this sort have been described, categorized, and studied under the rubric of organizational citizenship behavior (OCB; cf. Podsakoff et al. 2000) and contextual performance (CP; Borman & Motowidlo, 1993; Motowidlo, 2000).

Transformational leadership and LMX are thought to be particularly effective in eliciting OCB by establishing respect and *trust* between leader and follower (Bass, 1985; Deluga, 1994, 1995; Liden & Graen, 1980). Indeed, in a meta-analysis of the trust literature, Dirks and Ferrin (2002) report mean correlations of trust with transformational leadership and LMX of .79 and .77 respectively, and mean correlations between trust and OCB dimensions ranging from .13 (civic virtue) to .25 (conscientiousness, courtesy).[4] From a social-exchange theory perspective (cf. Cole, Schaninger, & Harris, 2002; Liden, Sparrowe, & Wayne, 1997), subordinates experiencing higher-quality exchanges with their leaders meet mutual obligations of reciprocity by going beyond formal position requirements (e.g. extra-role) and voluntarily performing acts which benefit the organization (Deluga, 1994).

A distinguishing characteristic of transformational, charismatic, and visionary theories is that they all build on the relationship between leaders and followers as discussed in LMX theory (Avolio, Sosik, Jung, & Berson, 2003). Wang, Law, Wang, & Chen (2001) contend that transformational leadership is more distally related to OCB than is LMX, because, as a leadership style, it is rooted in the personality and charisma of the leader. In contrast, they contend that LMX is more dynamic, changing continuously according to the "role-making process" (Graen & Scandura, 1987; Graen & Uhl-Bien, 1995). Wang, Law, Wang, and Chen (2001) found that LMX mediated the relationship between transformational leader behaviors and followers' performance and OCB.[5]

The preceding discourse establishes a rationale for examining, in some detail, the nature and extent of the relationship between LMX and OCB/CP. But is the rationale behind an LMX-OCB link generalizable to Eastern cultures? In particular, 21st century China is expected to be home to the world's fastest growing economy. As a new member of the World Trade Organization (WTO), it must open domestic markets to foreign competition. The competitive pressures for well-run businesses are on a steady and steep incline. With an accompanying rapid rise in foreign investment through joint ventures, the demand for effective organizational leaders will significantly outstrip supply. Attempts to fill the leadership gap are being met through expatriate assignments and training and development of local talent. Do the assumptions and prescriptions of LMX theory apply to China, a culture traditionally noted for its hierarchical authoritative structures and collectivist values? Is the conceptualization, and the content domain of OCB/CP, similar in China and the West? Does the rationale for an LMX-OCB link hold for China?

This chapter addresses these questions. First, we provide a brief overview of how LMX has been most commonly conceptualized and measured. We then do the same for OCB/CP. This provides the necessary framework within which to interpret subsequently presented empirical findings on the LMX-OCB link. Next, a review and interpretation of the empirical literature on the LMX-OCB relationship is undertaken. This is followed by an examination of LMX, OCB, and their association from a Chinese cultural perspective. The chapter is concluded with a discussion of unresolved issues that provide direction for future research.

LMX THEORY: AN OVERVIEW

While leadership can be exercised laterally and from the "bottom-up," LMX theory, as originally conceptualized, treats leadership as a "top-down" phenomenon (Dansereau, Graen, & Haga, 1975; Graen, 1976).[6] The basic premise of LMX theory is that supervisors establish fairly stable differential dyadic relationships with their subordinates, ranging from high quality (in-group members) to low quality (out-group members). Understanding how these relationships form, evolve, and impact work-related attitudes and outcomes has been a central aim of LMX research (cf. Gerstner & Day, 1997; Graen & Uhl-Bien, 1995; Schriesheim, Castro, & Cogliser, 1999).

What is LMX?

Fundamentally, LMX theory is premised on notions of social exchange, reciprocity, and equity (cf. Cole et al., 2002; Deluga, 1994). Specifically, each party brings to the relationship different kinds of resources for exchange. By behaving in ways that advance the cause of the leader, followers receive benefits of value to them (cf. Liden, et al. 1997).

In lower-quality exchanges, the leader exercises formal authority, allocating standard benefits in return for fairly standard job performance. As very little affective/personal "bonding" occurs, a predominantly economic exchange sustains the relationship. In higher quality relationships, however, a personal bond is established and social exchange is moved to a higher level, nourished by mutual trust, respect, and obligation. In return for exemplary supervisor-enhancing work performance (e.g. consistently volunteering to work extra hours to meet project deadlines), followers receive special privileges (e.g., access to key personnel or information), career-enhancing opportunities (e.g., special work assignments), and increasing levels of discretion in doing their jobs. Higher-level social exchange relationships engender stronger feelings of personal obligation, gratitude, and trust than do predominately quid pro quo economic exchanges.

We draw from Blau's (1964) framework in describing low-quality LMX relationships entailing predominantly an economic exchange, and high quality LMX relationships entailing predominantly a social exchange. In distinguishing economic from social exchange, Blau (1964) noted: "only social exchange tends to engender feelings of personal obligation, gratitude and trust; purely economic exchange as such does not" (p. 94). Social exchange engenders these feelings because it involves obligations that are diffuse and unspecified, whereas economic exchange specifies precisely how and when each party is to fulfil their obligation. Finally, social exchange lacks a standard of value against which gifts, favors, or contributions can be measured, whereas in economic exchanges, the equivalences are much clearer (Liden et al. 1997, p. 79). This distinction between economic- and social-exchange parallels Rousseau's (1990, 1995) distinction between employment and psychological contract, respectively.

But how do LMX relationships start and evolve? Examining closely the stages of LMX development and maturation builds the foundation for our later discussions on the applicability of LMX theory to the highly relationship-oriented Chinese culture.

LMX: Stages of Development

The following summary of the stages of the relationship-making process is taken from a more detailed description provided by Graen and Uhl-Bien (1995). Essentially, the relationship-building process is described as consisting of three stages. In Stage 1 there is a coming together of "strangers" occupying interdependent organizational roles. Interactions between leader and follower are characterized as formal, where the exchange is purely contractual and mostly immediate. Leaders communicate performance requirements, and followers oblige. In Stage 2, the two parties become "acquaintances." Leader and followers begin to share resources on a professional *and* personal level. This is considered an intermediate, "testing" stage, where each party expects an equitable return of "favors" within short time periods. Relationships that evolve into Stage 3 are described as "mature." Exchanges in this stage are highly developed, in that rather than being predominantly an economic quid pro quo contractual arrangement, these exchanges are more personal and socially-based. Exchanges are "in-kind" within broader time frames, with each party expressing loyalty and support, nourished by mutual *respect, trust* and *obligation.* The impact of leadership is considered greatest during this stage.

In all three stages, reciprocity governs the relationship. However, in Stage 3, the exchange is heavily social, less well specified (implicit), and less time-bound. From Stage 1 through to Stage 3, followers are given increasing levels of responsibility and undertake them without expecting any short-term payoff. At Stage 3, according to Graen and Uhl-Bien (1995)

> followers are willing to exert extra effort by engaging in activities that are not specifically prescribed by the organization, exercising personal initiative, exercising personal leadership to make their work unit more effective, taking career risks to accomplish assignments, being *good organization citizens* and so forth. (p. 233)

Accordingly leadership evolves from being transactional (Stage 1), to transformational (Stage 3). It is in Stage 3 that the "transformation" is said to occur, a transformation from a concern for self-interest to a concern for collective interests. Here, satisfaction of one's own interests is achieved through satisfying the interests of others, with the leader-follower relationship potentially becoming one of "partnership" between *peers*.

LMX Measurement, Correlates & Dimensionality

Schriesheim, Castro, & Cogliser (1999) provide a comprehensive review of the evolution of LMX measures. They note considerable diversity of opinion over how many dimensions underlie LMX, and how LMX is best measured. In a quantitative review (meta-analysis) of the LMX literature, Gerstner & Day (1997) show that the LMX-7 (reported in Scandura & Graen, 1984) is the most widely used measure of leader-member exchange. They also show that it has the highest internal consistency (coefficient alpha reliability) across studies, as compared to a category of "other LMX scales" (.89 versus .83 respectively, when completed by subordinate)[7].

Gerstner and Day (1997) further demonstrated that LMX-7, as compared to the "other category" of LMX measures, has the highest correlations with performance ratings and work-related attitudes. As would be expected, the mean sample-size-weighted correlation between LMX-7 scores and supervisory ratings of employee performance was significantly higher when the LMX-7 ratings were provided by the supervisors (ρ = .49) than when they were provided by the subordinates (ρ = .31). LMX-7 also correlated (mean, sample-size weighted) positively with objective measures of performance (ρ =. 11), satisfaction with supervision (ρ =.74), overall satisfaction (ρ =.50), organizational commitment (ρ =.38), and role clarity (ρ =.44). It correlated negatively (mean, sample-size weighted) with role conflict (ρ = -.40) and turnover intentions (ρ = -.27). Surprisingly, the Gerstner and Day (1997) meta-analysis did not include OCB, despite OCB being *centrally* implicated in past and current conceptualization of LMX theory (cf. Liden et al., 1997)! In light of the relatively high internal consistency and the convergent and discriminant validity of the LMX-7, Gerstner and Day (1997) and Graen & Uhl-Bien (1995) recommend it to researchers who are interested in an overall assessment of exchange quality.

Despite their recommendation to use only the aggregate scores from the LMX-7, Graen and Uhl-Bien (1995) contend that three dimensions underlie the LMX-7—*respect, mutual trust,* and *obligation*.[8] Dienesch and Liden (1986), however, conceptualize LMX as comprising the three dimensions of *perceived contribution to the exchange, loyalty,* and *positive affect.* Schriesheim, Neider, Scandura, and Tepper (1992), developed a six item scale (LMX-6) to measure each of these three dimensions and Schriesheim, Scandura, Eisenbach, and Neider (1992) provided further support for the psychometric integrity of this scale. Liden and Maslyn (1998) developed a 13-item scale (LMX-MDM) to measure these same three dimensions along with a fourth LMX dimension—"*professional respect.*" In addition to showing strong internal psychometric properties for the LMX-MDM, Liden and Maslyn (1998) provide evidence for *differential* relationships between the dimension scores and work attitude and outcome measures.

The merits to calculating separate LMX subscale scores rests heavily on being able to empirically demonstrate their differential relationships with other variables of theoretical interest. For example, Maslyn and Uhl-Bien (2001) reported differential relationships between LMX-MDM dimension-scores of subordinates and: (a) subordinate perceptions of how much effort their leaders invested in the LMX relationship; and (b) subordinate reports of their own efforts toward relationship building. Research of this kind can refine and enrich our understanding of the LMX relationship building process. If the different, additive components of LMX are enhanced in different ways, this has clear implications for training supervisors on how to develop high-quality LMX relationships—different behavioral strategies are required depending upon the LMX component you are seeking to enhance.

However, as most of the research on the LMX-OCB relationship used the LMX-7, or a variation thereof, it is appropriate to provide a context around the three dimensions that purportedly underlie this scale. *Respect* is required in the initiation of an LMX relationship. Members must respect one another's professional capabilities and believe that these capabilities are adequate to meeting or exceeding each other's job expectations. Next, once one's respect for the capabilities of the other is affirmed through mutual expectations being met, each member comes to *trust* the other to demonstrate commitment and support for the relationship. Finally, as trust for one another builds, LMX members develop a sense of mutual *obligation*, unconstrained by expectations of specific and short-term personal payoffs. High-quality LMX relationships are characterized as being high on all three components (Uhl-Bien et al., 2000, p. 156).

As there is no published research showing which of the three proposed dimensions each of the LMX-7 items represent, scores from the LMX-7 should be used in the aggregate only, as recommended by Graen and Uhl-Bien (1995). When dimensional LMX scores are required, the LMX-MDM (Liden & Maslyn, 1998) or the LMX-6 (Schriesheim, Neider, Scandura, & Tepper, 1992) appear to be better choices. Whether the LMX-6 or LMX-MDM composite scores are substitutable for composite LMX-7 scores is unresolved. While total scores from these scales tend to be highly and positively related (cf. Maslyn & Uhl-Bien, 2001; Schriesheim, Neider, Scandura, & Tepper, 1992; Schriesheim, Scandura, Eisenbach, & Neider, 1992), they do not consistently show the same pattern of results when used in the same study (cf. Maslyn & Uhl-Bien, 2001). This is not surprising, given that the LMX-MDM and LMX-7 are defined in terms of different dimensions.

Is Relationship Quality "In the Eyes of the Beholder"?

Separate from which scale to use, is the issue of whether to assess LMX from the perspective of the leader or follower. The two perspectives do not converge well. Gerstner and Day (1997) report the mean sample-weighted correlation between leader and member reports of LMX as .29 (.37 when corrected for leader and member unreliability). This lack of convergence was evidenced for both the LMX-7 and the category of "other" LMX measures. Moreover, the correlations between LMX and performance ratings are significantly stronger when LMX is measured from the leader's perspective than from the follower's perspective.

These results suggest that different constructs are being measured by the LMX-7, as a function of whether ratings are taken from the leader or follower (cf. Brower, Schoorman, & Tan, 2000). Accordingly, aggregate scores from the LMX-7 do not represent the quality of the leader-member exchange relationship per se. Rather, they represent a perception of the quality of the relationship taken from the perspective of an invested party (typically the follower).

Conceptual Link Between LMX and OCB

OCB figures prominently in the conceptualization of LMX theory. Graen and Wakabayashi (1994) noted: "within mature leadership relationships (high LMX), leaders and members experience reciprocal influence, *extra-contractual behavior*, mutual respect and liking, and internalisation of common goals" (p. 419). High LMX leaders "can rely on the followers to take on extra assignments without pay or provide honest constructive criticism in situations others may find intimidating" (Graen & Wakabayashi, 1994, p. 423). "It is this trust, respect and confidence in leaders that encourage followers to grow beyond a formalized work contract, to grow out of their jobs" (Graen & Wakabayashi, 1994, p. 423). High-quality LMX employees trade or contribute behavior "above and beyond the job description" in return for influence with the leader (Cole et al., 2002, p. 150; Liden et al. 1997). The "contribution" dimension of Liden and Maslyn's (1998) four-dimensional conceptualization of LMX is operationalized in terms of extra-role behavior. The two items used to measure this dimension are: (1) "I do work for my supervisor that goes beyond what is specified in my job description;" (2) "I am willing to apply extra efforts, beyond those normally required, to further the interests of my work group" (Liden & Maslyn, 1998, p. 56). OCB has been described in relation to the *trust* and *obligation* characteristic of social exchange (Bateman & Organ, 1983; Konovsky & Pugh, 1994; Moorman, 1991). As OCB is so central to LMX theory, it is important to examine the LMX-OCB link. It is for this reason that the omission of OCB from the Gerstner and Day (1997) meta-analysis is so puzzling. Before turning our attention to the LMX-OCB relationship, however, a brief overview of the OCB/CP literature is in order.

OCB/CONTEXTUAL PERFORMANCE

Earlier we stated that in order to be an effective leader one must know: (1) how to transform individual interests into collective interests, and (2) what is behaviorally expected of employees in their contributions to the collective interest.

Member behaviors contributing to the collective interests of an organization are those that enhance organizational productivity.

This is so for both profit and non-profit organizations, though the indicators of productivity are likely to differ between the two. Organizations are productive to the degree to which they are effective *and* efficient in achieving short- and long-term organizational objectives. They are *effective* if goals are accomplished, and *efficient* if the costs incurred to achieve the goals are minimized. Individual contributions to organizational productivity come from each member behaving in ways that are valued by management. Ideally, the behaviors valued by management (e.g. those selected for, trained for, and rewarded) are instrumental to achieving (efficiently) organizational goals (Motowidlo, 2003). Members who engage in more of these behaviors, at least cost to the organization (e.g. time, errors) will be the most productive, in the absence of constraining situational forces (e.g. faulty equipment or machinery). The productivity of each member, then, contributes to the aggregate productivity of the organization (Hackett, 2002; Motowidlo, 2003).

Contextual Performance

Personnel psychologists build predictive models of performance to identify from among a candidate pool the individuals most likely to contribute to organizational productivity. Historically there has been a focus on predicting how well the person will carry out the core task requirements of the position, identified through a task/job analysis. Task performance is comprised of behavioral activities that directly transform raw materials into the goods and services of the organization, as well as behaviors that support and maintain these technical core activities (e.g., purchasing, distribution, planning, coordinating, supervising) (cf. Motowidlo, 2003). In the last decade, the performance domain in these predictive models has been expanded to include behaviors outside the formal job description that *support* task proficiency (Borman & Motowidlo, 1993). Though the importance to productivity of these non-task-specific behaviors has been recognized for some time (cf. Katz, 1964; Katz & Kahn, 1978), they have historically been given relatively little weight in selection models.

Borman, Motowidlo, and their colleagues have referred to these non-task-specific behaviors, which support task proficiency, as "contextual performance" (Motowidlo, Borman, & Schmit, 1997), which they define as "behaviors that contribute to organizational effectiveness through their effects on the psychological, social and organizational *context* of work" (Motowidlo, 2000, 2003). Further, they classified contextual performance behaviors into three broad categories: *interpersonal support, organizational support,* and *job/task conscientiousness* (cf. Borman, Buck, Hanson, Motowidlo, Stark, & Drasgow, 2001; Borman, Penner, Allen, & Motowodilo, 2001; Coleman & Borman, 2000). *Interpersonal support* includes behaviors that help, support, and motivate others, with sub dimensions of helping, cooperating, courtesy, and motivating. *Organizational support* consists of behaviors that defend and promote the organization. It consists of the sub-dimensions of: "representing the organization," loyalty, and compliance. Finally, *conscientious initiative* includes behaviors that exemplify persistence of effort in completing tasks and developing self, with sub dimensions of persistence, initiative and self-development.

The behaviors listed in the above typology are considered prototypical of behaviors that are expected to contribute toward enhancing the psychological, social, and organizational context of work. Motowidlo (2003) notes that some behaviors may well contribute to both task and contextual performance. For example, persisting with extra effort despite difficult conditions and taking initiative to do all that is required to get a task done contributes to contextual performance, in as much as it may inspire others to do the same. Specifically, this behavior helps establish and reinforce norms that support and encourage similar behavior in others (Motowidlo, 2003). Simultaneously, however, this behavior directly enhances the individual's contribution to the production of organizational goods and services. Clearly, some behaviors have consequences both for producing goods and services (task performance) and for maintaining and enhancing the psychological, social and organizational context of work (contextual performance) (Motowidlo, 2003).

Within the personnel selection paradigm, research on contextual performance has focused primarily on identifying unique predictors of contextual- and task-performance. Empirical findings generally support predictions that individual differences in personality relate more strongly to contextual performance than to task performance. There is mixed support for the contention that individual differences in cognitive ability relate more strongly to task performance than to contextual performance (Borman & Motowidlo, 1993, 1997; Motowidlo & Van Scotter, 1994; Van Scotter & Motowidlo, 1996). Other research has examined the relative impact of contextual- and task-performance in supervisory-ratings of overall performance (Borman, White, & Dorsey 1995; Motowidlo & Van Scotter, 1994; Van Scotter & Motowidlo, 1996). The evidence here suggests that supervisors weigh task- and contextual-performance about equally when judging employees' overall performance (Borman & Motowidlo, 1997). However, Rotundo and Sackett (2002) have shown, using a policy capturing approach, that the weight managers gave to task- and contextual-performance in ratings of overall performance of their employees varied by manager.

Organizational Citizenship Behavior

Whereas the study of "contextual performance" was initiated by personnel psychologists with an interest in broadening and enriching the measurement of performance (Borman & Motowidlo, 1993), research into OCB evolved from an interest in understanding how job satisfaction relates to people's inclination toward helpful, cooperative behaviors in the workplace (Motowidlo, 2000; Organ, 1997; Smith, Organ, & Near, 1983). Behavioral domains overlapping with OCB have been variously labelled *pro-social organizational behavior* (Brief & Motowidlo, 1986; George, 1990, 1991; George & Bettenhausen, 1990; O'Reilly & Chatman, 1986), *organizational spontaneity* (George & Brief, 1992; George & Jones, 1997), and *extra-role behavior* (Van Dyne, Cummings, & McLean Parks, 1995). According to Organ's (1988) original definition, OCB consists of individual discretionary behaviors that are not directly recognized by the formal reward system, and (in the aggregate), promote organizational effectiveness. However, given the conceptual and operational difficulties with maintaining that OCB be discretionary and non-rewarded, Organ (1997) redefined OCB to be more in-line with Borman and Motowidlo's (1993) definition—"as contributions to the maintenance and enhancement of the social and psychological context that supports task performance" (Organ, 1997, p. 91).

Not surprisingly, there is considerable overlap in the behavioral content and proposed underlying structure of OCB and contextual performance (cf. Borman, Penner, Allen, & Motowidlo, 2001; Coleman & Borman, 2000; Podsakoff et al. 2000). Consistent with their origins, however, the contextual performance literature has traditionally given more attention to personality (individual differences model) as a predictor while the OCB literature has traditionally given greater attention to attitudinal predictors (rooted in cognitive appraisals of one's work environment or affective mood states; cf. Lee & Allen, 2002). While neither personality nor attitudinal variables are likely to predict specific, situation-bound behaviors very well, they do predict aggregations of thematically related behaviors across varied situations and reasonable time intervals (Epstein, 1980).

OCB Dimensionality, Measurement, and Correlates

The most common conception of OCB is Organ's (1988) five-dimensional typology, consisting of:

1. *altruism* (behavior directly intended to help a specific person, such as voluntarily orienting new people to their work and assisting others with heavy workloads);
2. *conscientiousness* (a generalized compliance with internalized organizational norms, such as punctuality and not wasting time);
3. *sportsmanship* (not complaining about trivial matters or "going along with" something which may be personally disagreeable to "keep the peace");
4. *courtesy* (consulting with others before taking action); and
5. *civic virtue* (keeping up with matters affecting the organization; making suggestions for organizational improvements).

The Organizational Citizenship Behavior Scale (OCBS) developed by Podsakoff, MacKenzie, Moorman and Fetter (1990) has become the standard for measuring Organ's five OCB dimensions.

Williams and Anderson (1991) have proposed that these five OCB dimensions can be sorted into two distinct subgroups, based on whether the most direct beneficiary is the individual (OCB-I; altruism and courtesy) or the organization (OCB-O; sportsmanship, civic virtue, and conscientiousness). This separation of OCB into OCB-I and OCB-O aligns well with Coleman and Borman's (2000) sorting of contextual performance behaviors into "interpersonal support" and "organizational support" noted earlier.[9] Accordingly, there appears to be a "coming-together" of the contextual performance and OCB literatures (Motowidlo, 2000).

Four meta-analytic reviews of the OCB literature have been published (Organ & Ryan 1995; Podsakoff, MacKenzie, & Bommer,

1996; Podsakoff et al. 2000; LePine, Erez, & Johnson, 2002). The LePine et al. (2002) review essentially consolidates the findings of the three earlier meta-analyses, and has shown that:

a. excepting for "sportsmanship," the OCB dimensions are highly related to one another, with inter-correlations closely approaching or exceeding generally accepted minimum values for internal consistency ($\rho =. 67$);
b. the OCB dimensions have equivalent relationships with job satisfaction, organizational commitment, fairness, leader support and conscientiousness;
c. predictive relationships with *overall* OCB as the criterion were as good as, or superior to, those with the narrower OCBdimensions; and
d. no differential relationships between the common OCB predictors and OCBI and OCBO scores (created by "dummy variable").

Meta-analytically derived mean correlations between overall measures of OCB and the five commonly studied predictors were: job satisfaction ($\rho =.24$), organizational commitment ($\rho = .20$), fairness ($\rho =.23$), leader support ($\rho =.32$) and conscientiousness ($\rho =.23$).[10] Research also suggests that the effect of OCB performance on overall supervisory ratings of performance is at least equal to that of task proficiency (Podsakoff, MacKenzie, & Hui, 1993; Podsakoff et al. 2000).

The results by LePine et al. (2002) calls into question the merits of determining separate OCB dimension scores, and suggests that the five OCB dimensions are simply imperfect behavioral manifestations of the same underlying construct—"positive cooperativeness at work" (Motowidlo, 2000; Organ, 1997). More specifically, perhaps OCB is best viewed as a multidimensional latent variable (Law, Wong, & Mobley, 1998), either trait- (personality) or state-based (situation-determined), reflecting a willingness to cooperate with, and help work colleagues, (Motowidlo, 2003; Organ, 1997). Organ and Ryan (1995) suggests that the latent variable is a "general morale" factor—"a basic psychological state vis-à-vis the workplace" (p. 794). LePine et al. (2002) do offer alternative explanations for their results, however, including correlated method variance in assessments of OCB, inadequate breadth of predictors and/or OCB criteria studied, and low statistical power for detecting differential relationships in their meta-analyses.

Particularly relevant here, however, is that of all the variables studied in relationship to OCB, leadership measures *consistently* emerge among the strongest predictors. Of the five correlates of "overall OCB" studied by LePine et al. (2002), leader support was the strongest (ρ = .32); next highest was job satisfaction (ρ = 24). In the meta-analyses reported by, Podsakoff et al. (2000), overall OCB correlated with "trust in leader" (ρ = .39), and with LMX (ρ = .30), again among the strongest of the relationships they investigated. The variable sets that Podsakoff et al. (2000) examined, as correlates of OCB, included: employee attitudes, dispositional variables, employee role perceptions, demographic variables, employee abilities and individual differences, task characteristics, organizational characteristics and leadership behaviors. Of these variable sets, the correlations between leader behaviors and OCB dimensions, and job satisfaction and OCB dimensions, showed the most consistent and strongest *pattern* of relationships. Of the leadership variables, transformational leadership behaviors, contingent-reward, "supportive leadership," and LMX showed the strongest and most consistent pattern of relationships with OCB. This pattern of results is clearly evident from Table 2 of Podsakoff et al. (2000, pp. 527-529), leading the authors to conclude, "leaders play a key role in influencing citizenship behavior" (p. 532). Podsakoff et al. (2000) interpret these findings as being consistent with the notion that: (a) inspiring others to perform above and beyond expectations is central to transformational leadership; and (b) OCBs play a key role in the reciprocal social exchange process of LMX.

As noted many times throughout this paper, a central assertion of LMX theory is that higher quality LMX relationships result in higher incidences of OCB. Yet, we know very little about the relationship of LMX to OCB. The two meta-analytically derived mean correlations reported by Podsakoff et al. (2000) for LMX and "overall OCB" (ρ =. 30), and LMX and OCB-altruism (ρ = .36) were based respectively on three and four studies. Moreover, meta-analyses of the LMX and the OCB literatures provide no information on how much unique variance each correlate explains in predictive models. Likewise, we know little about potential mediators or moderators of a proposed LMX-OCB relationship. In this regard, a careful review of the primary studies reporting relationships between LMX and OCB is warranted.

LMX-OCB: A REVIEW OF THE EMPIRICAL LITERATURE

Method

Literature Search

The PSYCINFO (1970-2003) and ABI (1970-2003) databases were electronically searched using the search term "leadership," "VDL" (vertical linkage model), "LMX," and "leader-member exchange" *in conjunction with* "OCB," "organizational citizenship," "contextual performance," "pro-social behavior," and "extra-role behavior." Additional studies reporting LMX-OCB relationships were identified through an awareness of other scholars doing research in this field, who sent us their working papers. In total, 18 studies reporting empirical data on LMX-OCB relationships were identified.

Meta-Analysis Strategy

We followed the procedures developed by Hunter and Schmidt (1990). Each study included in the meta-analysis contributed one correlation between subordinate-provided LMX ratings and supervisor-provided OCB-ratings. Moreover, each study provided all the information required allowing us to correct each individual correlation for statistical artifacts. Correlations were disattenuated for measurement unreliability in both LMX and OCB.

We examined the "overall" relationship between LMX and OCB, wherein we attempted to use the most stable and "complete" measure of OCB. Here, each of 18 studies contributed one LMX-OCB correlation. When primary studies provided individual relationships between different dimensions of LMX (e.g., using LMX-MDM subscale scores) and OCB (e.g., altruism, courtesy, etc.) without providing a correlation between composite scores for either LMX or OCB, we calculated linear composites following suggestions by Hunter and Schmidt (1990, p. 457).

We had several reasons for following this strategy. First, we wanted to assess an "overall" relationship between LMX and OCB, drawing from as many independent studies as possible, with each study contributing a single correlation.[11] Second, the results of LePine et al.'s (2002) meta-analysis suggests that the dimensions of OCB be considered as somewhat imperfect indicators of the same underlying construct (e.g. a general tendency to be cooperative and helpful in organizational settings). They noted: "when OCB is the focal construct of interest, scholars should avoid focusing on the specific dimensions of OCB when conducting research and interpreting results." (p. 61). Moreover, if the different ways in which "overall OCB" was represented in our meta-analysis impacts the magnitude of the LMX-OCB relationship, our results will suggest the presence of moderators. Indeed, Hunter and Schmidt (1990) recommended that one should first account for variance in a sampling distribution that can be attributed to statistical artifacts before commencing a search for moderators. Finally, we had no theoretical basis for expecting differential relationships between LMX and the OCB dimensions.

Table 1 presents the contributing studies. It shows for each study, LMX and OCB reliabilities, zero-order correlations, and disattenuated correlations.

In order to estimate the overall effect size in our meta-analysis, we followed recommendations by Hunter and Schmidt (1990, p. 148)

TABLE 1
Studies Contributing to the Meta-analysis of the Relationship between LMX and Organizational Citizenship Behavior

	Contributing Study	r	r_{yy}	r_{xx}	N	r_c
1.	Basu & Green (1995)	.42	.87	.90	223	.47
2.	Deluga (1998)	.28	.93	.88	123	.31
3.	Hofmann et al. (2003)	.40	.96	.94	94	.42
4.	Hui et al. (1999)	.21	.75	.73	347	.28
5.	Kraimer et al (2001)	.19	.81	.93	213	.22
6.	Manogran et al. (1994)	.17	.93	.91	282	.18
7.	Masterson et al (2000)	.31	.65	.89	651	.41
8.	Murphy et al. (2003)	.16	.91	.90	226	.18
9.	Settoon et al (1996)	.42	.81	.96	95	.48
10.	Song & Law (2002)	.34	.81	.86	142	.41
11.	Tansky (1993)	.42	.80	.85	70	.51
12.	Tierney & Bauer (1996)	.35	.87	.93	205	.39
13.	Uhl-Bien & Maslyn (2003)	.33	.90	.90	232	.37
14.	Wang et al (2001)	.14	.79	.86	203	.17
15.	Wang et al (2002)	.37	.91	.85	168	.42
16.	Wayne et al (1997)	.26	.86	.90	252	.30
17.	Wayne et al (2002)	.20	.83	.89	211	.23
18.	Zhong & Farh (2002)	.12	.83	.72	188	.16

Notes: r = observed correlation (uncorrected); r_{yy} = reliability of OCB measure; r_{xx} = reliability of LMX measure; n = sample size; r_c = observed correlation corrected for unreliability of both LMX and OCB.

and weighted each disattenuated correlation by the product of its corresponding sample size and its squared compound attenuation factor, thereby giving more weight to studies that used larger sample sizes and more reliable measures.

In addition to the estimate of the overall effect size, we calculated a chi-square statistic in order to test the homogeneity of effect sizes across primary studies (see Hunter & Schmidt, 1990, p. 110-112). This test assumes a random effects (heterogeneous) model, which is appropriate given our desire to generalize our conclusions to the research domain as a whole and not restrict our findings to the studies included in our meta-analysis (Field, 2001). However, researchers can never be certain of whether the true effect size is random or fixed (homogeneous) across individual studies. Accordingly, we calculated a second homogeneity statistic (Q) that assumes a fixed effect model (Hedges & Olkin, 1985) and decided that homogeneity would be supported if the tests based on the random and fixed models each yielded non-significant results.

Some researchers have advocated the removal of statistical outliers in an attempt to achieve homogeneity of effect sizes and determine a more reliable estimate of the true population effect size (Hedges, 1987; Hedges & Olkin, 1985; Huffcutt & Arthur, 1995). We conducted a statistical outlier analysis by ordering the contributing effect sizes with regard to their deviations from the mean effect size and sequentially eliminating the largest outlier until both homogeneity statistics were non-significant (indicating homogeneity across effect sizes), or until 20% of the contributing studies were removed (see Hedges & Olkin, 1985, pp. 256-257). On the basis of the work of many statisticians, Hedges (1987) recommended a 20% cut-off as a rule of thumb for concluding whether heterogeneity across effect sizes was attributable to a few aberrant values.

Meta-Analytic Results

As shown in Table 2 the population estimated correlation representing the LMX-OCB relationship was .32. Both homogeneity statistics were significant, suggesting heterogeneity across contributing effect sizes. Since we had no a priori moderator hypotheses, we proceeded with the statistical outlier analysis and found that only three studies had to be removed (representing less than 20% of all studies) to obtain homogeneity across effect sizes. Interestingly, the resulting population estimated correlation was the same as when the outliers were left in the meta-analysis. Overall, these findings

TABLE 2
Meta-Analytic Results of Overall LMX-OCB Relationship

	K	N	$\bar{r}$	ρ	χ^2	Q	95% CI
With all Primary Studies	18	3,925	0.27	0.32	28.13*	38.08**	.29 to .35
With Outliers Removed	15	3,311	0.27	0.32	17.99	23.33	.29 to .35

Notes: K = total number of studies; N = total sample size across primary studies; $\bar{r}$ = weighted mean correlation (uncorrected); ρ = weighted mean correlation (corrected); $\chi^2 b$ = random effects model homogeneity statistic; Q = fixed effect model homogeneity statistic; 95% CI = 95% confidence interval.
* $p < .05$
** $p < .01$

suggest that the corrected average correlation between LMX and OCB is stable and therefore generalizable.

While our estimate of the LMX-OCB relationship of .32 is lower than the .36 population estimate of the LMX-altruism relationship reported by Podsakoff et al. (2000), their analysis was based on four studies only, and an aggregate sample size of 502. The .32 we report also approximates the population correlation estimate of .30 between member-provided LMX ratings and supervisory ratings of performance (sample-size weighted, disattenuated for LMX-ratings only; Gerstner & Day, 1997). Moreover, the magnitude of the LMX-OCB relationship appears to be similar to that of the relationship between OCB and other leadership style variables, such as leadership support ($\rho = .32$, LePine et al., 2002).

Though our analyses suggest a stable, non-moderated relationship of .32 between LMX and OCB, the possibility of the relationship being moderated by OCB-dimension cannot be ruled out. However, there were too few studies for separate meta-analysis by LMX-OCB dimension to provide for reliable results, and no theoretical grounds for expecting differential relationships by OCB dimension. Still, based on the results of our analyses, and the results of LePine et al.'s (2002) meta-analyses showing very high inter-correlations among OCB dimensions, and a lack of differential relationships with other commonly studied variables in organizational behavior, we contend that the best estimate of the relationship between LMX and "overall OCB" is .32.

A limitation of our meta-analysis, however, is that it does not provide information on the amount of unique variance in OCB explained by LMX in comparison with other predictor variables. To better determine the relative and unique contributions to variance explained, and to more fully understand the processes (paths) by which LMX uniquely, or in combination with other variables, influences OCB, we consider the individual studies.

Individual Studies: Analysis of Variance

Wayne and Green (1993) had nurse managers rank their subordinates in terms of the quality of their LMX with each. The nurses reported the frequency in which they engaged in OCB (altruism and compliance). LMX rankings were categorized into "high," "medium," and "low" (though "cut-off points used in determining these categories are not clear"). Self-reported altruism was significantly higher for nurses with high- and middling-quality LMX relationships than for nurses with low-quality LMX relationships. LMX-ranking correlated .25 ($p < .05$) and .03 ($p > .05$) with altruism and compliance respectively. These correlations were not included in the meta-analysis because OCB measures were based on self-ratings.

Drawing on data provided by 232 manager-subordinate dyads of a large international service organization located in the South-eastern United States, Uhl-Bien and Maslyn (2003) used cluster analysis to group subordinate ratings of the quality of the dyadic exchanges. Clustering was based on Gouldner's (1960) three components of reciprocity:

1. *immediacy* (time between receipt of an exchange and "repayment"),
2. *equivalence* (the extent to which the amount "repaid" is equivalent to what was received), and
3. *interest* (motive of the exchange, whether self-interest, mutual interest or other-interest).

As expected, *lower* quality LMX (whether measured by manager or subordinate) was associated with relationships high in immediacy, equivalence and self-interest. A multivariate analysis of covariance (MANCOVA) was done, using cluster membership as the categorical variable. (e.g. negative reciprocity, low-quality reciprocity, and high-level reciprocity), and altruism, perceived organizational support, organizational commitment, conscientiousness, and supervisory performance ratings as the dependent variables. The clusters representing the higher quality exchange relationships were associated with higher levels of perceived organizational support and OCB-altruism (manager-reported) as compared to the clusters representing low-quality, and negative reciprocity dyad groups. Lower levels of performance and OCB-conscientiousness (rated by the manager) were evident only for the cluster representing negative reciprocity relationships.

Individual Studies: Regression Analyses

Tierney and Bauer (1996) assessed the "longitudinal" impact of LMX on "extra-role behavior" (altruism).[12] The sample consisted of 205 professional employees from a wide cross-section of U.S. companies. Subordinates provided LMX-7 ratings at Time 1 and attitudinal measures at Time 2. Supervisors at Time 2 rated OCB-altruism. Simultaneous regressions of altruism onto organizational tenure, LMX, job satisfaction and organizational commitment revealed LMX and job satisfaction as significant predictors.

Drawing on data from 75 supervisor-subordinate dyads from the subsidiary of a Fortune 100 company, Tansky (1993) found that subordinate-provided LMX-7 ratings predicted each of the five OCBS dimensions (supervisor-rated), after controlling for demographic variables (education, sex, supervisory position, and age). Specifically, LMX accounted for incremental variance in altruism (13%), conscientiousness (14%), sportsmanship (9%), courtesy (9%), and civic virtue (13%). While employee measures of perceived overall fairness, job satisfaction and organizational commitment were taken, no analyses were presented controlling for these variables.

Deluga (1994) analyzed data from 86 supervisor-subordinate dyads from across U.S. organizations, and across managers, professionals, technical, trade, and clerical workers. Supervisors rated subordinates on all five scales of the OCBS (Podsakoff et al., 1990) and subordinates rated the quality of LMX with their supervisors using the Information Exchange Scale (Kozlowski and Doherty, 1989). Each of the five OCB dimensions were regressed separately on in-role performance (step 1) and LMX (step 2). LMX accounted for incremental variance in OCB-conscientiousness (4%, $p. < .05$), sportsmanship (6%, $p. <. 01$), courtesy (10%, $p. <. 01$) and altruism

(5%, p. < .01). Demographic variables were *not* controlled for in these analyses.

Based on a sample of 127 supervisor-subordinate dyads drawn from managerial, professional, trade, technical and clerical groups, Deluga (1998) showed that LMX predicted incremental variance (5%, p. < .05) in OCB-total scores beyond that explained by demographic variables (sex, age, organizational tenure, and years with supervisor) alone. Supervisors provided the OCB ratings (OCBS; Podsakoff et al., 1990), and subordinates provided the LMX ratings (Information Exchange Scale; Kozlowski & Doherty, 1989). OCB-total scores were used reportedly because of high inter-correlations among the five OCB scales.

Song and Law (2002) studied 142 supervisor-subordinate dyads from a cigarette-manufacturing factory in Mainland China. They investigated whether LMX predicted unique variance in measures of job dedication and job facilitation, after controlling for demographic variables (age, gender, education, organizational tenure, and tenure with supervisor). LMX accounted for significant incremental variance in both job dedication (6%, p. < .05) and interpersonal facilitation (14%, p. < .05). Further, the relationships between collectivism (cf. Triandis & Gelfand, 1998) and both job dedication and job facilitation were partially mediated by LMX and moderated by emotional intelligence (cf. Wong & Law, 2002).

Commentary: ANOVA and Regression Studies.

The above studies show that there has been no consistent set of control variables. While demographic variables were controlled for in some studies (Deluga, 1998; Song and Law, 2002; Tansky, 1993), they were not in others (Deluga, 1994; Uhl-Bien & Maslyn, 2003). Moreover, the specific demographic "controls" varied by study, with some studies more inclusive (Deluga, 1998; Song & Law, 2002) than others (Tierney & Bauer, 1996). "In-role" performance was controlled in only two of the above studies (Deluga, 1994; Uhl-Bien & Maslyn, 2003), as was tenure with supervisor (Deluga, 1998; Song & Law, 2002). Finally, in some studies job satisfaction and/or organizational commitment was controlled for (Tierney & Bauer, 1996; Uhl-Bien & Maslyn, 2003) while in others it was not (Deluga, 1994, 1998; Song & Law, 2002; Tansky, 1993). Job satisfaction is particularly important to hold constant, given its high correlation with LMX. Accordingly, the research has not been well coordinated.

Collectively, these studies preclude any definitive, generalizable statements on the unique variance in OCB explained by LMX. This reveals the need for a guiding, integrative theoretical model of the LMX-OCB relationship around which empirical studies can be focused. Indeed, few of the above studies provided a clear rationale for the control variables selected. Recently, studies employing multivariate structural equation modelling of the LMX-OCB relationship have been undertaken. These studies have attempted to contribute to the literature by providing insights into the paths by which LMX impacts OCB.

Individual Studies: Structural Equation Modelling

Ten studies modelled the LMX-OCB linkage and applied structural equation modelling (SEM) to test for model fit. In five of these studies, LMX mediated the relationship between a third variable and OCB (Hui, Law, & Chen, 1999; Manogran, Stauffer, & Conlon, 1994; Masterson, Lewis, Goldman, & Taylor, 2000; Wang, Law, Chen, & Wang, 2001; Wayne, Shore, & Liden, 1997). In four studies, LMX related directly to OCB (Kraimer, Wayne, & Jaworski, 2001; Podsakoff & MacKenzie, 1993; Settoon, Bennett, & Liden, 1996; Wang, Law, & Chen, 2002). In the remaining study, both the direct and indirect paths between LMX and OCB were statistically non-significant (Wayne, Shore, Bommer, & Tetrick, 2002). In all studies, supervisors provided OCB ratings, and subordinates provided LMX ratings.

Of the five studies in which LMX mediated, two showed that LMX mediated between interactive justice and OCB (Manogran et al, 1994; Masterson et al, 2000). Interactive justice refers to the degree to which employees believe that they are treated fairly in their interactions with their supervisor (e.g. supervisor provides adequate consideration, applies criteria consistently, and is truthful; cf. Folger & Bies, 1989; Moorman, 1991).

Wayne et al. (1997) showed that "liking" of subordinate, salary growth expectations for subordinate, and dyad tenure directly and positively predicted LMX. LMX, in turn, predicted OCB-altruism. Their broader and more inclusive structural model showed that perceived organizational support (POS) and LMX were predicted by different sets of variables, and were differentially related to outcome variables, suggesting two different types (levels) of employee exchanges (supervisor and organization). POS refers to the degree of support employees perceive the organization providing (cf. Eisenberger, Huntington, Hutchison, & Sowa, 1986). The direct path between LMX and POS was .73, $p < .01$ (reverse path = .42, $p < .01$), and the direct path between POS and OCB-altruism was .22 ($p < .01$). Hence, this study showed that LMX related to OCB-altruism both directly and indirectly (through POS).

Hui et al. (1999), drawing on a sample of 386 supervisor-subordinate dyads of a Mainland Chinese manufacturing company, showed that LMX mediated between negative affectivity (NA) and OCB. Also drawing on a sample of workers from Mainland Chinese organizations, Wang, Law, Wang, and Chen (2001) showed that LMX-MDM mediated between transformational leadership and OCB.

Kraimer et al. (2001), found direct effects of LMX on both task performance and expatriate "contextual performance." Expatriate contextual performance assessed the expatriate's adaptation to the foreign facility's business customs and norms, the degree to which the expatriate established relationships with key host-country business contacts, and the expatriate's degree of interaction with co-workers.

Podsakoff and MacKenzie (1993) re-analyzed data from Tansky (1993) and reported that the relationship of LMX to OCB-courtesy and OCB-civic-virtue was fully mediated by perceived fairness (firstly) and job satisfaction (secondly). LMX had direct paths to OCB- conscientiousness, sportsmanship and altruism.

Settoon et al. (1996), reported direct paths between LMX and OCB (path = .48, $p. < .01$) and in-role behavior (path = .39, $p. < .01$), and a reciprocal relationship between perceived organizational support and LMX. Wang et al. (2002) reported a direct path from LMX-MDM "affect" to two facets of contextual performance, "interpersonal facilitation" and to "job dedication." They also reported a *direct* path between LMX-MDM "contribution" to "job dedication."

Finally, Wayne et al. (2002) reported that supervisor-contingent rewards and dyad tenure, directly predicted LMX, which in turn, predicted overall performance ratings, but not OCB. Distributive justice and non-contingent punishment did not predict LMX, as hypothesized.

Commentary: Structural Equation Modelling Studies.

Clearly, there is no clear pattern in the paths investigated, perhaps because there has been no widely agreed-upon model to test. As with the earlier studies reviewed, there is little consistency across studies in the variables included in the models tested. What we can conclude from these studies is that LMX appears to relate both directly and indirectly to OCB. Furthermore, though there are different paths by which LMX relates to OCB, involving different variable sets, there is no strong empirical support for the dominance of any one path.

SO, WHAT *DO* WE KNOW ABOUT THE LMX-OCB LINK?

Considering the meta-analytic findings, and a more in-depth analysis of the individual studies, it is clear that the quality of the LMX relationship is positively related to OCB, in about the same magnitude as the relationship between LMX and supervisory ratings of performance (.30). It also appears that OCB and task performance contribute about equally in explaining overall supervisory performance ratings. We also know from meta-analytic reviews that the strongest and most consistent correlates of *both* LMX (cf. Gerstner & Day, 1997) and of OCB (LePine et al. 2002) are "affect-laden" variables (job satisfaction, organizational commitment).[13]

Perhaps theory and results of meta-analyses can be drawn upon in building a more complete, inclusive causal model of the LMX-OCB relationship. As overall job satisfaction emerges as among the strongest correlates of LMX (.50) *and* OCB (.20), and because the OCB literature emerged from efforts to understand the consequences of job satisfaction, this variable should figure prominently in any modelling of the LMX-OCB relationship (e.g. mediator?). Surprisingly, job satisfaction has appeared only once in a causal model of LMX-OCB (Podsakoff & MacKenzie, 1993), and this involved a re-analysis of an earlier data set (Tansky, 1993). They found that LMX related to perceived fairness, which in turn predicted OCB through job satisfaction. Unfortunately, there has been no published attempt to replicate these findings. A key challenge in modelling the LMX-OCB relationship is that OCB can both contribute to, and result from, high-quality LMX.

Finally, a key variable to consider as a potential moderator of the LMX-OCB relationship is culture. Is what we know about LMX, OCB and the link between these two variables transferable from Western- to Chinese- cultures? This is an important issue, given that the need for management training and development is growing exponentially in China, with China's recent entry into the WTO, and its dearth of managerial talent. Exploring the nature of the relationship between LMX and OCB is of particular interest because of the characterization of China as a high "relationship-oriented" and collectivist culture.

LMX, OCB, AND CHINESE CULTURE

LMX in Chinese Cultural Context

Are the fundamental premises of LMX theory applicable to a Chinese cultural context? Cross-cultural research has pointed out several fundamental cultural differences between the East and the West (China and the United States in particular) (e.g., Hofstede, 1980; Hsu, 1981; Trompenaars, 1993). Whereas in the West the cultural assumptions emphasize individualism, egalitarianism, universalism, justice, and individual rights, the East espouses values of familism, submission to authority, particularism, and duties and obligations. These cultural differences have profound implications for leadership because leaders cannot choose their styles at will and what works for a leader depends to a large extent on cultural context. For example, in high power-distance cultures there is a greater tendency for subordinates to defer to authority and respect hierarchical relationships, and expectation for bosses to be benevolent and autocratic (e.g. paternalistic) (Farh & Cheng, 2000). In high collectivist cultures, maintenance of harmonious relationships is very important and the values of the group of which one is a member supersede individual personal values (Triandis, 1994). In such cultures, there is often a greater demarcation between the social boundaries of "in-groups" and "out-groups," with norms of felt-obligation (moral duty) and reciprocity differing by group-membership status (Tsui & Farh, 1997).

There is reason to expect the fundamental tenets of LMX theory to apply to the leader-follower relationships in Mainland China. In the traditional Chinese culture, norms of reciprocal obligation ("bao") are particularly intense and heavily shaped by the hierarchically structured network of social relations ("guanxi") in which people are embedded (Hwang, 1987; King, 1991; Tsui & Farh, 1997; Yang, 1957). The notion of exchange of "renqing" (social obligation or interpersonal favor and generosity) plays a much more significant role in governing relationships in traditional Chinese culture relative to other cultures (Hwang, 1987; King, 1991). This rule of "renqing" provides the normative standard for regulating social exchange as well as provides for a social mechanism individuals can use to strive for desirable resources within a stable and structured social network. Cultivating "renqing" is said to be a prerequisite to establishing or sustaining the relationship among friends (Tsui & Farh, 1997).

In a relation-centered world, different rules of social exchange govern the social interactions of relationships varying in intimacy (e.g. "in-group" versus "out-group"). More specifically, Hwang (1987) described three levels of social exchange corresponding to the degree of relationship intimacy:

1. *instrumental tie*,
2. *mixed tie*, and
3. *expressive tie*.

These three levels share some similarities to the LMX stages of *stranger, acquaintance,* and *partner* (maturity) respectively, with the nature of the exchange moving from instrumentally based to affectively-based. With instrumental ties, the exchange is quid pro quo, often fleeting or temporary, and the terms of the exchange are clearly defined. For example, instrumental ties exist between salesmen and customers, bus-drivers and passengers, and nurses and their patients. Universality in fairness and equity, as well as impersonality, governs these relationships. In mixed ties, more stable exchange partnerships are developed, with the relationship taking on an affective/expressive component. This kind of relationship commonly occurs among neighbors, classmates, relatives, and work colleagues. Mixed ties last as long as each party in the relationship interacts with each other frequently, and rather than being governed by universal laws of equity and fairness, allow for special treatment to sustain and nurture the relationship (i.e., the principle of "renqing"). Finally, expressive ties are relatively permanent and the most highly affectively based in which the welfare of the other is part of one's duty. The general rule of exchange is one that one must do his or her best to attend to the other's need with no or little expectation of return in the future. Expressive ties occur mostly among members of such primary groups such as family, close friends, and other congenial groups. As with high-quality LMX relationships, the currency of the exchange becomes less tangible, less time-bound, and less aimed at gratifying self-interests than on being dutiful in meeting socially prescribed role obligations.

Given the paramount importance of reciprocal obligation underlying social relationships in traditional Chinese culture, and the parallels between the three levels of LMX and the three levels of relationship ties among the Chinese as described by Hwang (1987), there are strong grounds for expecting the basic tenets of LMX theory to generalize to the Chinese context. Potential differences lie in leader-member roles being more socially prescribed by the hierarchical social order among the Chinese, compared to being negotiated over time through successive reciprocal exchanges within Western cultures. That is, the respect, loyalty, mutual-obligation and trust of the subordinate toward the leader—essential to LMX and "guanxi," may be more "earned" in Western cultures, but more prescribed within Chinese cultures (e.g. one's moral duty). Likewise, supervisor benevolence toward subordinate is socially prescribed among the Chinese (Farh & Cheng, 2000), but must be earned among Westerners. However, these cultural influences among the Chinese do not preclude instrumental ties developing into mixed ties, and mixed ties developing into expressive ties, where relationships assume increasing importance, stability and longevity. Likewise, failure to meet expectations of reciprocity in leader-member relationships among the Chinese can result in weakening of the social tie over time. Recent research on Chinese leadership shows that Chinese leaders tend to classify their subordinates as either "zijiren" (in-group members) or "wairen" (out-group members) based on "guanxi," loyalty, and competence, and to treat them accordingly (Cheng, Farh, Chang, & Hsu, 2002).

Despite these parallels, however, the currency of exchange in LMX may differ in Chinese versus Western cultures, with the Chinese valuing more security, pay, benefits, and good working conditions, and Westerners valuing more personal growth, achievement, autonomy, and influence (Triandis, 1994). In return for these provisions, traditional Chinese supervisors may expect compliance, obedience, and loyalty (Farh & Cheng, 2000), whereas supervisors in the West may expect initiative, proactive behavior, independent decision-making and openly constructive criticism. Also, in the higher power-distance culture of the Chinese, it is unlikely that mature LMX relationships would reach a "partnership among equals"—used to describe mature LMX relationships in Western cultures. Accordingly, even if the LMX-OCB relationship holds-up across Western and Eastern cultures (c.f. Graen and Wakabayashi, 1994), the currency and "moral tone" of the exchange may still differ.

OCB in Chinese Cultural Context

In high collectivist cultures, norms and prescribed social roles, rather than personal attitudes, play a more important role in regulating social behavior. Also, the interdependent self takes precedence over the independent self, and in-group goals are prioritized over personal goals (Markus & Kitayama, 1991). Moreover, as compared to more individualistic cultures, individuals in collectivist cultures experience more of a moral obligation to contribute to the welfare of the collective. Their self-efficacy is enhanced through contributions they make to the social group of which they are a member (Earley, 1993). In collectivist cultures, then, OCB is more likely to be considered by subordinates as an inherent part of their work roles. Stated alternatively, collectivists, as compared to individualists, are likely to define their work roles more holistically (Smith, Misumi, Tayeb, Peterson, & Bond, 1989). Research by Lam, Hui, and Law (1999) found that Hong Kong and Japan employees would be more inclined to regard some categories of OCB as an expected part of the job than were participants from the western cultural context.

Using an inductive approach, Farh, Zhong, and Organ (in press) found that the Chinese formulation of OCB differs from Western counterparts. They identified 10 OCB dimensions, with at least one dimension not evident at all in the Western literature, social welfare participation, and four that do not figure importantly in established OCB measures:

1. self-training,
2. protecting and saving company resources,

3. keeping the workplace clean, and
4. interpersonal harmony.

They also found five other OCB dimensions:

1. taking initiative,
2. helping coworkers,
3. voice,
4. group activity participation, and
5. promoting company image,

which are similar to those that have been empirically investigated in the Western OCB literature. Moreover, organization type was found to have a strong influence on the reporting of OCB on several dimensions. Compared to employees from privately- or foreign-invested enterprises, state-owned enterprise employees tended to report more social welfare participation and fewer incidents of taking initiative and protecting and saving company resources. These differences are consistent with the expectation that state employees are more susceptible to the legacy of pre-reform policies of the communist government. They reasoned that state employees probably participated more in social welfare activities because their companies were more dependent on the state and were less concerned about taking initiative and saving company resources because they were partially shielded from the full force of market competition.

Farh et al. (in press) shows that what is considered to be OCB varied markedly across cultural boundaries. Culture conditions our belief about what behaviors contribute to organizational effectiveness. Because the Chinese believe that conflict is harmful to organizations, interpersonal harmony emerges as a major form of OCB in the PRC. Culture also shapes our criteria for organizational effectiveness. In the tradition of the PRC, state-owned enterprises are expected to support government promoted social causes. Employee participation in social welfare activities that help their firm fulfill such an obligation naturally contributes to organizational effectiveness and is considered OCB.

In addition, culture may moderate the relationship between OCB and its antecedents. As traditional Chinese societies underwent industrialization and modernized, they went through revolutionary changes in institutional patterns as well as in people's values and attitudes. Such change is of course not uniform across the fabric of Chinese societies; i.e., while some Chinese still hold on to traditional attitudes and values despite the onslaught of modernization, others have embraced modernization and its accompanied individualistic and egalitarian values (Yang, 1996). Farh, Earley, and Lin (1997) found that organizational justice related less strongly to OCB for Chinese holding traditionalist Chinese values than for Chinese holding more Westernized values in Taiwan. They explained this in terms of the more broadly defined work role expectations held-by the traditionalists, and their stronger sense of obligation to behave in accordance with their perceived roles in the work context. Research also has shown that collectivists, as compared to individualists, are less likely to engage in social loafing and shirking and are more likely to help others (Earley, 1989). Taken together, these findings suggest that individuals holding traditionalist Chinese (collectivist) values may be inclined toward OCB regardless of their treatment by their supervisors (e.g. strong situation). This further suggests that OCB is less a currency of exchange within an LMX relationship, and more an outcome of normative social expectations. Still, we would expect that individuals falling short of meeting these "citizenship" expectations would, over time, receive less favorable treatment from their supervisors than would the "good citizens," eventually giving rise to a positive relationship between LMX and OCB. Where norms of reciprocity are violated by unmet expectations, the relationship will be adversely affected.

LMX-OCB: Chinese Samples

The results of our meta-analysis suggested a non-moderated relationship between LMX and OCB, and a breakdown by Chinese versus Western samples produced highly similar results ($\rho = .28$, $K = 5$, $N = 1048$; $\rho = .33$, $K = 13$, $N = 2877$, respectively).

CONCLUSION

LMX and OCB are moderately positively related, and the magnitude of the relationship is very comparable across Chinese and non-Chinese samples. Generally, employees reporting high-quality LMX with their supervisor appear to contribute more OCB as compared to those in low quality LMX relationships. Little is known about the processes underlying this relationship, however. Since employee affect (e.g. job satisfaction, organizational commitment) relates strongly to both LMX and OCB, perhaps LMX influences OCB by means of enhancing employee affect; with OCB, in part, being an expression of this affect. Conceivably, OCB is both an antecedent and a consequence of high LMX, with the influences being reciprocal and iterative. More research needs to be done to understand the psychological processes underlying the LMX-OCB relationship, and to determine whether the same processes, and currencies of exchange, apply to both Chinese and Western samples. While acknowledging the correlational nature of much of this research, it's a "safe bet" that supervisors in Western and Chinese cultures who develop high-quality LMX relationships with their subordinates are likely to reap personal and organizational benefits.

Acknowledgments: We gratefully acknowledge the financial support for this project provided by the Hong Kong University of Science and Technology (DA602/03M46) and the Social Sciences and Humanities Research Council of Canada (SSHRC #410-96-0893).

NOTES

1. By "collective," we refer to team, department, and/or organization. In a well-managed organization, of course, there would be a unifying culture and management systems to ensure that the goals of these three units are in alignment.

2. Transformational leaders develop a closer relationship (than transactional leaders)—one founded more on *trust* and *commitment* than on contractual agreements. (Jung & Avolio, 1999).

3. Tierney and Bauer (1996) liken a low-quality LMX relationship to an *economic* exchange, and a high-quality LMX to a *social* exchange. They suggest that transformational leaders have a high LMX and that transactional leaders have a low quality LMX.

4. Sample-size weighted and corrected for attenuation.

5. Gerstner and Day (1997) rightly called for an integration of LMX and transformational leadership, noting many parallels between the two.

6 LMX is founded in Vertical Dyad Linkage theory (VDL), but has been extended to exchanges and relationships that are not necessarily vertical. For example, dyadic partners can be team member and teammates, employees and their competence networks, joint venture partners etc. (cf. Graen and Uhl-Bien, 1995, p. 225).

7. The coefficient alphas were lower for LMX ratings provided by leaders, and did not differ significantly between LMX-7 (.78) and the category of "other" LMX measures (.76).

8. The "centroid" item from their scale is: "How would you characterize your working relationship with your leader? (Five point Likert scale from "extremely ineffective" to "extremely ineffective").

9. Almost all the research on OCB and contextual performance has been based on Western samples. Research done in the "East," and in particular, with ethnic Chinese samples, suggests that while three of the OCB dimensions (civic virtue, altruism, and conscientiousness) from the West appear to be applicable to the ethnic Chinese, two are not (sportsmanship and courtesy). Two other OCB dimensions (interpersonal harmony and protecting company resources) were identified as particular to ethnic-Chinese (Farh, Earley, & Lin, 1997). These findings will be discussed in greater detail later in the Chapter when we consider LMX and OCB from an ethnic-Chinese cultural perspective.

10. Sample-size weighted, corrected for unreliability in predictor and criterion.

11. Where more than one correlation from the same study contributes to the sampling distribution, this will lead to an underestimation of the adjustment for sampling error. It is recommended that where multiple correlations from the *same* study are reported between the two variables of interest, that the *mean* of these correlations be used, along with the simple sample size for that study (c.f. Hunter et al., 1982, p. 118).

12. Unfortunately, the time interval between Time 1 and Time 2 date collection is not reported.

13. These affective-laden variables, collectively, have been referred to as a "morale" factor; see Organ, 1997).

REFERENCES

Note: Studies contributing to the meta-analysis of the relationship between LMX and organizational citizenship behavior are indicated with "*" before the name of each first author in the references.

Avolio, B. J., & Bass, B. M. (1995). Individual consideration viewed at multiple levels of analysis: A multi-level framework for examining the diffusion of transformational leadership. *Leadership Quarterly,* 6(2), 199-218.

Avolio, B. J., Sosik, J. J., Jung, D. I., & Berson, Y. (2003). Leadership models, methods and applications. In W. C. Borman, D. R. Ilgen & R. J. Klimoski (Eds.), *Handbook of psychology* (Vol. 12). Industrial and Organizational Psychology, 277-307. New York: John Wiley & Sons.

Bass, B. M. (1985). *Leadership and performance beyond expectations.* New York: The Free Press.

Bass, B. M. (1997). Does the transactional-transformational paradigm transcend organizational and national boundaries. *American Psychologist,* 22, 130-142.

*Basu, R. & Green, S.G. (1995). Subordinate performance, leader-subordinate compatibility, and exchange quality in leader-member dyads: A field study. *Journal of Applied Social Psychology, 25*(1), 77-92.

Bateman, T. S. & Organ, D. W. (1983). Job satisfaction and the good soldier: The relationship between affect and employee citizenship. *Academy of Management Journal, 26,* 587-595.

Blau, P. M. (1964). *Exchange and power in social life.* New York: John Wiley & Sons.

Borman, W. C., Buck, D. E., Hanson, M. A., Motowidlo, S. J., Stark, S., & Drasgow, F. (2001). An examination of the comparative reliability, validity and accuracy of performance ratings made using computerized adaptive rating scales. *Journal of Applied Psychology, 86,* 965-973.

Borman, W. C., & Motowidlo, S. J. (1993). Expanding the criterion domain to include elements of contextual performance. In N. Schmitt, & W. C. Borman (Eds.), *Personnel selection in organizations* (pp. 71-98). San Francisco: Jossey Bass.

Borman, W. C. & Motowidlo, S. J. (1997). Task performance and contextual performance: The meaning for personnel selection research. *Human Performance, 10,* 99-109.

Borman, W. C., Penner, L. A., Allen, T. D., & Motowidlo, S. J. (2001). Personality predictors of citizenship performance. *International Journal of Selection and Assessment, 9,* 52-69.

Borman, W. C., White, L. A., & Dorsey, D. W. (1995). Effects of ratee task performance and interpersonal factors on supervisor and peer performance ratings. *Journal of Applied Psychology, 80,* 168-177.

Brief, A. P., & Motowidlo, S. J. (1986). Prosocial organizational behaviors. *Academy of Management Review, 11,* 710-725.

Brower, H. H., Schoorman, F. D., & Tan, H. H. (2000). A model of relational leadership: The integration of trust and leader-member exchange. *Leadership Quarterly, 11*(2), 227-250.

Bryman, A. S. (1996). The importance of context: Qualitative research and the study of leadership. *Leadership Quarterly, 7,* 353-370.

Burns, J. M. (1978). *Leadership.* New York: Harper & Row.

Cheng, B. S., Farh, J. L., Chang, H. F., & Hsu, W. L. (2002). Guanxi, zhongcheng, competence, and managerial behavior in the Chinese context, *Chinese Journal of Psychology, 44,* 151-166.

Cogliser, C. C., & Schriesheim, C. A. (2000). Exploring work unit context and leader-member exchange: a multi-level perspective. *Journal of Organizational Behavior, 21,* 487-511.

Cole, M. S., Schaninger, W. S., & Harris, S. G. (2002). The workplace social exchange network: a multilevel, conceptual examination, *Group and Organization Management, 27*(1), 142-167.

Coleman, V. I., & Borman, W. C. (2000). Investigating the underlying structure of the citizenship performance domain. *Human Resource Management Review, 10*(1), 25-44.

Dansereau, F., Graen, G., & Haga, W. J. (1975). A vertical dyad approach to leadership within formal organizations, *Organizational Behavior and Human Performance, 13,* 46-78.

Deluga, R. J. (1994). Supervisor trust building, leader-member exchange and organizational citizenship behavior. *Journal of Occupational and Organizational Psychology, 67,* 315-326.

Deluga, R. J. (1995). The relation between trust in the supervisor and subordinate organizational citizenship behavior. *Military Psychology, 7*(1), 1-16.

*Deluga, R. J. (1998). Leader-member exchange quality and effectiveness Ratings: The role of subordinate-supervisor conscientiousness similarity. *Group & Organization Management, 23*(2), 189-216.

Dienesch, R. M., & Liden, R.C. (1986). Leader-member exchange model of leadership: A critique and further development. *Academy of Management Review, 11,* 618-634.

Dirks, K. T., & Ferrin, D. L. (2002). Trust in leadership: Meta-analytic findings and implications for research and practice. *Journal of Applied Psychology, 87*(4), 611-628.

Earley, P. C. (1989). Social loafing and collectivism: A comparison of the United States and the People's Republic of China. *Administrative Science Quarterly, 34,* 565-581.

Earley, P. C. (1993). East meets West meets Mideast: Further explorations of collectivistic and individualistic work groups. *Academy of Management Journal, 36,* 319-348.

Eisenberger, R., Huntington, R., Hutchison, S., & Sowa, D. (1986). Perceived organizational support. *Journal of Applied Psychology, 71,* 500-507.

Epstein, S. (1980). The stability of behavior: Implications for psychological research. *American Psychologist, 35,* 790-806.

Farh, J. L., & Cheng, B. S. (2000). A cultural analysis of paternalistic leadership in Chinese organizations. In J. T. Li, A. S. Tsui, & E. Weldon. (Eds.), *Management and Organizations in the Chinese Context* (pp. 84-127). London: Macmillan Press.

Farh, J. L., Earley, P. C., & Lin, S. (1997). Impetus for action: A cultural analysis of justice and organizational citizenship behavior in Chinese society. *Administrative Science Quarterly, 42,* 421-444.

Farh, J. L., Zhong, C., & Organ, D.W. (in press). Organizational Citizenship Behavior in the People's Republic of China. *Organization Science.*

Field, A. P. (2001). Meta-analysis of correlations: A Monte Carlo comparison of fixed- and random- effect methods. *Psychological Bulletin, 6*(2), 161-180.

Folger, R., & Bies, R. J. (1989). Managerial responsibilities and procedural justice. *Employee Responsibilities and Rights Journal, 2,* 79-90.

French, J. R. P., & Raven, B. (1959). The bases of social power. In D. Cartwright & A. Zander, (Eds.), *Group Dynamics* (pp. 150-167). New York: Harper & Row.

George, J. M. (1990). Personality, affect, and behavior in groups. *Journal of Applied Psychology, 75,* 107-116.

George, J. M. (1991). State or trait: Effects of positive mood on prosocial behaviors at work. *Journal of Applied Psychology, 76,* 299-307.

George, J. M., & Bettenhausen, K. (1990). Understanding prosocial behavior, sales performance, and turnover: A group-level analysis in a service context. *Journal of Applied Psychology, 75,* 698-709.

George, J. M., & Brief, A. P. (1992). Feeling good-doing good: A conceptual analysis of the mood at work-organizational spontaneity relationship. *Psychological Bulletin, 112,* 310-329.

George, J. M., & Jones, G. R. (1997). Organizational spontaneity in context. *Human Performance, 10,* 153-170.

Gerstner, C. R., & Day, D. V. (1997). Meta-analytic review of leader-member exchange theory: Correlates and construct issues. *Journal of Applied Psychology, 82*(6), 827-844.

Gouldner, A. W. (1960). The norm of reciprocity: A preliminary statement. *American Sociological Review, 25,* 161-177.

Graen, G. (1976). Role-making processes within complex organizations. In M. D. Dunnette (Ed.), *Handbook of industrial and organizational psychology* (pp. 1201-1245). Chicago: Rand McNally.

Graen, G. B., & Scandura, T. A. (1987). Toward a psychology of dyadic organizing. In L. L. Cummings & B. M. Staw (Eds.), *Research in organizational behavior* (Vol. 9, pp. 175-208). Greenwich, CT: JAI Press.

Graen, G. B., & Uhl-Bien, M. (1995). Relationship-based approach to leadership: Development of leader-member exchange (LMX) theory of leadership over 25 years: Applying a multi-level multi-domain perspective. *Leadership Quarterly, 6*(2), 219-247.

Graen, G. B., & Wakabayashi, M. (1994). Cross-cultural leadership making. Bridging American and Japanese diversity for team advantage. In H. C. Triandis, M.D. Dunnette, & L.M. Hough (Eds.), *Handbook of industrial and organizational psychology* (2nd Ed., Vol. 4, pp. 415-446). New York: Consulting Psychologist Press.

Hackett, R. D. (2002). Understanding and predicting work performance in the Canadian military. *Canadian Journal of Behavioral Sciences, 34*(2), 131-140.

Hedges, L. V. (1987). How hard is hard science, how soft is soft science? The empirical cumulativeness of research. *America Psychologist, 42,* 435-455.

Hedges, L. V., & Olkin, I. (1985). *Statistical methods for meta-analysis.* Orlando, FL: Academic Press.

*Hofmann, D. A., Morgeson, F. P., & Gerras, S. J. (2003). Climate as a moderator of the relationship between leader-member exchange and content specific citizenship: Safety climate as an exemplar. *Journal of Applied Psychology, 88*(1), 170-178.

Hofstede, G. (1980). *Culture's consequences.* Sage Publications, Newbury Park, CA.

Hsu, F. L. K. (1981). *Americans and Chinese: Passage to differences* (3rd Ed.). Honolulu: University of Hawaii Press.

Huffcutt, A. I., & Arthur, W., Jr. (1995). Development of a new outlier statistic for meta-analysis data. *Journal of Applied Psychology, 80,* 327-334.

Hunter, J. E., & Schmidt, F. L. (1982). *Meta-analysis: Cumulating research findings across studies.* Beverly Hills, CA: Sage.

Hunter, J. E., & Schmidt, F. L. (1990). *Methods of meta-analysis: Correcting for error and bias in research findings.* Newbury Park, CA: Sage.

*Hui, C. Law, K. S., & Chen, Z. X. (1999). A structural equation model of negative affectivity, leader-member exchange, and perceived job mobility on in-role and extra-role performance: A Chinese Case. *Organizational Behavior and Human Decision Processes, 77*(1), 3-21.

Hwang, K. K. (1987). Face and favour: The Chinese power game. *American Journal of Sociology, 92*(4). 944-974.

Hwang, K. K. (1998). Two moralities: Reinterpreting the findings of empirical research on moral reasoning in Taiwan. *Asian Journal of Social Psychology, 2,* 211-238. [Au: pls. cite in text or delete.]

Jung, D., & Avolio, B. (1999). Effects of leadership style and followers' cultural orientation on performance in-group and individual task conditions. *Academy of Management Journal, 42,* 208-218.

Katz, D. (1964). The motivational basis of organizational behavior. *Behavioral Science, 9,* 131-146.

Katz, D., & Kahn, R. L. (1978). *The social psychology of organizations.* New York: Wiley.

King, Y. C. (1991). Kuan-hsi and network building: A sociological interpretation. *Daldalus, 120,* 63-84.

Konovsky, M. A., & Pugh, S.D. (1994). Citizenship behavior and social exchange. *Academy of Management Journal, 37,* 656-669.

Kozlowski, S. W. J., & Doherty, M. L. (1989). Integration of climate and leadership: Examination of a neglected issue. *Journal of Applied Psychology, 74,* 546-553.

*Kraimer, M. L., Wayne, S. J., & Jaworski, R. A. (2001). Sources of support and expatriate performance: the mediating role of expatriate adjustment. *Personnel Psychology, 54,* 71-99.

Lam, S. K., Hui, C., Law, K. S. (1999). Organizational Citizenship Behavior: Comparing perspectives of supervisors and subordinates across four international samples. *Journal of Applied Psychology. 84*(4), 594-601.

Law, K. S., Wong, C. S., & Mobley, W.H. (1998). Toward a taxonomy of multidimensional constructs. *Academy of Management Review, 23,* 741-755.

Lee, K., & Allen, N. J. (2002). Organizational citizenship behavior and workplace deviance: The role of affect and cognitions. *Journal of Applied Psychology, 87*(1), 131-142.

LePine, J. A., Erez, A., & Johnson, D. E. (2002). The nature and dimensionality of organizational citizenship behavior: A critical review and meta-analysis. *Journal of Applied Psychology, 87*(1), 52-65.

Liden, R. C., & Graen, G. (1980). Generalizability of the vertical dyad linkage model of leadership. *Academy of Management Journal, 23*(3), 451-465.

Liden, R. C., & Maslyn, J. M. (1998). Multidimensionality of leader-member exchange: An empirical assessment through scale development. *Journal of Management, 24*(1), 43-72.

Liden, R. C., Sparrowe, R. T., & Wayne, S. J. (1997). Leader-member exchange theory: The past and potential for the future. In G. R. Ferris (Ed.), *Research in personnel and human resource management*, (Vol. 15, pp. 47-119). Greenwich, CT: JAI Press.

*Manogran, P., Stauffer, J., & Conlon, E. J. (1994). Leader-member exchange as a key mediating variable between employees' perceptions of fairness and organizational citizenship behavior. *Academy of Management Best Paper Proceedings, 54*, 249-253.

Markus, H. R., & Kitayama, S. (1991). Culture and the self: Implications for cognition, emotion, and motivation. *Psychological Review, 98*, 224-253.

Maslyn, J. M., & Uhl-Bien, M. (2001). Leader-member exchange and its dimensions: Effects of self and other effort on relationship quality. *Journal of Applied Psychology, 86*(4), 697-708.

*Masterson, S. S., Lewis, K., Goldman, B. M., & Taylor, M. S. (2000). Integrating justice and social exchange: The differing effects of fair procedures and treatment on work relationships. *Academy of Management Journal, 43*(4), 738-748.

Moorman, R. H. (1991). Relationship between organizational justice and organizational citizenship behavior: Do fairness perceptions influence employee citizenship? *Journal of Applied Psychology, 76*, 845-855.

Motowidlo, S. M. (2000). Some basic issues related to contextual performance and organizational citizenship behavior in human resource management. *Human Resource Management Review, 10*(1), 115-126.

Motowidlo, S. J. (2003). Job performance. In W. C. Borman, D. R. Ilgen, & R. J. Klimoski (Eds.). *Handbook of psychology* (Vol. 12, pp. 39-53). *Industrial and Organizational Psychology,* John Wiley & Sons: New York.

Motowidlo, S. J., Borman, W. C., & Schmit, M. J. (1997). A theory of individual differences in task and contextual performance. *Human Performance, 10*, 71-83.

Motowidlo, S. J., & Van Scotter, J. R. (1994). Evidence that task performance should be distinguished from contextual performance. *Journal of Applied Psychology, 79*, 475-480.

*Murphy, P. J., Liden, R. C., & Wayne, S. J. (2003, April). Interactional justice, group cohesion, and LMX: Combined impacts on outcome. Poster session presented at the 18th annual meeting of the Society for Industrial-Organizational Psychology, Orlando, Florida.

O'Reilly, C., III, & Chatman, J. (1986). Organizational commitment and psychological attachment: The effects of compliance, identification, and internalisation on prosocial behavior. *Journal of Applied Psychology, 71*, 492-499.

Organ, D. W. (1997). Organizational citizenship behavior: It's construct clean-up time. *Human Performance, 10*, 85-97.

Organ, D. W. (1988). *Organizational citizenship behavior: The good soldier syndrome.* Lexington, MA: Lexington Books.

Organ, D. W., & Ryan, K. (1995). A meta-analytic review of attitudinal and dispositional predictors of organizational citizenship behavior. *Personnel Psychology, 48*, 775-82.

Podsakoff, P. M., & MacKenzie, S.B. (1993). Citizenship behaviors and managerial evaluations of employee performance: A review and suggestions for future research. *Employee Responsibilities and Rights Journal, 6*, 257-268.

Podsakoff, P. M., MacKenzie, S. B., & Bommer, W. H. (1996). Transformational leader behaviors and substitutes for leadership as determinants of employee satisfaction, commitment, trust, and organizational citizenship behaviors. *Journal of Management, 22*(2), 259-298.

Podsakoff, P. M., MacKenzie, S. B., & Hui, C. (1993). Organizational citizenship behaviors and managerial evaluations of employee performance: A review and suggestions for future research. *Research in Personnel and Human Resources Management, 11*, 1-40.

Podsakoff, P. M, MacKenzie, S. B., Moorman, R. H., & Fetter, R. (1990). Transformational leader behaviors and their effects on followers' trust in leader, satisfaction, and organizational citizenship behaviors. *Leadership Quarterly, 1*, 107-142.

Podsakoff, P. M., Mackenzie, S. B., Paine, J. B., & Bachrach, D. (2000). Organizational citizenship behaviors: A critical review of the theoretical and empirical literature and suggestions for future research. *Journal of Management, 26*(3), 513-563.

Rotundo, M., & Sackett, P. R. (2002). The relative importance of task, citizenship and counterproductive performance to global ratings of job performance: A policy-capturing approach. *Journal of Applied Psychology, 87*(1), 66-80.

Rousseau, D. M. (1990). New hire perspectives of their own and their employer's obligations: a study of psychological contracts. *Journal of Organizational Behavior, 11*, 389-400.

Rousseau, D. M. (1995). *Psychological contracts in organizations: Understanding written and unwritten agreements.* Sage: Thousand Oaks.

Scandura, T. A., & Graen, G. G. (1984). Moderating effects of initial leader-member exchange status on the effects of a leadership intervention. *Journal of Applied Psychology, 69*, 428-436.

Schriesheim, C. A., Castro, S. L., & Cogliser, C.C. (1999). Leader-member exchange (LMX) research: A comprehensive review of theory, measurement, and data-analytic practices. *Leadership Quarterly, 10*(1), 63-113.

Schriesheim, C. A., Neider, L. L., Scandura, T. A., & Tepper, B. J. (1992). Development and preliminary validation of a new scale (LMX-6) to measure leader-member exchange in organizations. *Educational and Psychological Measurement, 52,* 135-147.

Schriesheim, C. A., Scandura, T. A., Eisenbach, R. J., & Neider, L.L. (1992). Validation of a new leader-member exchange scale (LMX-6) using hierarchically-nested maximum likelihood confirmatory factor analysis. *Educational and Psychological Measurement, 52,* 983-991.

*Settoon, R. P., Bennett, N., & Liden, R.C. (1996). Social exchange in organizations: Perceived organizational support, leader-member exchange and employee reciprocity. *Journal of Applied Psychology, 81*(3), 219-227.

Smith, C. A., Organ, D. W., & Near, J.P. (1983). Organizational citizenship behavior. Its nature and antecedents. *Journal of Applied Psychology, 68,* 653-663.

Smith, P. B., Misumi, J., Tayeb, M., Peterson, M. F., & Bond, M. (1989). On the generality of leadership style measures across cultures. *Journal of Occupational Psychology, 62,* 97-108.

*Song, L. J., & Law, K. S. (2002). Effects of collectivism and leader-member exchange on contextual performance: A field study. Paper presented at the 25th International Congress of Applied Psychology (ICAP), Singapore.

*Tansky, J. W. (1993). Justice and organizational citizenship behavior: What is the relationship? *Employee Responsibilities and Rights Journal, 6,* 195-207.

*Tierney, P., & Bauer, T.N. (1996). A longitudinal assessment of LMX on extra-role behavior. Academy of Management Best Paper Proceedings, (Organizational Behavior Division, pp. 298-302).

Triandis, H. C. (1994). Cross-cultural industrial and organizational psychology. In H. C. Triandis, M. D. Dunnette, & L. M. Hough (Eds.), *Handbook of industrial and organizational psychology.* (2nd. Ed., Vol. 4, pp. 103-172). Palo Alto, CA: Consulting Psychologists Press.

Triandis, H. C., & Gelfand, M. J. (1998). Converging measurement of horizontal and vertical dimensions of individualism and collectivism: A theoretical and measurement refinement. *Cross-Cultural Research, 29* (3), 240-275.

Trompenaars, F. (1993). *Riding the Waves of Culture.* London: Nicholas Brealey.

Tsui, A. S., & Farh, J. L. (1997). Where Guanxi matters: Relational demography and Guanxi in the Chinese context. *Work and Occupations, 24,* 56-79.

Uhl-Bien, M. Graen, G. B., & Scandura, T.A. (2000). Implications of leader-member exchange (LMX) for strategic human resource management systems: relationships as social capital for competitive advantage. *Research in Personnel and Human Resources Management, 18,* 137-185.

Uhl-Bien, M., & Maslyn J.M. (2003). Reciprocity in manager-subordinate relationships: components, configurations, and outcomes. *Journal of Management, 29*(4), 511-532.

Van Dyne, L., Cummings, L. L., & McLean Parks, J. M. (1995). Extra-role behaviors: In pursuit of construct and definitional clarity (A bridge over muddied waters). In L. L. Cummings & B. M. Staw (Eds.), *Research in organizational behavior* (Vol. 17, pp. 215-285). Greenwich, CT: JAI Press.

Van Scotter, J. R., & Motowidlo, S. J. (1996). Interpersonal facilitation and job dedication as separate facets of contextual performance. *Journal of Applied Psychology, 81,* 525-531.

Waldman, D. A., Bass, B. M., & Yammarino, F. J. (1990). Adding to contingent reward behavior: The augmenting effect of charismatic leadership. *Group & Organization Studies, 15,* 381-394.

*Wang, H., Law, K. S., & Chen, Z. X. (2002). A structural equation model of Leader-Member Exchange, task and contextual performance and work outcomes. Paper presented at the Society for Industrial and Organizational Psychology, Toronto, Ontario Canada.

Wang, H., Law, K. S., Chen, Z. & Wang, D. X. (2001). Relationship between LMX and performance appraisal: The moderating effects of leadership style. Academy of Management Meeting, August, Washington, DC.

*Wang, H., Law, K. S., Wang, D. X., & Chen, Z. X. (2001). The linkage role of LMX: a mediating effect of LMX on the relationship between transformational leadership and followers' performance and OCB. Paper presented at the Annual Conference of the Academy of Management, Washington, DC.

Wayne, S. J., & Green, S. A. (1993). The effects of leader-member exchange on employee citizenship and impression management behavior. *Human Relations, 46*(12), 1431-1440.

*Wayne, S. J., Shore, L. M., Bommer, W. H., & Tetrick, L. E. (2002). The role of fair treatment and rewards in perceptions of organizational support and leader-member exchange. *Journal of Applied Psychology, 87*(3), 590-598.

*Wayne, S. J., Shore, L. M., & Liden, R. C. (1997). Perceived organizational support and leader-member exchange: A social exchange perspective. *Academy of Management Journal, 40,* 82-111.

Williams, L. J., & Anderson, S. E. (1991). Job satisfaction and organizational commitment as predictors of organizational citizenship and in-role behaviors. *Journal of Management, 17,* 601-617.

Wong, C. S., & Law, K. S. (2002). The effect of leaders' and followers' emotional intelligence on performance and attitudes: An exploratory study. *Leadership Quarterly, 13*(3), 243-274.

Yang, K. S. (1996). Psychological transformation of the Chinese people as a result of societal modernization. In M. H. Bond (Ed.), *The handbook of Chinese psychology*. Hong Kong: Oxford University Press.

Yang, L. S. (1957). The concept of *pao* as a basis for social relations in China. In J. K. Fairbank (Ed.), *Chinese thought and institutions* (pp. 291-309). Chicago: University of Chicago Press.

*Zhong, C. B., & Farh, J. L. (2002). Work autonomy as situational constraint of organizational citizenship behavior. Paper presented at the Annual Meeting of the Academy of Management. Denver.

Rick D. Hackett is Professor of Human Resources Management at the Michael G. DeGroote School of Business, McMaster University, in Hamilton, Ontario, Canada. He is Past-President of the Canadian Society for Industrial-Organizational Psychology (CSIOP) of the Canadian Psychological Association, a professional association of approximately 260 Canadian industrial-organizational psychologists. He is "Fellow" of the Canadian Psychological Association and is past Editor of the *Canadian Journal of Administrative Sciences* (Human Resources Division). Rick was Guest Editor of a special issue of *Canadian Psychology*, (focus, I/O Psychology) published in 1998; member of *International Who's Who of Professionals*; and member of *Who's Who In Canadian Business*. He is co-author of a book entitled *Recruitment and Selection in Canada*, which is published by ITP Nelson in 2001 (2nd Ed.). From July 1, 2001 to June 30, 2003, Rick was a Visiting Scholar at the Hong Kong University of Science and Technology, Hong Kong, PRC. Rick has published in the leading journals of his field, including the *Academy of Management Journal, Journal of Applied Psychology, Personnel Psychology, Journal of Vocational Behaviour*, and *Organizational Behaviour & Human Decision Processes*. His primary research interests are leadership, work attitudes, employee commitment, contextual performance and absenteeism.

Jiing-Lih (Larry) Farh is professor in the Department of Management of Organizations at the School of Business and Management at the Hong Kong University of Science and Technology. He obtained PhD in business administration from Indiana University at Bloomington. He currently serves as the Associate Editor-in-Chief for *Journal of International Business Studies* and on the editorial boards of *Human Relations* and *Asian Pacific Journal of Management*. He has also served on the review boards of *Academy of Management Journal, Journal of Management, Personnel Psychology*, and *Leadership*

Quarterly. He has authored or co-authored over 40 articles in the leading international journals of management such as *Administrative Science Quarterly, Academy of Management Journal, Organization Science, Journal of Applied Psychology, Personnel Psychology, Journal of International Business Studies, Journal of Management, Journal of Vocational Behavior,* and *Organizational Behavior and Human Decision Processes*. His current research interests focus on guanxi and managerial networking, paternalistic leadership, organizational justice, organizational citizenship behavior, and values and business ethics in Chinese organizations.

Lynda J. Song is a doctoral candidate in the Department of Management of Organizations at Hong Kong University of Science and Technology. She holds an MA in industrial/organizational psychology. Her current research interests revolve around leadership, organizational culture, and emotional intelligence.

Laurent M. Lapierre is an Assistant Professor of Organizational Behaviour and Human Resources Management at the University of Ottawa's School of Management, in Ottawa, Ontario, Canada. Previously, Laurent was an instructor at McMaster University's Michael G. DeGroote School of Business in Hamilton, Ontario, Canada, and worked full-time as a management consultant. In his consulting role, Laurent helped several large organizations redesign and implement human resource management processes, including selection, performance management, and employee attitude surveying. Laurent's research currently addresses leader-subordinate work relationships, family-work balance, and employee mistreatment. His work has been published in the *Journal of Vocational Behavior*.

Printed in the United States
40355LVS00005B/30